The New Private Practice

Therapist-Coaches Share Stories, Strategies, and Advice

Also by Lynn Grodzki
Building Your Ideal Private Practice:
A Guide for Therapists and Other Healing Professionals

A NORTON PROFESSIONAL BOOK

The New Private Practice
Therapist-Coaches Share Stories, Strategies, and Advice

Lynn Grodzki, *Editor*

W.W. Norton & Company
New York • London

An earlier version of "When the Therapist Neeeds a Coach" by Lynn Grodzki (pp. 211–225) appeared as "Taming the Jungle" in the *Family Therapy Networker* (2000, April).

For information about permission to reproduce selections from this book, write to Permissions, W. W. Norton & Company, Inc., 500 Fifth Avenue, New York, NY 10110

The text of this book is composed in Caslon
with the display set in Frutiger
Composition and book design by Paradigm Graphics
Manufactured by R. R. Donnelley, Haddon Bloomsburg

Library of Congress Cataloging-in-Publication Data
The new private practice : therapist-coaches share stories, strategies, and advice / edited by Lynn Grodzki.
      p. cm.
   "A Norton professional book."
   Includes bibliographical references.
   ISBN 0-393-70379-7
   1. Counseling. 2. Psychotherapy. 3. Therapist and patient.
4. Mentoring. I. Grodzki, Lynn.

RC454.4.N494 2002
361'.06–dc21   2001055762

W. W. Norton & Company, Inc. 500 Fifth Avenue, New York, N.Y. 10110
www.wwnorton.com
W. W. Norton & Company Ltd., Castle House, 75/76 Wells Street, London W1T 3QT
1 2 3 4 5 6 7 8 9 0

Contents

Acknowledgments   vii

OVERVIEW: THE NEW PRIVATE PRACTICE   1
Lynn Grodzki

What is this thing called coaching? Here is a clear analysis of the differences and similarities between coaching and therapy from an insider's point of view.

PART I: EXECUTIVE COACHING

Therapists who coach executives must shift aspects of their professional identities and adopt different skill-sets to fit into the corporate, fast-paced, show-me-results business world.

1   Coaching CEOs and Executive Teams   25
      Robert Niederman

2   The Leadership Edge   37
      Hannah S. Wilder

3   Dysfunction or Discovery: A Former Therapist   51
      Becomes an Executive Coach
      Patrick Williams

4   The Role of the Family-Business Coach   67
      Kacie LaChappelle

5   Coaching Professional Women to Speak Up   87
      Linda D. Tillman

6   The Hardiness Factor: Heightening Executive   100
      Productivity
      Carole D. Stovall

PART II: PERSONAL COACHING

Personal coaches work outside of a traditional medical model, enjoying a sense of freedom and autonomy not always possible while engaged in the practice of therapy.

7   Beyond Insight to Vision   115
           Susan Shevlin

8   Using Lightness and Humor to Coach Highly   128
           Creative People
           Roz Van Meter

9   A Spiritual Approach to Coaching   145
           Debbie Call

PART III: PEAK-PERFORMANCE COACHING

Coaching to enhance performance means knowing how to be both tender and tough, to help clients stretch far beyond their normal abilities and perform at levels of excellence.

10   Uncommon-Sense Coaching   161
           Carol Sommer

11   Coaching Amateur Athletes: From Frozen to Fearless   178
           Wendy Allen

12   Coaching Professional Athletes: Alignment 101   192
           Audrey Penn

PART IV: SPECIAL NICHES COACHING

Giving in to a strong "itch to niche," some coaches build practices around a particular passion or expertise and attract a specialized clientele.

13   When the Therapist Needs a Coach   211
           Lynn Grodzki

14   The Money Coach   226
           Lynne M. Hornyak

15   Celebrating Success with Special College Students   240
           June Bond

16   Coaching Lawyers   256
           Ellen Ostrow

Acknowledgments

In the summer of 2000, my publisher Deborah Malmud proposed that I edit a collection of essays by therapists who had successfully transitioned from therapy to coaching. Together, we envisioned a book that would take readers behind the scenes into the coaching profession, inviting these therapist-coaches to share stories, advice, and trade secrets—who they coached, how they worked, what they charged, and how they broke into the field. I put out a call for contributors via three large coaching organizations and within a month received about 100 responses from a wide array of therapist-coaches, all eager to take on the challenge of writing a chapter. Space decreed that I could select only a small fraction of those who volunteered to write essays so I opted for diversity, to show the fascinating variety of coaching done by therapists. The result is this groundbreaking book that takes an up-close and personal look at the world of coaching through therapists' eyes.

I thank Deborah for her ideas, intelligence, keen editorial eye, and the pleasure of her friendship. I also thank Regina Dahlgren Ardini, who edited this book with care and meticulousness. My husband, Tad, is a writer's dream of a spouse, always supportive, interested, and encouraging. Above all, I want to express my deep appreciation and admiration to the fifteen other therapist-coaches who generously contributed their time, energy, and professional experience to write their stories. Their efforts help to define the art of the coaching profession of today, and the frontier of the new private practice of tomorrow.

The New Private Practice

Therapist-Coaches Share Stories,
Strategies, and Advice

Overview:
The New Private Practice
Lynn Grodzki

In 1929 Cole Porter asked, What is this thing called love? and then proceeded to wonder in that lilting song whether attempting to unravel love's mystery might make a fool of him. This song plays in my mind when therapists who know that I work as both a therapist and a coach ask me a series of questions: What is this thing called coaching? Is coaching a passing fad or a new profession? What are the distinctions between coaching and therapy, from a therapist's point of view? Do you have to stop being a therapist to become a coach, or is there a way to combine the two professions? Do coaches charge more than therapists? What does it take to get a coaching practice up and running? Who are the successful therapist-coaches and how did they build their practices?

This book began as an attempt to answer these questions, but when read as a whole it does more than just characterize what it means to work as a coach: It highlights a turning point in the field of therapy, by describing a *new* kind of private practice.

This new private practice appeals to therapists who are searching for different ways to work with clients, and attracts clients who are searching for untraditional ways to achieve personal growth. This new private practice operates outside of a medical model, outside of the constraints of managed care, and outside of the conventional limitations of psychotherapy. This new private practice incorporates the essence of what therapists do best and adds to it, so that therapists can reposition themselves to become first-rate coaches.

Transitioning from therapist to coach doesn't follow a single, established route; more often it's a twisting, turning path—one that looks illusive at the start. Knowing how to build a coaching practice, adopt a coaching mind-set, and determine the needs of the growing coaching market can be confusing. I hope that this book unravels whatever mystery exists in making the therapist-to-coach transition. However, during the unraveling process I wondered, similar to the sentiments in the Cole Porter song, if it might make a fool of me. Fortunately, I had the best of help. The team of therapist-coaches who contributed chapters have produced a collected work that offers a clear and insightful look at the many ways that therapists succeed at coaching. After reading these inspiring stories, case studies, and practical advice, therapists will understand what is involved in both the art and business of coaching, and be better prepared to transition into the coaching profession.

The book is simple in format: I asked former and current therapists now working as coaches to share their professional and personal narratives, take us behind the scenes into their workdays, and mentor those thinking about entering the coaching field. I wanted this stellar group of therapist-coaches to spell it all out: why they decided to become coaches, how they built their coaching practices, and what it took for them to flourish in the coaching field. Don't hold back, I shouted from my editing sidelines. Be transparent! Reveal your best ideas and strategies for others to consider! I wanted to demonstrate the diversity of therapists who coach, so the book covers the waterfront by including executive coaches, personal coaches, peak performance coaches, and some with special niches. To understand the choices these therapist-coaches made in developing their practices, it helps to first examine the origins of coaching.

This Thing Called Coaching

Before coaching was defined as a profession, it was understood as a style of relating, one that has been used in a variety of settings (sports, business, and, of course, therapy) for decades. Daniel Goleman, author of *Emotional Intelligence,* writing in the Harvard Business Review (2000, March-April), defines the coaching style as consistently positive, constructive, motivational, inspiring, and effective. Coaching is action-oriented. It gets the client moving. Coaches assist their clients to reach further, go faster, expand their vision, think big, and develop their future potential. Coaches use accountability; they want to see evidence of progress. They not only advise and consult, they also engage in ongoing relationships with clients that offer support and collaboration until the goals get implemented. Coaches help clients learn new skills, expand existing strengths, heighten self-awareness, and achieve measurable success in easier, more elegant, and faster ways than a client could alone.

During the early 1980s, due to a sea-change in the business world, this style of relating generated a separate profession. The relentless corporate downsizing saw a disappearance of a corporate culture of in-house mentoring relationships. Gone were the important executive coaching relationships of years past, where senior executives targeted junior executives and groomed them to succeed. Both senior and junior executives found themselves isolated and dealing with chaos, needing more than good advice. They needed guidance in the form of an ongoing relationship that would provide meaningful interaction. But if mentoring were to exist, it would have to be outsourced. Enter the executive coach in the role of mentor.

Corporations first hired executive coaches to groom senior executives and improve problem managers. Executive coaches helped clients achieve corporate goals: develop better communication with staff, build more productive management teams, do strategic planning for a division, manage rapid change and multiple layoffs happening around them. But as the coaching relationships matured, the coaching became personal.

The executive/personal coach was a confidant—a trusted, independent advisor who counseled his or her executive clients how to create a balanced life and cope with emotional stress while navigating the political labyrinths of the office. Coaches heard about far more than work issues. They listened as clients discussed family problems, fears about retirement, or a search for meaning and purpose. The coach listened nonjudgmentally, asking probing questions, offering advice, solutions, encouragement, and ideas in a way that helped the executive feel supported, yet powerful.

In the 1990s, the concept of coaching found its way into the business media. Now the question being heard at some business roundtables wasn't

"What is a coach?" but "Who is your coach?" With articles about coaching appearing in *Time, Newsweek,* and *New Age Magazine,* interest in coaching spread beyond the corporate world. Entrepreneurs, students, artists, retirees, and working moms hired a coach to transition from one stage of life to another, to achieve peak performance, or to have a trusted sounding board.

As the millennium approached, the democratization of coaching was helped by several mass-media events, including coach Cheryl Richardson's best-selling *Take Time for Your Life,* Tony Robbins's motivational late-night coaching infomercials, and Oprah Winfrey's year-long "lifestyle makeovers" on her talk show. A mass audience became more familiar with the language and concepts of coaching.

Substantial energy and resources from the International Coach Federation (ICF), the professional association of the coaching world, helped build public awareness and create a market of clients for the hundreds of coaches who were graduating from coach training programs. Over a two-year period, from 1998–2000, 1000 mentions and stories were placed in national magazines and newspapers about coaching, aided by a media campaign spearheaded by the ICF and Coach University, a large coach-training organization. These organizations and others helped hundreds of their members get quoted in newspapers, interviewed on TV, and featured on radio and in magazines. As a result, during the past decade coaching developed a buzz and became the "new new thing."

The difference between a trend and a fad is that one lasts and the other doesn't. As the market for coaching grew, therapists, human resource and personnel managers, retired executives, and a wide variety of others signed up for coach training. Industry experts now estimate the total number of personal and business coaches at 10,000 and growing. Concerned about the need to make coaching a lasting profession, the ICF wisely began a catch-up effort to establish certification guidelines for coaches that would bring all the various coaching institutions into agreement in terms of who could rightly be called a Professional Certified Coach (PCC) or a Master Certified Coach (MCC). A PCC must have logged 125 hours in an accredited coaching program; been coached by a PCC or an MCC for a minimum of 10 hours over a three-month duration; have 750 hours of direct coaching experience with clients; have letters of sponsorship from a PCC or MCC; and complete a written and oral examination. MCC requirements go further, including experience of 2500 hours of coaching. While one does not need to be certified to work as a coach, in the future certification may become an important marker for establishing serious coaches from dilettantes. And as more coaches want to meet the ICF guidelines, more PCCs and MCCs will need to be on board to guide them through the requirements.

Training programs for coaches are not standardized at this time, although the ICF has attempted to bring programs under its accreditation. (At the time of this printing, only eight programs have received ICF accreditation.) Coaching programs have different ideas regarding curriculum and duration. Some training programs consider a student to be sufficiently trained after a few weekend workshops; others have a three-month curriculum; still others have classes and requirements that take several years to finish. Since the field is so new, no formal analyses of comparisons of training curriculums exist. Therapists wanting to become coaches have to rely on researching the existing programs themselves and then selecting the training that meets their needs.

THE THERAPIST AS COACH

Because of their expertise in helping people change, therapists seem naturally positioned to become first-rate coaches. According to Warren Bennis, professor of business administration at the University of Southern California business school, in an article by B. Morris (*Fortune,* 2000, February 21), "A lot of executive coaching is really an acceptable form of psychotherapy. It's still tough to say, 'I'm going to see my therapist.' It's okay to say, 'I'm getting counseling from my coach." The *New England Financial Journal* (Doherty, W., & Wylie, M. S., 1995, November), echoes this, calling executive coaches "part therapist, part management consultant."

What is now considered a coaching style showed up in the therapeutic literature starting in the post-war era of the 1950s. As therapists shifted from a Freudian, psychoanalytic view to embrace the human potential movement, they adopted behavioral and humanistic methods of therapy (Warren, C., *Family Therapy Networker,* 2000, January). Carl Rogers's client-centered approach to therapy using positive regard was an early example of the style of relating considered coaching. Abraham Maslow's hierarchy of needs promoted self-actualization, a state of fulfillment and high personal achievement—essential goals of coaching. Virginia Satir's approach to therapy removed the traditional boundaries between therapist and client; a Satir therapist functioned like a coach, becoming more real with clients and communicating openly and honestly. Milton Erickson espoused the idea of the unlimited potential and possibilities in clients, sometimes unlocking the most amazing "cures" within a single session, with the right question asked in the right way, at the right time. Therapists of the sixties and seventies followed suit and many became specialists in possibility thinking, seeing the unlimited potential of their clients. Therapy sessions focused on helping clients change present and future situations, as skill-based methods came into vogue. In the eighties and nineties, solution-focused therapy methods and the many dramatic so-called "alphabet" therapies—NLP, EMDR, TFT, EFT, and others—help clients make rapid change in just one or two sessions by using methods that draw on each client's inherent resources. The therapists using these methods naturally adopt a facilitator stance, positioning themselves as coaches and therapists.

TRANSITIONING FROM THERAPIST TO THERAPIST-COACH

Depending on how therapists have been trained and how they work, the shift from therapist to coach may be a short hop or a sizeable leap. If therapists have been trained to use proactive, directive, solution-focused methods, if they give advice, assign homework, and like to see evidence of change in the therapy session, if they teach classes, lead workshops or run time-limited groups, if they conduct training in business settings or consult for organizations, if they speak in public and are comfortable being out in the community educating others about their work—chances are they are probably using a vast array of coaching skills. For these therapists, making a decision to become a coach often feels like a natural and logical step. Therapists who have been trained analytically may find that they also would like to become coaches, but adopting a coaching mind-set of proactive, pragmatic, optimism and the tools that further strategic goal setting will require additional training.

Sometimes becoming a coach is a way to integrate disparate but complementary aspects of one's professional life. In my case, I wanted to bridge two careers—a current one in therapy and a former one in business. From 1980–1986 I worked in the family business as general manager of a large scrap metal company. I entered the job as the boss's daughter with an art degree and a sprinkling of undergraduate business courses. I found the work both fascinating and disheartening. I loved helping to run a multimillion-dollar business and learning about profit, management, and sales, and I found I was pretty good at business. But I struggled to fit into the rough and tumble world of a scrap yard. A large part of me went unfulfilled, and in 1983, beset by increasing stress and chronic health problems, I found a gifted psychotherapist (Marilyn Ellis, in Virginia) who helped me deal with an underlying depression that was contributing to my poor health.

Psychotherapy was a revelation to me. I cherished the potential for change that therapy offered. The thought of becoming a therapist, helping others as Marilyn had helped me, tantalized me, although it seemed out of reach. I was a single parent with sole custody of a young son, and felt dependent upon a job that could give me benefits and financial security. But with Marilyn's unfailing optimism that I, too, could have a career that nourished me, and with her steady, practical coaching, I felt able to take some big, life-changing steps and become a therapist.

In 1988, masters degree in hand, I opened a solo private practice. After a few years, I found myself counseling people not only about their relationships and personal lives, but also occasionally about their problems at work. One afternoon, when I mentioned to a colleague in a peer supervision group that I was spending an increasing amount of time with a client helping him strategize how to get a promotion at work, she said, "That's really not psychotherapy."

"What would you call it?"

"Business coaching," she said.

Now that I knew what to call it, I looked for training to help me to do it better. In 1996 I enrolled in Coach University (affectionately called

CoachU by its students and staff), a large coach-training organization with a curriculum that emphasized business. This was a virtual training program, meaning that all my classes, over 600 hours, would be conducted by phone via teleclasses—long-distance group conference calls. Each week at an assigned time I phoned in for an hour class and began to meet other student coaches from all over the country or—as the program expanded— the world. It was fun to meet virtually on telephone bridgelines.

The core curriculum consisted of 36 classes, each one month long, organized into six areas of study: an introduction to coaching including an overview of the basics of both personal and business coaching; specific coaching skills, such as strategizing, challenging, and advising; a series of personal coaching skills for the students to use to improve their own lives including how to develop a vision, find a personal path, become financially independent, and get "buff"— a class that upped the ante on having it all; the specific objectives for coaching a variety of client types, from artists to entrepreneurs to CEOs; solid models of business coaching to use, including how to help a new business become highly profitable and the principles behind organizational coaching; finally, practice-building tips and strategies for building a coaching business of one's own. The materials for following along with the teleclasses at home came in the form of an eleven-pound, loose-leaf textbook full of self-tests, diagrams, and detailed explanations of terms and concepts. The curriculum, as well as new courses added each year on topics such as "Personal Evolution" or "The Million-Dollar Coaching Practice," took me three years to complete, but I began to use the tools and concepts immediately in my practice.

The coach training had some overlap with my therapy training. Both emphasized the value of helping clients build sound, balanced, happy personal lives. Both devoted time to honing the skills necessary to develop a good relationship with clients—how to listen closely, empathize, ask good questions, challenge, and advise. But even with these basic skills, I soon developed a coaching style that was different from what I was doing as a therapist.

In an initial session with a client as a therapist, I listen for symptoms and problems, paying close attention to my client's emotions and to my own nonverbal, body-based reactions. I listen without solutions in mind, letting my mind be blank, staying open to vague impressions, images, and feelings—the transmittal of unconscious information that can occur between client and therapist. Therapy sessions last 50 minutes and I work long-term with clients, so I can be patient and let things play out. I trust that the deeper, core issues of each client will surface, given enough time. As a therapist I freely make interpretations, or sit in silence with a client when appropriate. I watch for and welcome the emergence of transferential material or projective identification, which often further my goal of helping my clients better understand how their personal history may be influencing their current thinking, feelings, or behaviors. Since insight often brings affect, I have a toolbox of therapeutic techniques learned over many years that I use to help clients process deep feelings.

As a coach, I listen differently. I pay primary attention to a client's value system and ego strength, noting behavioral patterns that are obstacles to achievement, but not delving into their origins. Instead of listening blankly, I silently consider strategies. I ask questions designed to help clients expand their vision. I help them focus and stay on track, rather than encouraging free association. I make specific requests for action each session. I challenge clients to go beyond their comfort level to achieve more, faster. I avoid an exploration of childhood issues and don't make psychological interpretations. I know, of course, that my coaching clients have their own set of psychological issues; I just don't explore them by saying, "I hear a lot of pain and anger in your voice as you berate yourself. Who taught you to think so negatively about yourself? How far back does this go?" Or "Do you notice how that pattern of negative thinking plays out, even between the two of us?" Instead I diffuse the transference, opting for more mutuality, and direct the focus to the future, saying, "All of us have to deal with negative self-talk from time to time. Your negative self-talk is clearly getting in your way when you sit in meetings. As your coach, I'd like to support you to think more positively about yourself and have a confident demeanor. What's the best way to start?"

In coaching sessions we talk a lot about money, achievement, balance, success, the future, and passion. I float broad concepts that I hope will stimulate out-of-the-box thinking: abundance, vision, integrity, legacy, and effortlessness. I brainstorm with clients to strategize their way through sticky business problems, make needed corrections, work smarter instead of harder, or get comfortable with a new level of professional success. We talk about topics that don't often have a chance to surface in therapy, such as optimizing one's life with grace and ease. I find that I rely on humor to help lighten up the coaching sessions, so we laugh a lot.

I know that my persona is different when I am coaching than when I am being a therapist. As a therapist, I've been told I seem serious, empathic, and nondirective. As a coach I present as optimistic, proactive, and strategic. It's wonderful to have a practice of both coaching and therapy, which allows me to stretch and work in different ways.

The Distinctions Between Coaching and Therapy

The public, the coaching community, the media, and even some therapists would like an easy explanation of the difference between coaching and therapy. I have heard the following sound-bite definitions offered in newspaper articles or at various coaching conferences to explain the difference between therapy and coaching: Therapy deals with a person's past, coaching deals with a person's future; therapy provides understanding, coaching creates action; therapy focuses on resolving a person's pain, coaching focuses on helping a person achieve pleasure. The definitions may satisfy nontherapists looking for a way to distance coaching from therapy, but it's not possible to reduce the field of therapy, a vast, hundred-year-old profession of many schools of thought and hundreds of methods, to a pat phrase. The differences and similarities between coaching and therapy take more than a sentence to clarify and can be better understood by exploring the following five categories: who, what, where, how, and why.

Who (Population)

The majority of people who seek therapy come at a low point in their lives, in pain or facing a high degree of distress. The issues are often entrenched and tough to address for both the therapist and the client. Traditional training for therapists follows a medical model for dealing with this level of distress and pain—the therapist is a medical expert who diagnoses, treats, and hopefully cures the client or patient. Clients range in functioning from seriously impaired to well-functioning, but regardless of how well a particular client is functioning, he or she seeks therapy for the part of his or her life that is dysfunctional, wounded, or hurting.

Coaches attract that segment of the population economists call the "worried well"—higher-functioning adults who would rate themselves as "content," but want more or feel blocked in some area of their lives. In a panel discussion at the American Association of Family and Marriage Therapy National Conference (2000, November), Marisa Domino, Assistant Professor of Health Economics at University of North Carolina, reported that 85% of the worried well don't seek psychotherapy or counseling even when they have personal problems, because they don't identify themselves as psychologically "ill." When the worried well want help with relationship problems, parenting concerns, career changes, boredom, or unhappiness—the same issues that cause others to seek counseling or therapy—they look for other kinds of help. The worried well, underserved by therapy, are considered a target market for coaches.

Coaching clients can be more demanding than therapy clients, bringing high expectations about the outcome of their sessions. Coaching clients don't "see" a therapist for treatment, they "hire" a coach for results, and they want to see evidence of the results. Most like to be challenged and have less patience for the slow tempo, long silences, or vague language of a process-oriented therapist. To satisfy this type of client, therapist-coaches need to be skillful, direct, get their points across clearly, and pick up the pace.

WHAT (PURPOSE)

The purpose of therapy is hard to sum up briefly, but in 1995, Martin Seligman, writing for *The American Psychologist* (1995, December) on the effectiveness of psychotherapy, tried to do just that. He defined psychotherapy as "concerned with the improvement in the general functioning of clients/patients, as well as amelioration of a disorder and relief of specific, presenting symptoms." When therapy works, he wrote, clients report robust improvement with treatment in the specific problem that got them into therapy, as well as in personal growth, insight, confidence, well-being, productivity at work, interpersonal relations, and enjoyment of life.

However, the progress of therapy is rarely linear; some aspects of a person's functioning improve while other aspects stay the same or change more slowly. When the goal is to help a person gain insight, heal emotional wounds, eliminate self-destructive behaviors, or bring about characterological development, therapists must use a broad perspective to evaluate progress, one that takes into account the complexity of the problem and the intractability of the system in which it occurs. A therapist might consider the therapy successful if, after treatment, a client has made substantial internal shifts in thinking, feeling, and behaving, even if the client is still functioning in the world in a low to moderate level. A coach uses a different assessment and might see success only if a client has made substantial external change and is functioning at a high level.

Thomas Leonard, author of *The Portable Coach* and one of the early founders of the coaching movement, defines coaching as a threefold process that helps people set and reach better goals, do more than they would have done on their own, and focus better so as to produce results more quickly. According to Leonard (www.CoachU.com, 2000), coaches position themselves not as experts, but as equals with their clients. They see themselves as collaborative partners, ready to work in tandem with a client to solve an interesting challenge. The issues that coach and client address are rarely life-and-death, so the coach uses a less diagnostic, analytical approach. In coaching, emphasis is placed on a person's present state of mind and future potential. Action is the byword of coaching. Most coaches rely on markers for concrete outcomes, since coaching is less about process, and more about doing.

Harriett Simon Salinger, Master Certified Coach (and a former therapist), sees the distinctions between therapy and coaching as the "therapy-to-coaching continuum" (personal communication, 2000). At one end of the continuum is the traditional version of psychotherapy, say psychoanalysis, and at the other end the traditional version of coaching, say sports coaching. Just looking at the ends of the continuum, one can easily discern many differences between the two approaches. In psychoanalysis, there is little expectation for a patient to take action or meet goals; uncovering unconscious material and developing insight is tantamount. The analyst is a neutral presence, is nondirective, and wants to help the patient weaken defenses as a way to develop self-awareness and feel repressed emotions.

Contrast this to sports coaching, on the other extreme end of the continuum. The feelings and inner desires of the athlete are not examined; winning is the sole focus. The coach is tenaciously influential, directive, opinionated, and expressive, trying to strengthen—not weaken—defenses.

But as one starts to move toward the middle of the continuum, away from the classic approaches of psychotherapy and coaching toward the middle ground, the differences begin to blur. Helping a client to feel happy, self-actualized, and more productive? Building a person's confidence, self-awareness, or ability to have better relationships? These goals could fit into the stated purpose of either therapy or coaching. At the very center of the continuum we might see an area of shared common territory simply described as "personal growth."

Although the differences between therapy and coaching tend to overlap in the center of the continuum, many coaches and therapists use methods that place them more toward the ends. The distinctions between therapy and coaching become sharper when we add to the discussion of "who" and "what" the other categories of where, how, and why.

WHERE (SETTING)

Most therapists agree that to provide optimal therapy they need a controlled, consistent, private setting so that they can have confidential face-to-face sessions with a client at regular, anticipated intervals. Licensed therapists adhere to the ethical and legal guidelines of their professions to protect the client and promote safety and trust. The therapist-client relationship is usually a hierarchical one for good reason; sometimes the therapist, in the role of expert, needs to make a hard call to protect the life or well-being of the client, or to set a course of immediate medical action. The hierarchy also encourages the emergence of transference, one of the powerful methods that some therapists use to help clients work through unconscious material.

Coaching is notable for its flexibility in regard to setting. Coaching sessions can take place in the coach's office, the client's office or workplace, a hotel, restaurant, in the field, on the phone, or over the Internet. It's not necessary for a coach and his or her client to have ever met face to face for the sessions to be effective. Sessions may be regular, infrequent, or packaged to fit the terms of a specific contract.

The coach may purposefully keep the professional boundaries of the relationship loose, revealing more about self, for example, in order to diffuse transference. Traditional therapeutic guidelines such as confidentiality may or may not apply in coaching, depending on whether the coach is hired by an individual or by that individual's employer. In coaching, dual relationships may exist—the life coach may be a social friend or business associate of a client, the executive coach may play golf with a client after hours, the peak performance coach may open his or her home to house a client during a training season. For this reason, coaches often seek to keep relationships authentic and mutual, to make it possible to work within varied and changing conditions.

HOW (SKILL-SET)

Postmodern therapists and coaches both rely, at least in part, on standard cognitive-behavioral methods—asking questions, listening carefully, establishing rapport, reframing, giving advice, making suggestions, proposing assignments—to help clients think and behave differently. Whereas therapists draw on a century of methodology and development, coaches have limited approaches upon which to draw, because the field is still in its infancy. As a result, coaches often borrow from other disciplines. What distinguishes a method as a coaching tool versus a therapy tool is not just the skill-set, but also how it is applied, in what setting, with what population, for what intention, and with what results.

Some coaches use a set coaching model that has been developed by a coaching organization. Most coach-training organizations provide students with a lot of coaching tools (assessments, checklists, exercises, programs). Other coaches design or collect their own tools and approaches. Similar to therapists, some coaches work eclectically while others use a structured approach based on pre-and post-measurements and assessments. An eclectic coach might borrow techniques from organizational development, human resources, psychotherapy, psychology, personal growth, sports, career counseling, movement specialties, or spiritual meditative practices.

Let's imagine a therapist-coach with an understanding of family systems therapy who wants to work inside corporations. She might start with what she knows about a systems model and then adapt it to theory from the field of organizational development, develop a program of how to work with executives or teams, purchase a variety of assessments and measures that work in a corporate culture, read business magazines to become familiar with corporate language, and then begin to test out her approach by getting small contracts.

Therapist-coaches pick and choose from a long list of methods developed for therapy that work equally well within the parameters of coaching— EMDR, guided imagery, relaxation, reframing, paradox, self-administered tests, solution-therapy protocols, neurolinguistic programming, or stress-release exercises, to name only a few.

Therapists decide how to position themselves as coaches usually in one of three ways:

- *Reorient.* Therapists who reorient cease working as therapists and use the professional title of "coach." They may work in a corporation as the resident coach, for an organization as a consultant or subcontractor, in a coaching firm, as a sole proprietor in a private practice, or they may sell products that augment individual or group coaching (studies, assessments, trainings, etc. They may travel a lot to see clients, work from an office, or work from home.
- *Diversify.* Therapists who diversify have a therapy practice and a coaching practice operating side by side. Their practices allow them to switch back and forth between professions, being a coach one day (or one hour) and a therapist the next. Some completely separate the two practices, working out of separate offices with two different business set-ups. Others have both practices under one roof, working more fluidly. The ability to diversify and shift roles back and forth successfully relies on having clear boundaries and well-articulated services.

- *Integrate.* Therapists who integrate complete a coach-training program but continue to work only as therapists, using their coaching skills as yet another skill set. In this case, the coaching skills allow them to offer an expanded set of therapy services for a broader population. These therapists find that their coaching skills come in handy for retaining clients because they have an expanded menu of services to offer those clients who progress from "ill" to "well" and still want to keep growing and learning.

WHY (INTENT)

Intention is key in terms of determining the difference between coaching and therapy. A therapist-coach can use the same skill, say guided imagery, with a therapy client or with a coaching client and, based on her intention, create dramatically different results. This means that a therapist-coach needs to determine first, his or her intention. If the intention is to help a person further his or her progress, take action, set and reach better goals, do more, focus better, and produce results fast, the therapist-coach will make choices that will reflect a coaching style. If the intention is to help a person heal, get in touch with feelings, resolve past issues, or relieve symptoms, the choices will be more reflective of therapy. Each therapist-coach is presented with choice-points several times during each coaching sessions, and needs to be clear on his or her intention in order to successfully set the framework for coaching.

SHIFTING IDENTITIES

Because coaching is a newly emerging profession, therapists who transition sometimes get confused about their professional identities. Well-seasoned therapists graduate from a coach-training organization and mistakenly think that they need to abandon their "therapy smarts"—their professional knowledge base and demeanor—in order to be a coach. Years of hard-won professional confidence and competence, refined relational skills, expertise at helping clients make behavioral change, and awareness regarding the complexities of interpersonal dynamics are cast aside. These newly minted coaches draw a blank at their first coaching session, and ask me what to say to a client or how to react because they want to make sure they are "being a coach, not a therapist." A sense of dissociation settles over them and they forget what they know best—how to simply *be* with a client.

Any coach-training program that does not recognize the expertise in empathic, relational, and strategic skills that most therapists already have does a disservice to the confidence of new coaches. Therapists do need to set aside some of their previous training and mind-set—the medical model so many are taught to use to diagnose, the hierarchical stance, the passive neutrality—and learn to be more "coach-like." They need to normalize behaviors, put aside a pathological framework and adopt a mind-set of wellness and possibility. They need to be consistently positive, action-oriented, focused, expansive, optimistic, nonjudgmental, and nonhierarchical. They need to understand about holding a vision and learn to think strategically.

As one who mentors new therapist-coaches, I find that whether or not a new coach will successfully build a coaching practice rests partially on his or her reason for making the transition. Some therapists shift to coaching because they feel financially frustrated due to the difficulties in operating a healthcare private practice. These therapists soon recognize that it is not necessarily any easier to build a coaching practice than it is to rebuild a failing therapy practice. Adding the word "coach" to a therapy business card will not automatically attract clients or insure that the therapist creates a bustling, fee-for-service practice. Building a coaching practice, just like building a therapy practice, requires investment, planning, time, networking, and, yes, marketing.

It's an easier transition if therapists see becoming a coach as part of a logical progression, one that fits how they already define themselves professionally. Therapists who naturally gravitate toward a coaching style of working, look to incorporate an array of talents and skills under one professional title, or simply want a change of career tend to find success in becoming a coach.

One of the common questions I hear from therapists who consider becoming coaches is whether or not the role of therapist and coach can ever be combined, or whether the two roles must always be kept separate. For example, is it possible to switch roles with a single client and be that person's therapist for a while and then, later, his or her coach? How much sequential overlap is permitted?

Therapist-coaches need to be mindful about the potential problems inherent in having multiple relationships, so that they adhere to the ethics of their licensure and don't place themselves or their clients in compromising situations by exploiting them or developing a conflict of interest.

Therapists usually have styles, boundaries, and policies that differ from those used by coaches, so the idea of crossover can be problematic. For example, in the coaching profession it is not unusual to find executive coaches who make friends with their clients, socialize with clients, or have additional business interests with clients. In these cases, it would strain the ethical boundaries of psychotherapy to try to go from executive coach to therapist with a client or vice versa. Another issue to consider is that the normal transference encouraged in a therapy relationship would be impossible to contain or undo, once the shift into a coaching relationship is established.

Because I have a diversified practice and work as both a therapist and a business coach, I have had occasion to be asked to crossover by clients. Much of my coaching is on a national or international format, which means I am often working by phone and e-mail. Virtual contact brings limitations; I would not try to do therapy over the phone with a client I have never met face-to-face, so my phone-coaching clients understand that I will refer them for psychotherapy when needed in order to make our coaching relationship possible. When a psychological issue comes up in the coaching call that feels beyond the scope of what I want to address, I might say, "I think this is something you need to take to therapy and work on, in order for us to be able to progress with your coaching."

Occasionally a coaching client's personal problems become too obstructive for us to proceed and then I suggest that we end the coaching relationship so that he or she can focus on getting the therapy that's needed. Sometimes a coaching client will ask me to "put on my therapist hat" for a single session and offer some advice or direction on how to deal with a personal issue, say a problem with depression, or some feelings of heightened anxiety. If the issue persists, I refer the coaching client for therapy with someone other than me to keep my role clearly defined.

Similarly, sometimes a therapy client will ask me to put on my coaching hat for a session to talk about an issue at work. Again, if it involves extensive coaching, I simply refer out to another coach. Working as both a therapist and a coach, I need to evaluate what services I am willing to offer, to whom. Sometimes a person comes to see me in person for executive coaching and at the initial session it becomes evident that he or she needs psychotherapy rather than coaching. In a these cases I may say, "This session seems more like psychotherapy and less like coaching. I think you could use some psychotherapy around this issue. If you'd like, I would be willing to work with you, but only as your therapist."

Therapist-coaches who continue to practice as therapists must take care to be highly professional in all of their client-based relationships. Their licensure usually requires that they adhere to the highest standards of their ethical and legal professional duties whether working as a therapist *or* a coach.

Some who review the issues of coaching offered by mental health professionals advise that the therapist-coach consult with an attorney for clarifications of the issues and always err on the side of caution. According to Amos Martinez, Colorado Administrator for the Department of Regulatory Agencies, in an article he wrote for the *Mental Health Professions Newsletter* (www.dora.state.co.us/Mental-Health/newsletter.pdf, 2001–2001), mental health professionals working as personal coaches, even those using disclaimers stating they are not providing psychotherapy, may still be subject to the jurisdiction of their psychotherapy regulatory boards. He states that it is incumbent upon a personal coach to know and understand the regulations that govern psychotherapy practice, because these regulations may also be applied to his or her coaching practice. For example, regulatory boards, when reviewing a grievance, can find that a coach did not provide a mandatory disclosure statement to clients or may have practiced outside his or her area of training, experience, or competence. Martinez cautions that there can be severe consequences of liability or malpractice for therapist-coaches. He gives one example that he believes would leave a coach open to such consequences: a personal coach who promises, through an advertisement, to provide clients with "the opportunity to create the most wonderful life possible."

For this reason, it is not uncommon to see therapist-coaches with diversified practices maintaining identical boundaries and identical policies whether working as a coach or a therapist. These therapist-coaches have clear, consistent ethical, professional, and financial boundaries with all clients. They engage in only professional, well-boundaried relationships. They don't socialize with clients or undertake additional business ventures with clients. They don't step outside of normal therapeutic behavior with clients by making "friendly" gestures, such as initiating spontaneous phone calls or sending gifts. They may use a partnership model of coaching, but don't disclose inappropriately about themselves.

It's important to remember that even when we therapist-coaches keep our roles completely separate, there is a natural blending of perspective and knowledge that informs us no matter what our current role. I call this the "added value" component. The fact that I am a therapist is an added value for my coaching clients, and the fact that I am trained as a coach provides something extra for my therapy clients.

I believe that the best-informed therapists have been through their own therapy, and the best coaches have been coached. My first coach, Pam Richarde, helped me look at the lack of vision in my life, find more purpose, and gave me a lot of great advice about balancing my compulsion for hard work with more play. I hired writing coaches who helped me untangle confusion and feel more confident while working on writing projects. I hired an entrepreneurial business coach who had a lot to teach me about money, setting up my business, and having more fun in the process. Similar to getting continuing education as a therapist, I attend coaching conferences, take courses, and stay connected to a community of coaches.

The experience of being a client who pursues her own therapy *and* coaching feels like swimming in the Caribbean Sea. Coaching moves me through the water at a rapid pace: I stay buoyant on the surface, keeping one eye on the horizon, moving purposefully and watching for rough currents. Therapy pulls me to the bottom now and then in dramatic bursts: Once there I swim in cloudy depths that eventually, with effort, become clearer. I recognize long-lost parts of myself in the depths, and I work to integrate these parts. Then pop! Back to the surface, moving with more ease, pleasure, and calm. In my experience, the process of therapy and coaching enhance each other. Each helps me develop different aspects of my life.

The therapist-coaches you will meet in the chapters in this book demonstrate in detail the variations and distinctions possible in today's coaching practices. Following in the coaching tradition, each author writes as a mentor, hoping to make the journey easier for other therapist-coaches who follow behind. My hope is that readers will use this book to become more knowledgeable about coaching and to take the next step toward creating their new private practices.

Part I

Executive Coaching

1

Coaching CEOs and Executive Teams

Robert Niederman

Ten years after becoming a therapist, I became interested in sports psychology and coaching. I began reading and thinking and talking to people in the field. Then one Friday afternoon when I got home from work, I had the opportunity to try out a few ideas with one of my children. Joe was 10 years old at the time and a gifted athlete. He was frequently the best player on his team, no matter what the sport. However, on this day he was not acting like a powerful athlete. He was in front of the house shooting free throws and in a very black mood. He had just completed basketball camp and, as I soon found out, he was one of the poorer free-throw shooters on his team. This was a source of great embarrassment. Others had sunk 7 or even 8 out of 10 tries and the most he could muster was 3! He was angry and looked wounded. I stood around for a while and watched him shoot. Sure enough, one went in, the next went out. He'd start over and then it would go in, then the next in, then the next out. I watched this routine for about 10 minutes. Then I said, "Joe, I'd like to try something. Are you willing to try something out?" Joe agreed.

So I said, "I would like you to do just as I ask for a few minutes. Are you willing to do that?" He shrugged in agreement. (Joe rarely agrees so compliantly to my requests, but in this instance he may have been so desperate he was willing to do anything.) I said, "Okay, after each shot I want you to start over. Okay?" He looked like he didn't understand me. Then he shrugged an agreement. He shot and the ball went in. I positioned myself under the basket so I could catch the ball. I then threw it back to him and said, "Okay, start over."

"What?"

"Start over!"

He shot the next one and it went in. He said, "Two in a row." In a friendly and nonchalant way, as if it were always true, I replied, "No, we started over. That one didn't count. Start over again."

The next one also went in. "Three in a row!" he said.

"No, that didn't count. Remember? We started over. It's now zero. Now let's start again." So we did start over. Over and over and over.

That afternoon Joe sank 18 free throws in a row before he missed one. He had no idea what happened. What's more, he didn't want to talk about it. He went into the house looking dazed, as though he didn't believe what just happened. I couldn't believe it either, but I was hooked. I had followed a coaching idea I had read about and applied it to this situation. The idea was to look for patterns in behavior. Find out what is working and make that happen more often.

When I tell this story to audiences, I ask them to explain the performance improvement. Many say, "He was able to relax because he started over. His anxiety went down." I reply, "That's very true. However, that would probably account for a small improvement, perhaps two or three more baskets but it would not account for an exponential improvement." Something else had to be taking place in order for Joe to perform at six times his former success rate.

Here's what happened: Frequently there are a set of rules a person follows as he or she goes about doing a task. Many times people are not aware of these rules; they are tacit and unexamined. These rules are often difficult to change but they may be used to improve performance. Rules may be identified by noticing a fixed pattern of response. The pattern I noticed that afternoon as I watched Joe shoot was that his first shot always went in, his next shot often did not, and his third shot rarely went in. But when he started over, his first shot always went in. What I did in my intervention was make all of his shots first shots. After that, they all started going in.

After my experience with Joe, I got excited. If this kind of performance enhancement can happen with a 10-year-old boy, surely it can happen with adults in places where it matters far more than free shots on a Friday afternoon! This is when I went after coaching in a serious way.

I studied a number of books on coaching, practiced on my clients and friends, and looked around for a coaching job. Eventually I found one working with TECWorldwide, a company that coaches CEOs and brings them together into groups. My job was to meet with them face to face and to facilitate them in groups. I loved groups so this was an ideal position for me. I was thrilled to be working with CEOs, particularly in Silicon Valley, the center of the technology revolution. Now I could truly gain experience helping the most powerful members of the business community. But I soon noticed that I needed to change some of my own habits if I was going to become an expert coach. The most obvious habit was pace. I thought my job was to understand the mind of the CEO, and I was used to the pace of a therapist. I used my old bag of therapy techniques. I listened, asked questions, formulated my thoughts, tested them against what I heard, and finally, when the proper moment arrived, I delivered my well-formed interpretation. But I noticed that my CEOs were not as complacent as my patients. They did not want to wait calmly for my thoughts. They were moving quickly and they wanted me to be on the same train. Speed was essential to the work. And they were not interested in interpretations. They wanted results, and they wanted them quickly. They were not interested in the "inner world"; they wanted something to happen in the outer world, where it counted. This was intimidating. This would truly put me to the test. It meant that I had to change my style.

I realized that I needed to learn a confrontational style, which was very different from the style I used in therapy. In therapy, I was mostly hidden. Clients did not see my reactions. I kept them under control. But in coaching this didn't work. CEOs were not interested in what I thought unless it helped them move forward toward their goal. Through being coached by others, I began to realize that I needed to use the same internal experience I had developed in therapy but in a much more interactive and interpersonal arena. I needed to learn how to translate my inner experience into a language that would make a difference in my clients' actions. And I needed to be present at any moment for the opportunity to coach.

For example, one day I was waiting for Sam, an imposing CEO and founder of a regional banking firm with revenues of about 30 million dollars. I was in the waiting room when he came to get me. As I got up he disappeared down a long hallway. He was moving extremely fast and I was trying to catch up to him. He never turned to greet me or inquire how I was. I felt left in the dust. In my race to close the gap between us, I remembered a little boy I used to see when I drove to work. He was a kindergartner and his father walked him to school. But the father kept such a rapid pace that he was always half a block ahead, never turning to find his son; the little boy struggled just to keep the gap from widening.

We turned several corners and went down another long hallway until we finally reached our meeting room. Sam sat down with full command, opened his book and began to march down his agenda. I realized that if I did not take control in that moment I would be unable to pay attention to anything in the meeting. So I said, "Sam!" He looked up, startled by this interruption. I waited until I had his full attention. "I want to tell you something. I want to tell you how I felt just now walking down that hall with you. Would you be open to hearing about that?" He seemed surprised but nodded that he was interested. "It reminded me of being a little kid; it was as if my big father is charging ahead because he is much more important, and his time is so much more valuable than mine. It made me feel that you believe that you are very important but that I'm not."

Sam looked stunned. For a moment he did nothing. Then he seemed to reflect on something. I asked, "What are you thinking?"

"I am remembering something my CFO said to me earlier this week. He hasn't been speaking to me for three months and this week he told me why. He said it was because I was so arrogant and he couldn't take it."

"It must have really hurt you to hear that."

Sam was moved and he nodded thoughtfully. I asked if we could talk about this relationship and again Sam nodded agreement. We then examined at some length the situation between himself and the CFO and the difficulties, the struggles, and some of the painful conversations. We also developed an action plan to deal with the CFO. At the end of this conversation I said, "I'm curious about something. Was your CFO on your agenda today?" He looked down at his notes, then pursed his lips in embarrassment. "No, he wasn't. But it is the most important thing going on in my organization right now."

Being alert for the coaching opportunity, whenever it strikes, is a key factor in becoming a competent coach and includes making the following observations:

- What is going on internally?
- What is going on externally?
- Is my internal response linked to the external conditions? In what way?

When I can answer these questions, my next step is to comment on the external condition, my internal response, and the link in such a way that the client is able to learn something valuable from the interchange.

This process assumes that what is happening to me as a coach is also happening to many of the other people who encounter my client. My reaction is a sample of the kind of responses that my client evokes in others. If I can articulate this reaction in a language my client can grasp, then I give the client information that is usually unavailable to him or her. To avoid the possible claim that I may be evoking the response, or selectively attending to particular responses, I use my reaction as a starting point of inquiry rather than proof of a judgment about the client. If the client accepts my observation, we frequently can reveal a whole new territory for learning.

I used this process also with George, a CEO of an 8 million dollar software firm. After our first handshake, George launched into a litany of concerns, troubles, difficulties, and confusions, showing how one problem led to much bigger problems, which spawned several even greater problems in an unending plethora of difficulties. I felt myself quickly swept into a current of confusion and my mind began to spin. This is a very uncommon occurrence for me. In order to slow things down, I intervened to ask a question, but George was in the middle of a domino-effect type of story that seemed to have no end. And it gained momentum as it went. Despite the fact that it caused him pain and agony in the telling, he did not seem capable of letting it go. He was overwhelmed and yet his style of speech was overwhelming himself even more. At this point I was also at the point of becoming overwhelmed. I interrupted him in the middle of his story (a story without end is always in the middle) and asked him to stop. Eventually he did. Then I said, "I am having a very difficult time keeping up with you. Would it be okay with you if I explained my difficulty?" He nodded and said, "Sure."

I then said, "When I asked one question, you began to answer but then you shifted to a new topic. That topic then led to another and then another. Very soon I became lost and I can't remember what it was we were trying to talk about. I wonder if that has been a problem with other people you see."

George laughed. "Every day! Marie, my director of marketing, comes in here and we have discussions for hours and hours and when we get done I feel like we just wasted all of our time chasing our tails. We never get anything done and we don't end up understanding each other any better at the end than we did at the beginning."

I nodded. "I was starting to have that same feeling. I was having such a hard time following the discussion that my mind began to spin. Would you be willing to talk about how we might work on that problem of creating confusion in conversation?"

"Absolutely! It is one of the biggest problems I have—getting people to understand what I mean and getting them to do it!"

I then explained the concept of "framing" to help him understand what might be missing in his conversation. "Do you see that picture over there on the wall?" He nodded. "Do you see that it has a frame around it?" He nodded again. "What do you think that frame is for?"

"To hold it up, to protect it, to give it a way to hang on the wall. I don't know!"

I said, "Yes, all those things are right. But there is something else. The frame is there to help you to see where the wall ends and the picture begins. It helps you define where the picture is so that you can look at it more closely if you want to. Do you agree that the frame also helps you to do that?" George nodded.

"You see, a picture is different than wallpaper. Wallpaper has no frame.

It's just all over the wall. After a while it's hard to see the wallpaper, it just blends in. Do you agree?" George nodded. "Well, ideas are the same way. When ideas run into each other, when they stack up on top of each other, they are like wallpaper. After a while you stop seeing them. If you want someone to pay attention to your ideas, you have to frame them one at a time. Like a picture. So to be an effective communicator, you need to have one idea and frame it by telling people what the idea is and why it's important. Then talk about that idea, just like you might talk about that very interesting picture of that green 1957 Chevy that you have over there in the corner. We could spend five minutes talking about just that picture. Then when we were finished, we could talk about another picture, which has its own frame, its own importance. Ideas are just like that. If you want someone to understand you, you must frame your idea and stay within that frame until you have explored it thoroughly and decided what you want to do with it. Then, when the discussion is complete, leave that idea and go to a new one with its own frame. What do you think of that idea?"

George was stunned. "I never thought about that before. All my life I had the feeling that I couldn't get through to people. I thought they just wouldn't listen to me. So I just spoke louder and more forcefully and kept pounding away at them. I never thought that what I needed to do was to 'frame' my ideas so that people could notice them. I really need to think about this. Maybe we can talk some more about this next time because it seems like this is a real shift in the way I do things."

Later that night I received an e-mail from George saying that our session was a mind-altering experience. Since then George has become much more conscious about how he speaks to people and how he frames his thoughts. He still has tremendous difficulties, but he is conscious of them and is working on them.

CEOs are the power center of their organization. They are the leader and, as such, are frequently the creator of the company culture, values, and strategic direction. Yet with all their power and prestige, I have found that working with them alone is not sufficient to change an organization. In order to do that, I must make a significant impact on the entire executive team. It is through them that the CEO's intentions are carried out. For this reason I now work intensively with CEOs and their executive team in order to foster communication and build the skills necessary for productive confrontation. I have found the following patterns in all organizations.*

1. CEOs base their key decisions on tacit assumptions and beliefs about the strategic goals of the company and the skill, performance level, and commitment of the executive team and employees.
2. The assumptions and beliefs of the executive team frequently differ dramatically from those of the CEO.
3. The executive team frequently covers up the divergence of assumptions because they view divulging differences as damaging their own future success in the company.
4. The greater the degree of divergence between the assumptions held by the CEO and those held by the executive team the poorer the performance of the company.

Most executive teams face a powerful dilemma: If they divulge their own beliefs, they may damage their personal future with the company; if they do not divulge their beliefs, they may damage the future growth of the company. Faced with this dilemma, many executives do not divulge their beliefs. As a result, many companies do not grow at optimal speed.

While I focus my work with CEOs in the context of their executive team, my client remains the CEO; I work with him or her in relationship with the whole company. This may mean that I will have individual sessions with members of the team in addition to those I have with the CEO. It also means that I "qualify" the CEO by testing his or her ability to respond productively when confronted. This capacity becomes crucial in group situations where I coach executives in how to effectively confront each other.

In order to obtain a context for an intervention, I first conduct a confidential individual survey with each member of the team. The survey is designed to uncover what each member believes to be true about what is working well in the company and what is not working well. The interview

---

*Much of the following is adapted from the work of Chris Argyris, *On Organizational Learning,* and from conversations with coach Don Rossmoore as a participant in his study groups.

explores in depth the assessments of the member and endeavors to obtain descriptions of specific actions or events to ground the assessments. The results of the survey are collected and analyzed for themes, insights, concerns, and roadblocks to success. Issues related to leadership, marketing, sales, operations, and strategic direction are specific targets of analysis.

I present the results to the whole executive team with the CEO present. This process raises the stakes for honesty. I confront the CEO on the major issues that have been expressed during the survey. The CEO then demonstrates productive defensiveness. This shows the team that the CEO can be confronted and it demonstrates exactly how to do it. I then encourage them to confront the CEO productively and to confront one another. I coach them to do it and to summarize what they hear before they respond. The results process requires the better part of a day, and as it proceeds, anxiety levels rise. Executives enter a new territory of honesty and vulnerability.

I recently received a phone call from Susan, a vice president of a regional software firm who was participating in the survey process. She was furious. She told me that her CEO, Tom, had agreed to lay off several of her people as part of a company-wide layoff. Then two days later, without her knowledge, he hired back one of her people—the very one she wanted gone forever. And he hired her back into Susan's department! The executive team had been working with Tom for months to let go of the reins so that they could be in charge of their own departments without his interference. He continually agreed. Now he was again intervening and destroying many of her plans. I summarized what she told me and inquired about how she might express her concerns directly to Tom. This terrified her—she was much too volatile and was worried she would blow up, particularly since he added insult to injury by complaining about her to a person who worked for her. Now she did not know where she stood with him. Is he considering letting her go too? I summarized what she had said and suggested that all of these concerns should be brought up directly with Tom in their next conversation. By the end of the call, Susan was ready to address her issues directly with Tom. She later told me that she felt confident and calm in her presentation and that Tom listened very carefully. She felt she had made a significant step in expressing herself fully to her boss under high-stress conditions.

In the above examples I have tried to demonstrate some of the ways I intervene as an executive coach. Many times this is done in a one-on-one context where the purpose is to help the executive recognize his own contribution to a hidden but highly significant problem. When I work with executive teams, most of my work focuses on helping them to deliver their points of view productively under difficult conditions. I also assist them in becoming able to listen to different views and summarize what they heard. When the executive team learns how to do this, there is a boost in morale and a deeper commitment to the strategic goals of the company.

PRACTICAL INFORMATION

ADVICE FOR NEW EXECUTIVE COACHES

1. CEOs are people. Our culture tends to idealize them. Partly this is because we worship money and partly it is because we have very powerful responses to all authority figures. These emotional reactions interfere with responding to CEOs in ways that can help them.
2. Most people do not give CEOs direct feedback, for reasons listed in number one. They are starved for this. If you can provide it, you will be highly valued.
3. If you can hold the CEO accountable, in the same way you expect him or her to hold others accountable, you will be highly valued. This means you need to learn the skill of confronting. And you need to find out if the CEO you work with is "confrontable." That is, you must answer the question: "Can this person productively respond to my confrontations?" This can only be answered empirically. You must confront him or her and find out if this confrontation leads to productive change.

ADVICE FOR NEW THERAPIST-COACHES

1. Coaching is different from, though related to therapy. Find an experienced coach to provide mentoring and coaching to you. Enroll in a certified coaching program to get training.
2. Find a support group of other coaches with whom to meet on a regular basis for study and case review.

MY FEES

I charge $300 per hour for individual consultations. I don't charge extra for phone calls or e-mails unless these become a burden. However, most of my work now is with executive teams. I do individual surveys with team members and then I report the results in a group context with the CEO present. I demonstrate how to confront the CEO in a productive way and I invite the executive team to bring their major issues to the table. I may survey 15 to 18 people. These would be members of the executive team and some of the people who report to them. It takes about one month to do the survey, analyze the data, and report it to the group. I charge $30,000 for the survey and $10,000 per month to coach the executive team through the next year.

WHAT I KNOW NOW

Coaching is very different from therapy. It is much more results-oriented. It is focused in reality and not in the intrapsychic world, and therefore requires strong abilities in the area of interpersonal influence, particularly in the area of how to give direct feedback and how to confront productively. These skills can be obtained in specially designed coaching groups.

A BRIEF BIOGRAPHY

I received a Ph.D. in educational psychology from University of California at Berkeley and did postgraduate work at Stanford University. I practiced psychotherapy for 13 years before becoming a coach. I gradually became interested in corporate coaching as a result of having several CEO clients. Through friends I found other psychologists who made the leap from therapist to corporate coach and inquired how they made that transition. Several of them suggested that I contact TECWorldwide, an international company that develops CEOs and corporate executives. I did that and received an interview and then an offer to join the company.

I was trained at TECWorldwide in how to market to CEOs, lead groups of CEOs, and how to coach them one-on-one. I later became a trainer of new coaches for this company. I also became a member of a consultation group, led by a master coach, Don Rossmoore, which engages in full consultations with CEOs and executive teams. I am currently involved in the

Newfield Network, a program specializing in the training of coaches at a variety of levels of experience.

Many people helped me get to where I am today. TECWorldwide had many mentors and coaches who were very helpful. I also had my own coach. Don Rossmoore has been an important mentor. David Bradford at Stanford Business School helped to train me to lead groups of MBA students. This was excellent training for interpersonal work. I also received much encouragement and direction from friends who are coaches.

CONTACT INFORMATION

Robert Niederman, Ph.D.
801 Church Street, Suite 1235
Mountain View, CA 94041
Phone: 650-966-1162
E-mail: bobn@batnet.com

2

The Leadership Edge

Hannah S. Wilder

What do tadpoles growing into frogs have to do with leadership coaching? As a child I lived near a stream, and spent hours watching tadpoles being born, swimming, and developing into frogs. I noticed them lose their tails and grow legs, so they could move not only in the water, but also come out on dry land and hop around, sticking out their long tongues to catch flies for dinner. I learned that growth and transformation are natural; they just require the right conditions. No one was giving these frogs a workshop on becoming amphibious. I also learned that taking them home in a jar, even with a hole punched in the lid "so they could breathe" didn't provide what they needed, and that when the conditions for nurturing life aren't present, living things lose their vitality and eventually die.

Frogs are lucky. Their natural instincts tell them most of what they need to know: that it's time to use those legs and hop around on the land, what to look for when they get there, how to survive and thrive. It's a whole new world, but one their nervous system somehow recognizes, acting as an inner guide for exploration and getting basic frog needs met. Some even become exceptional, like the one in Mark Twain's story, "The Celebrated Jumping Frogs of Calaveras County." And just as frogs evolve from tadpoles, the truth is that all leaders begin their lives as babies wearing diapers.

The difference between people and frogs is that we humans have cultural and mental obstacles to accessing our basic instincts. Our perceptions of reality are structured by culturebound ideas, to which we become so attached that we talk ourselves out of what we really know. One of the limiting ideas of our culture is that people can be sorted into two categories: those with "leadership potential" and "others." As anyone who has analyzed team behavior knows, there are many different kinds of leadership: bringing people back to task, building consensus, innovating, stimulating ideas, encouraging risk-taking, and so on. Like tadpoles, leaders need the right conditions for vitality, the time and space to transform into all that they can be. Then most of us, I believe, can develop and move from one situation to another, becoming, in our own way, "amphibious." Indeed, fast-paced corporate life and global expansion are making this adaptive quality a highly sought-after leadership skill. We excel in areas where our natural inclinations are nurtured, and develop in areas we find challenging, stretching ourselves beyond familiar territory.

Usually we get stuck or make mistakes when we talk ourselves out of what we really know. Much of my work as a leadership coach is about assisting my clients to reconnect with what they already know deep down, and bring it to the surface. It's my job to nurture the internal conditions for strengthening their instincts and trusting their authentic selves. Then, no matter what the challenge, they can go inside and come out with their best approach. Executives are moving up and facing new situations so quickly these days that this internal foundation is essential for maintaining equilibrium in the face of shifting external conditions. An encounter with a new situation or culture always brings us face to face with ourselves in a new way. We do best when we know our own core, and become comfortable with not knowing precisely what is around the next corner, where the next "growing edge" is heading our way.

CREATING THE STRUCTURE FOR NATURAL TRANSFORMATION

Rae was a corporate executive who called me because she was dissatisfied with her annual performance review. She'd seen an article I wrote and wanted to meet with me. At lunch she was open with me about some developmental areas that needed immediate attention. They were long-standing habits she perceived as interfering with her effectiveness. She described her working environment as politically complex with a lot of public exposure. She thought coaching might help and wanted to "try it for a month."

Internally, I smiled to myself. My years as a therapist had taught me well how people change, and that sooner or later something inside them, or the system around them, will resist change. That's when they need the most support, where a container for the growth relationship is essential. With her long-standing habits, I suspected that Rae was going to hit that wall fairly soon, and at that point she might give up on herself and coaching.

But I like a good challenge, have a strong belief in the power of coaching, and trust my instincts. I'm comfortable working with powerful people, and had a gut feeling that I was going to learn a lot here. If this was going to work, I would need to pull in everything I knew. And I had to begin by creating a clear structure for the coaching relationship, so that Rae could feel safe taking personal risks. I admired her courage in calling me, and felt honored that she had asked me to be her partner in making some maximal impact changes.

I told Rae that I had a three-month minimum and explained that it would take at least that long for her to know whether this coaching relationship was going to work. Together we created a contract stating how often we'd meet, what the areas of focus would be, and a few other operating principles. It also specified that I would be paid in advance for three months. This last part was unusual for her, but I was firm and she agreed. We shook hands and set up our first series of meetings.

Unlike the therapy relationship, where the client comes in wanting help with a problem and hoping that the professional has the answers, coaching, especially with leaders, is a partnership of equals right from the start. The client has all the answers, and the coach draws them out through artful questioning; together we create the best strategy for getting to where the client wants to go. It's designed for action in the present and future, rather than resolving things from the past. Sometimes successful present actions do resolve past patterns, but that's not the primary objective of coaching.

PEELING THE ONION

Rae had been criticized for not providing enough strategic leadership. As a woman, she felt particularly sensitive about this, so this part of her performance evaluation had hit a raw nerve. She'd always prided herself on being accessible to her managers and others in the organization, so she was excellent at operations and building good relationships, but tended to get overwhelmed and bogged down with requests for her attention. This cost her time and energy for strategic planning. All leaders face the challenge of gaining control of their own schedules and finding some balance, but this developmental challenge was at the top of the agenda for her.

After agreeing that she needed a high-level assistant who could assume some of the accessibility and project supervision pressure, and setting the hiring process in motion, we turned to her schedule. It was a process of peeling away layers to get at the heart of the matter. Since I knew she was chronically late for appointments, I asked: What kinds of boundaries do you have around starting and ending your appointments? At what point do you bring in your own agenda? What's the best way of concluding an appointment and moving on? My questions provided information for me, and raised her awareness about what the real issues were. Her answers provided clues to changes that needed to happen.

Rae saw that her chronic lateness and sense of feeling overwhelmed were a result of not introducing her own agenda at the beginning of a meeting. Priding herself on being accessible and responsive, she listened to the other person first, and brought her concerns or priorities in only at the end. This made her late for her next appointment and created a chronic feeling that she had to rush to make up for lost time. She became proactive in getting her own agenda addressed up front. We did some role-plays, bringing in her concerns and issues at the beginning so that they were handled, and she could then turn to what others in the meeting wanted. We also practiced giving others a five-minute warning to maximize getting their needs met before the appointment ended. If more time was required, she would schedule another time with that person and go on promptly to her next meeting. She was proud that she could now set some limits and manage her accessibility without offending people (one of her lifelong concerns).

When I next saw her in person, her face looked much lighter, her expression more relaxed. She reported that the feeling of being constantly overwhelmed had changed to a sense of choice and purpose. She was now able to listen more generously to others, so her connections with her subordinates and peers actually deepened and strengthened, even though she spent less time with them. "They respect me more now, and I'm more relaxed and responsive to them when it's appropriate. When I'm there, now I'm *really* there."

HITTING THE GREAT WALL

After just a few weeks, Rae had made substantial changes in some of her basic behaviors. She was also facing a major change in her perception of who she was in the world. As we worked together, I sensed that she was trying to operate in a mode that wasn't in sync with who she was. This is a common challenge for women executives, since the workplace culture has been shaped by men for decades and tends to emphasize competitiveness and aggression. So that she could become more aware of herself and where the fit wasn't working, I asked her questions like "What was going on then?" and "Who were you when this happened?" This allowed her to develop a dual-level reflective observation (sometimes challenging for action-oriented people). She began to see that her social conditioning as a woman had oriented her to sacrifice and self-effacement, whereas her leadership position called for self-confidence and clear priorities. She was having trouble creating and holding a "big picture" vision because her background had not entitled or trained her to do this. As we started to look at how this might change, she came up against some strong family and ethnic conditioning.

The pressure was on. Her progress was beginning to reach critical momentum, and she was both planning a retreat for her executive staff and approaching her next performance review. It was about this time that what I had predicted happened: She began to have doubts about continuing coaching. She began a session by saying, "Coaching feels like just one more thing I have to do! How many more sessions do we have?" My experience as a therapist had prepared me to stand for success when the client finds the going tough. I knew she had the capacity to sustain her awareness, continue developing her innate strengths, and tackle some of her biggest challenges, but at that particular moment, she didn't believe any of this in her bones. My job was to do that for her. I remember thinking, "This must be how an athletic coach feels when his players threaten to walk off the field."

Leadership coaching is not for the faint of heart. The qualities of an excellent leader and of a good leadership coach are very similar. Being able to hold a sense of stability and success for my clients when they are under pressure from all sides is crucial, just as holding that for followers is important for a leader. Years of working with therapy clients who were suffering, but not quite ready to give up the habits that created their suffering, had prepared me to stand fast. With both therapy and coaching clients, what I want is for them to feel successful and peaceful.

I calmly replied that she was halfway through her weekly sessions and we had six more that had been prepaid. I waited a few minutes and asked, "So, how can we make the best use of them?" She smiled and sighed (I'm still not sure whether in relief or resignation). After thinking for a few minutes, she said, "Well, my board of directors is not really working well together, and I don't know how to help them. Is there some way we can work on that?" "Aha," I thought to myself, "this is going to be fun!" My early academic research background in power and influence relationships had been very helpful in my counseling, consulting, and training career, and I was more than ready to jump in. "Sure, we could," I replied.

This turned out to be one of the most powerful themes in our coaching relationship, because a major shift occurred in her sense of what was her responsibility and within her control, and what wasn't. The persistent infighting and criticism among board members had been making her job difficult for years. She seemed to take this pattern on as her responsibility, thinking that if she did something differently, everyone would somehow work together harmoniously. But the persistence gave me a clue that it was rooted in the system itself, so I asked her questions that gave me information about that system and prompted her to reflect on what her responsibility did and didn't include: Who are the players and what are their behaviors? How does succession to leadership on the board come about? Was all this true before you came, or did it begin when you arrived?

Together we began to see that the succession structure itself made infighting and criticism inevitable. "I never saw that before," she said, with some surprise. "All this time, I kept thinking that it was me, that there was something I wasn't doing right." While she couldn't change the situation, her realization normalized the situation for her and allowed her to detach from some of the struggle.

I found myself wondering if her frustration with the situation had also been a result of her general discomfort with conflict, and asked her about that. She said that yes, as a matter of fact it had also been a long-standing pattern for her to try and manage conflict so that she felt safe. In my experience as a therapist, fear is usually a prime motivation for controlling behavior or an exaggerated sense of responsibility. As a therapist, I might have explored the roots of this discomfort in Rae's childhood, but that didn't seem necessary, since she was ready to move on. The infighting continued, but she was able to avoid getting hooked into or bandied about by the perpetual fray because she saw its source and her own relationship to it in a new light. Her detachment allowed her to be more comfortable with the fact that conflict was taking place.

I asked her to tell me about the members of the board and how they behaved, both individually and as a group. As she relayed her perceptions, I reflected back in summary form what I heard. "You've got it! They're really all over the place," she said. "So," I asked, "what kind of strategic alliances could you form to create some working relationships and counterbalance the infighting? Who's easiest for you to talk to and work with?" She came up with the names of two board members with whom spending some extra time just might make a difference. It worked. She partially neutralized some of the strife in how the members worked with one another. Forming these two strategic alliances paid off in another, unexpected, way. One was eventually appointed chairman of the board, and the fact that Rae had invested the time and energy to establish a good working relationship with him made her job much, much easier.

KICKING THE WORRY HABIT

Rae often stayed awake at night worrying about things at work, especially after a board meeting. Looking closely at her habit of worrying, we found two ways to change how she framed her relationship to her responsibilities. First, after taking whatever actions she could before going home, she learned to let go of work-related concerns at night by "making an appointment to worry" the next morning. When she was fresh and rested, the attention to the issue at hand took the form of realistic assessment instead of worry. Second, I knew from the initial interview that she was a Christian, so, in a light tone, I asked her if she thought that the other people in her organization had the same higher power she did. "Oh, yes," she replied. "Well then, do you think that you could hand over the responsibility while you get some sleep?" I asked. Rae assumed too much personal responsibility for everything that happened in her sphere of influence, a common pitfall for executives. She got the point, and used prayer as a way to release her worry each evening. It took some practice, but gradually the "appointments to worry" and the prayers took the place of her ruminations.

Anxiety and "busyness" have long been linked habits for Rae, and I find this is common for executives. Appearing busy is seen as a good thing in our culture, and if one is a leader, the busier the better. I shared with her some ways to use the power of the quiet mind to build a foundation of mental stability and clarity so that decision-making, time management, team leadership, and strategic planning could all flow much more easily. Gradually, she learned to sit quietly, focus on her breath, walk, and do everyday tasks in such a way that calm and thoughtfulness prevailed. Carrying this over into professional areas has made it possible for her to stay present with what she is doing, and move forward smoothly.

BALANCING WORK AND LEISURE

Dividing her attention between work and home life was another area where Rae reflected the executive's classic dilemma. She worked long hours, often on weekends, and almost never took enough leisure time or relaxation. We made a list of habits Rae could develop to keep herself in balance and move toward relaxing. Her "field work" between sessions included doing a minimum number of these per day. She found that walking helped her to clear her mind and solve problems or even leave thoughts of work behind. She also went to the gym and used the exercise bicycle, which helped her to think with a fresh mind. We also looked at setting up some vacations where she left her laptop, cell phone, and briefcase behind. Being completely off duty for a certain period of time is essential for everyone, but is especially challenging and important for executives, who tend to think that things at work will fall apart if they are not there running them. Discovering that life and work go on in their absence often helps them to delegate more effectively when they return.

During the next month, Rae created some time for planning, and worked on a proposal that she would present at an upcoming company retreat. To do this, she had to find a place to "hide out" in a quiet, inaccessible place for several hours a couple of times a week. She was able to come up with a strategic plan that laid out her company's path for the next year. She was really proud when she reported this to me, and I cheered with her.

It's true that it's lonely at the top, but having a trusted partner makes it much less so, and helps bring out the best in leaders. They feel that someone who really knows what they are facing each day is standing behind them. Often there is no one but the coach who really appreciates how much a particular accomplishment means to executives. Celebrating successes with my clients is one of the best parts of being an executive coach.

Going Forward

After another month and a half Rae had come to the point where the initial three-month commitment for our coaching partnership was ending. Since she had wanted to stop earlier, I fully expected that she would thank me and move on. We had accomplished a lot together, and she had reached her initial goals. I felt sure that she would do much better on her upcoming performance review, and made a mental note to ask her to let me know how that went.

We agreed to meet for lunch. I came feeling relaxed and prepared to review with her what she had accomplished. I had a list of areas for her to pay attention to on her own. Of course, I would offer that she could contact me for a session from time to time on an "as-needed" basis, something I am always willing to do with established clients.

To my amazement, she showed up with her file and the original client information form, which she had never finished filling out. She had also done a session prep form; while most of my clients do this weekly, this was a first for Rae. It includes sections on successes, challenges, opportunities, and focus for the session. "You know, doing this prep thing really was enjoyable," she said. "I learned a lot just by looking everything over and getting ready for today. Could we continue coaching?"

Her performance review went very well, and she began to look ahead to her future with a greater sense of choice and enthusiasm. Rae has continued to inspire me with her courage and willingness to take risks. She has examined what really excites her and made some major personal and professional changes.

After working in her field for over a decade on a salaried basis, she decided to go out on her own as a consultant. That transition was probably the most challenging step she'd taken in her life. When drawing a healthy salary, she didn't often think about what her contributions were worth financially, so as she began her own business she seriously underpriced her work. At one point I actually laughed and said, "Rae, do me a favor. Tell them you will get back to them about the price, and call me before you do, okay?" She needed some mentoring on making the shift from salaried executive to sole proprietor and turning what she did into a business.

Rae realized that there is really only one city where she felt at home, so she moved back there, found a life partner, and established a lucrative consulting business. She's become fascinated with leadership, her own and models that work for this time in history. "My life has really come together the way I want it," she said.

If Rae had come to me as a therapy client, I would have expected to see more concern over the origins of her "long-standing habits," and I might have worked with her in the mode of what I called "archeology of the heart," looking into her past for the roots of her current behavior. I was an unusual therapist in that I worked within a relational model. Though I didn't bring unresolved issues of my own into the relationship, I let my clients know that they affected me. I was never a "blank slate" to them, since I consider this stance disempowering. I was a real person who was present for their deepest moments of self-exploration. However, as a coach, I feel much freer to come forth, to challenge and question more directly, and to focus on actions for the present and future, to make requests (which can be rejected, accepted, or negotiated). It isn't the roots of the behaviors that we spend time on, but how to make changes that will serve the client better. In coaching, we don't need to unravel and reknit the client's life so thoroughly; instead, we figure out how to go from here to there, and "there" is defined by the client right from the beginning of our relationship and reconfigured as we progress.

Working with Rae, who has inspired me as much as I have her, I realized that leadership coaching was where I wanted to stay and deepen my experience. I've been a leader in my own life, worked with media leaders and government officials, and my Ph.D. was in the study of political behavior, including leadership. After becoming a coach, I decided that whatever was going on in this field, I wanted to know about it, learn from it, and contribute to it, so I looked around for a group to join. Since I didn't find one, I created it. The Leadership Coaching Special Interest Group, open to all leadership coaches regardless of training, has been meeting monthly by telephone for over a year and a half now. It's a forum for discussing resources and approaches for leadership and executive coaching and draws on models and coaches from all over the world.

I'm a firm believer that a leadership coach must also be a leader, so that she or he can walk beside clients with credibility and courage. Leaders have strong egos for the most part, and it's important to be both truthful and trustworthy. The best leaders are always learning, being led, exploring—as, I believe, are the best leadership coaches. We know that our client partnerships with leaders help them make a difference in the world by supporting them in being who they really are: people embracing life in the present by creating new agendas for the future.

PRACTICAL INFORMATION

ADVICE FOR NEW LEADERSHIP COACHES

1. A leadership coach needs to know how to facilitate demonstrable change and growth in both people and systems and how to focus on performance as well as self-fulfillment and balance between work and leisure.
2. To be effective and credible, a leadership coach needs leadership or executive experience and a good understanding of power and influence relationships. You must enjoy working with powerful people.

3. Leadership coaches have to understand and exemplify leadership development and be familiar with feedback instruments. They must also possess strong relational and communications skills and high ethical standards. Leadership coaches are strategic partners with executives and teams and, in some ways, function as "shadow" leaders.

4. Be a leader yourself, and one who is willing to be led. Your clients will know more about their own particular areas of leadership than you may, and you need to be a "quick study" in order to walk beside them. In this "fast company" world, you will be a good role model for your clients.

ADVICE FOR NEW THERAPIST-COACHES

1. Clarify your own basic values and narrow them down to two or three. Use these as a basis for setting up your life. Then, set up your practice to support your value-based life. This will support you in strengthening your personal and professional foundation.

2. Play from the strengths of the training you have in understanding human development, emotional processing, and compassion, and develop the ability to challenge and inspire your clients in ways that are more direct than you would use as a therapist.

3. Actively cultivate equanimity and joy in your life, so that you can balance being in the moment for yourself with being there for others.

MY FEES

$900 to $1500 per month per client (depending on the client and their constituency), or monthly retainer fee for volume contract coaching with corporations (setting aside a certain number of hours for that company's leaders). Work with executive teams is by contract and the fee depends on the specific circumstances and the number of people and amount of time involved.

WHAT I KNOW NOW

1. How much I already knew, and how much I love this work!

2. How useful mindfulness practice (stopping and looking deeply at the present moment) and my background in political behavior is in executive coaching. I'm much more relaxed and in my stride now, and this makes it easy to hit the ground running. Both the coaching relationship

and the client progress faster because I know the value of what I bring to the situation.

A BRIEF BIOGRAPHY

I have a lifetime interest in international leadership studies, power and influence relationships, and communication, and have explored these as I earned a Ph.D. in political behavior and communication from M.I.T. and an M.A. from Harvard University. I've been a leader myself in educational and professional settings where I've taught human services, women's studies, and social science (at six colleges and universities). I also served as executive director of a health education organization and as marketing coordinator for an international corporation in the semiconductor industry.

As a therapist I was a licensed clinical mental health counselor (LPCC) in two states, with 13 years in private practice and clinical programs. I taught at the university level in multicultural counseling, clinical assessment and intervention, ethics and internship supervision and served as coordinator of the Human Services Program at the University of New Mexico Taos Education Center.

I'm a graduate of Coach University, a member of the International Coach Federation, the Virginia Chapter of ICF, and the Central Virginia Personal and Business Coaches Alliance. I mentor coaches on three continents and currently lead two large virtual monthly special interest groups for coaches: Global Practice Coaching and Leadership Coaching. I am a certified teleclass leader, a teleclass leader trainer, and a faculty member at WomensU.com. I am the founding director of a global leadership coaching consortium and have trained facilitators at the Federal Executive Institute to lead virtual teams of high-level government executives. I've worked with leaders at AT&T Solutions and other corporations, national and international media organizations in east and west Europe and Africa, Planned Parenthood, professional health associations, municipal governments. Global, cross-cultural work has always inspired and enriched me, so I've made this a special interest in coaching.

Those who have been influential in where I am as a coach are: my coaches Denslow Brown and Cynder Niemela; my mindfulness teachers, Vietnamese Zen Master Thich Nhat Hanh, his niece Anh Huong Nguyen and her husband Thu Nguyen; my lifelong beloved friend, Laurens Monroe Vernon; many wonderful colleagues in the coaching profession (especially A. Gayle Hudgens, Denise Brouillette, Jay Perry, Michael Sheffield, Cheryl Weir and the coaches from the Global Practice, Leadership Coaching and ICF Women's Coaching Special Interest Groups); my partners in global executive transitions work and my wonderful clients, who are a constant source of inspiration and learning. My family heritage of spirituality and independence from the island of Nantucket has also contributed to who I am as a coach, and my company, Wiseheart Global Leadership Coaching, is named for my grandmother's grandmother, Charlotte Wiseheart, of Loudoun County, Virginia.

CONTACT INFORMATION

Hannah S. Wilder, M.A., Ph.D.
Phone: 800-267-2520 or 434-466-4606
E-mail: Hannah@Wiseheartcoach.com
Web sites: www.wiseheartcoach.com; www.globaleadershipcoaching.com

3

Dysfunction or Discovery: A Former Therapist Becomes an Executive Coach

Patrick Williams

Mike knew this was the end of the line. His company had referred him to an executive coach, and that must mean trouble. Mike's background, similar to many men's today, was "old school" and had taught him that seeking outside help meant you were weak. Strong men didn't do that. Strong men didn't need help. Capable managers didn't need executive coaches. Yes, he concluded, he was in trouble . . . and, at the very least, at a crossroads.

Mike had heard a little about coaching. But what *really* was an executive coach? Wasn't that just some psychologist in coach clothing? When we began our work, Mike had what I would call mild angst. Unanswered questions filled him with dread. What was happening to him, and where would all this lead? Was he on his way out of this company? If Mike had been referred to me as a therapist with this type of dread, I might have looked for the symptoms of anxiety or depression toward a *DSM-IV* diagnosis. As a coach, however, I assumed no pathology. If clinical symptoms arose I would refer him for therapy.

Mike was the chief financial officer of a growing robotics company. He had 6 other managers reporting to him and was responsible for two departments of about 28 employees as well as a large budget and financial information for the company's U.S. operations. It was a stressful job at times although a great company to work for, and he seemed happy to be part of the team. His previous jobs had ended either because of mergers or because he was unhappy in the job. He had been referred to coaching by the company CEO and the company was paying the bill. This is often the case in executive coaching and sets up a potentially sticky triangle with the company and the coachee.

Technically, the company was the client because they were paying the bill, but Mike was the client being coached. I always negotiate with the company up front, explaining that the details of the coaching conversations will be confidential and clarifying what kind of reporting the company needs and what outcomes they are expecting. Otherwise details are kept between my coachee and me.

Fueling Mike's wariness about coaching was his own employment history. He had recently moved to his current company from a similar high-level position in another company, and before that yet another company had terminated him coldly—a casualty of a messy merger. Then there was the position that just plain didn't work out, in another organization. Mike had been scorched. And now he was skeptical. Did this company really want him to improve his managerial skills, or was this all a big ruse to dismiss him later? The questions kept coming with no real answers.

A corporate trainer originally hired by Mike's high-tech company to work with their management team referred Mike to me. She was doing some organizational consulting and team-building with the management team. During the course of this training, it was soon obvious that all the training in the world would not benefit a team whose manager not only had an old-school mind-set, but also old-school management skills. Mike was effectively preventing the training from taking hold and yielding positive results—he was a micromanager, more of a "boss" than a leader. Quite literally, the buck stopped with Mike, and so did any growth of his team.

Not wanting to be herded out the door before what he thought was "due time," Mike reluctantly agreed to coaching. On the surface he was open to being coached, but still quite wary. My first meeting with Mike was in person. While much of executive coaching is conducted over the telephone, face-to-face meetings are often beneficial, especially in the early stages of coaching, and especially with someone like Mike. It was essential to establish his trust and achieve his buy-in. I explained how I work, and that I believe in the ability of people to discover their own personal brilliance and lead the most fulfilling life possible. I am a facilitator, one who could help him live the life of his dreams in all areas, not just those defined by his work role.

As a former therapist, what I didn't tell him was that this process might sometimes involve helping to heal wounds and eradicate major emotional blocks. The goal, however, is getting to the place where the client can develop and live the life he or she wants to live. My work does not involve just the workplace, though that is often the beginning focal point. It doesn't matter why I begin the coaching process with someone—to improve the client's work, help him or her move up the ladder, become a better manager, or make an important transition—life in general is improved. This is total life coaching, working with the client to create the total life he or she wants to live. Life coaching is the umbrella under which everything else resides and, in fact, I have developed and adopted this practice as a systematic methodology.

CREATING THE COACHING ALLIANCE

This kind of talk wasn't what Mike was expecting. He was prepared for a lecture, some sort of negative appraisal of his management skills and a psychological shakedown, along with a prescription for remedial work. Once Mike understood what I was about, he could understand what the coaching sessions were about. He could understand that his company was not pouring money into him to fire him. I could see Mike's wariness dim, and the life improvement prospect coming into clear and distinct focus. Soon, Mike thought all of this sounded pretty good, and he realized that he really did want to be a better manager and live a better life.

In this initial meeting I encouraged Mike to tell me about his work and home. I asked him a lot of questions, all targeted at the positive influences and experiences in his work and life. I wanted to know his career story, what he liked about his job, what was going well. I peppered him with questions designed to draw out his strengths, which is always my first focus. What is your perfect day? When are you at your best? What parts of your life and work are the easiest, the most joyful? It is only after exhausting all these possibilities that the talk is turned to the challenges. I avoid words like *issues, obstacles,* or *hurdles.* Coaching is always about the positive. This does not mean the negatives are ignored; it merely means they can become strengths if addressed properly, and not immediately labeled as weaknesses. When the positives are the framework of all coaching objectives, the transitions become much more powerful. The whole coaching process is focused on creating and becoming who and what one wants to be, and achieving goals for life and work.

In therapy, this process yields what is eventually called the "presenting complaint or problem." This "complaint" then becomes the issue around which therapy sessions are focused, with the underlying thought, in both the therapist's and the patient's mind, that they are working to overcome deficiencies. (Even in solution-focused therapy, which is less pathologically driven, it is assumed that a problem warrants a solution.) In coaching, however, complaints or desires become the "presenting objectives." This term is less pathological, and weaknesses then become targeted strengths. Instead of the paradigm of pathology, coaching presents the paradigm of possibility. It is here that I often see the client's proverbial light bulb not just flicker, but surge to life. A huge step has already been taken, perhaps the biggest of all.

I needed to obtain some basic information about Mike in order to work most effectively with him. I had developed an intake packet with instructions for clients to provide such things as basic contact information, their primary life goals, and just what they would like to accomplish as their first short-term projects. I encouraged Mike to provide me information about what makes him happy, what his long-term goals might be, what his unmet dreams were, and perhaps about some exciting ideas and goals that he had let go of in the past. I asked for his complete life narrative, a continuum of sorts, told in the way that worked best for him. He could write an autobiography about Mike, or just provide me with highlights and bullet points. It was up to him.

After giving Mike an opportunity to complete the intake packet, we met again to discuss his responses. Mike's light bulb was indeed on. I was fortunate to have a client who was very self-aware, and now not only willing, but also fired up and excited about using coaching to better himself in every possible way. The angst and the wariness were gone, replaced by eager anticipation for personal achievement.

Occasionally, however, a manager who is referred to an outside executive coach for "remedial" work will not have this kind of positive attitude about the process ahead. Mike started out wary, but was soon sold on coaching and worked hard to make it a positive experience for him. Some come to coaching grumbling and complaining, reminding me of the adolescents coming out of probation who were often referred to me in my therapy practice. They flat-out didn't want to be there, and made sure I knew it. For these people, the approach is a little different and sometimes a little more challenging, but usually even those with the boulder-on-the-shoulder syndrome come around. Interview questions may take a different tack. I may have to acknowledge that they are there because someone said they had to be there. But what do you want to be here for? If you were here of your own accord, what would you want to do? These conversations are meant to establish rapport with the client, to convince him that this just might be a good experience, not a forced and fruitless waste of time. Coaching is not like being sent to the principal's office, or to the therapist's office after probation. It is an opportunity, and the coach must quickly establish that this is a good thing. Coaching is always focused on what can be, even if it takes different directions and has different outcomes than first thought.

THE POWER OF INQUIRY

During our second meeting, Mike and I progressed a little deeper. As coach, I guided our discussion with questions that were evocative and powerful. I needed to know Mike the executive and Mike the person. I was not conducting analysis or looking for reasons for certain behaviors. Together we were building the foundation upon which Mike's coaching would be built in order for him to achieve his very best. I asked powerful questions like: What do you want? What big dream have you put aside? If you went to work tomorrow and everything was as you would like it to be, what would be different? What would be your ideal work environment? How could you teach your supervisor how to better manage you?

Coaching does not seek to understand problems, overcome a past, or heal unresolved issues, though such understanding can very likely be a side product as the sessions progress. The successful coach does not view the client as a therapy patient. One of the joys of coaching is the truly egalitarian partnership with the client. There is no hierarchical structure. Although therapists might try to create a feeling of partnership with their clients, there is an invisible and contextual hierarchy that is difficult to overcome. Similarly, patients do not generally consider their medical doctor a partner; there is a built-in assumption of expert knowledge and patients naturally place them on a pedestal. If a coach slips into the role of consultant or therapist and starts giving advice or solutions, he or she is no longer a partner. Suggestions and ideas may be part of brainstorming or possibility thinking with your client, but advice should be avoided. Coaching in its most ideal state is one of being curious and evocative with clients, in order to bring out their brilliance, or to tap into possibilities that are created and posited because of the nature of the coaching relationship. Therapists trained in solution-focused techniques experience a relationship closer to coaching, but a search for solutions assumes problems that need solving.

I feel privileged to be able to cocreate with my clients, and help elicit their best skills for their job and overall greatness for human being and doing. This might sound a bit lofty, but it is a powerful concept, vital to the coaching process. My singular stated goal may be to improve this person's effectiveness in the workplace, but the whole person will benefit. That is the pure nature of coaching.

Together, Mike and I had overcome that age-old stigma that plagues men in high-level positions. He saw that I was genuinely interested in bringing out his best and that he really had nothing "wrong" with himself. He really liked that I was willing to listen to him without judgment and help him make the changes that he could, and live with the situations that he could not change. Executive coaching is a positive step, an employee perk in Mike's case, with both corporate and personal objectives, not a sign of weakness or failure. Now we could get on with the business of coaching.

I had a brief but specific understanding of what was needed, and what was expected, as the outcome of my coaching with Mike. As I mentioned earlier, I had an agreement with a trainer who held the original contract with Mike's organization. This was a little unusual, since in most executive coaching arrangements the coach has a direct contract with either the sponsoring corporation or the individual being coached. The ideal is to contract directly with a corporation to coach a number of executives, not just one individual. In this case, however, I was what might be considered a third-party consultant, hired specifically to meet the needs of an individual leader—as they pertained to the corporate initiative.

The use of the word consultant here, however, is misleading, and really does not typify the work of a coach. There may be a contract for specific work, and it may be predicated by the results desired by the corporation, or the individual employee, but let's make this clear: A coach is not a consultant. A consultant stands back, evaluates a situation, and then explains the problem and how to fix it. A coach stands with the client, helps the client identify the challenges, and then works *with* the client to turn challenges into celebrated and shared victories

WORKING *WITH* THE COMPANY AND *FOR* THE CLIENT

Although Mike's company was paying the bill for my services, Mike understood that everything we did together was absolutely and always confidential. A company has the right to updates and progress reports about certain improvements, but the details of coaching sessions are never shared. Such progress might include improved scores on a management strengths survey or a 360-degree assessment completed by the coach or by an internal human resources consultant. Reports might also include self-reports of improvement by Mike in the specific behaviors or skill areas that were identified by his manager.

A contract may specify expected outcomes, internal measurements, quarterly reviews, and evaluation summaries, but it should also always plainly detail the necessity for total coach-client confidentiality. Knowing this helped Mike share with me much more openly and honestly, without fear of any corporate repercussions. On occasion, executive coaching contracts and areas of responsibility and confidentiality can become slightly sticky, especially if the organization is paying the bill. These are best spelled out up front in plain language so all parties understand the conditions. The coach can never violate client trust. This is perhaps the only area where therapy and coaching stand on common ground.

The contract term for Mike's work, which is considered a minimum in the coaching world, was for six months of sessions. The company wanted Mike to improve and to meet their corporate expectations. The company and I determined and agreed together that six months was the minimum amount of time to enable this to happen. They weren't looking for a complete overhaul, just for hidden strengths to surface. Initially, this meant one, one-hour coaching session every week—very standard, very traditional. Later, based on Mike's need for flexibility—he traveled frequently—we changed this to three appointments per month, with the agreement that some sessions could go longer than planned, if needed—and he could e-mail or fax me for "spot coaching" as needed or desired between sessions.

In all coaching agreements and schedules, flexibility is a must in today's fast-paced, quickly changing world. However, this should never—and never did in Mike's case—interfere with the regularity of contact. The coach must be as available as possible. A great deal of the energy of coaching goes on between scheduled calls, as clients process and incorporate information and innovations. I always made it a habit to respond to Mike with 24 hours, maximum. However, the coach also has a life, and must remember to model boundaries as well. So much of what I did as a therapist was often of an emergency nature that a personal life was often compromised As a coach, however, I am another professional with boundaries that are set, modeled, and appreciated by my clients—another similarity with therapy or counseling.

Over the course of the next few months, my work with Mike helped him to identify specific skills he felt needed improvement, such as communication with his team, appearing less aloof to his employees and colleagues, and more delegating while granting authority (less micromanaging). He had a tendency to do it all and to do it his way. He had to learn to delegate and grant the authority with the responsibility. This is an important distinction. Mike identified those areas for himself – I did not do it for him. And having done so, he was wholeheartedly pouring himself into his betterment. I recommended that Mike read a book titled *Jump Start Your Career*, by Lois Frankel. This is a wonderful resource, which identifies the eight most common reasons for career derailment executives experience in their professional lives. Mike was able to see that some of these applied to him. Further, he was actually comforted that there were others like him, experiencing the same difficulties. After the initial reading assignment of the first chapter, I asked Mike to rate himself. His was now developing a keen sense of self-awareness, and his responses provided discussion material for the next several weeks. He had highlighted three of those eight areas, and these became the focus of our coaching for the next few months.

A coach provides the tools for self-awareness and must have a well-stocked arsenal of resources to recommend to the client. I don't have all the answers—no coach does. But I have access to many ways to arrive at the answers, resources that ultimately benefit my clients. These resources might be tools and assessments from the Center for Creative Leadership or other leadership programs I have access to, as well as time-management tools, delegation skills, and skills to develop what Daniel Goleman has called *emotional intelligence* (*Working with Emotional Intelligence*). As we worked our way through some of those resources, Mike excitedly pinpointed several areas he wanted to work on: possibility thinking, brainstorming alternatives, and innovative methods. He recognized himself as an executive in a high-level management position, but one who also happened to be an introvert, with a long-standing negative mind-set. Through coaching Mike learned that he could still be a powerful leader, and that he had powerful things to say, but he needed to give those things powerful thought first. He also learned that he had some powerful listening to do as well.

In our early conversations, Mike tended to defend some of his original management behavior with classic executive excuses. For example, as an old-school manager, he often had the habit of running his department from behind a closed door. After all, he was a busy man; he had lots to do. He couldn't tolerate all those interruptions. I validated his behavior, and his excuses, before suggesting alternatives. Eventually Mike learned that he could get his work done and still maintain an open door. He communicated to his team that at certain times the door was closed on purpose, but when the door was open, he was available to them. He informed them—by telling the truth nicely—that although the door was open, he was still working, and they needed to respect that by asking about his availability, not assuming it.

Because of the open and honest nature of our coaching arrangement, Mike and I even discussed the possibility of whether he should stay at this company, or move on. His current employer, however, was extremely supportive, willing to work on lateral moves, skill development, or whatever would benefit both Mike and the company. While this kind of support is not typical, it is becoming more common. In today's corporate marketplace, training and retraining are expensive. Employee retention is the key to a healthy bottom line. When a coach can be brought in to facilitate this kind of mutual growth and benefit, the employer and employee both win. It is a win-win situation that the employer sees as a potentially trustworthy return on investment.

Sometimes a need for skill development can provide a challenge to the coach. The client may have a deficit in areas such as communication, delivering presentations, public speaking, or organization. The coach must decide if he or she has the required expertise in those fields. For this reason, an excellent network or master team of professionals with various areas of expertise must be maintained. That's how I came to be Mike's coach. I was in the original trainer's network. Someone else would have been called if Mike had stage fright—in other words, if he needed specific skill-training by another specifically experienced professional.

COACHING THE WHOLE PERSON

We continued working on specific goals within the framework of Mike's position, but then our focus shifted slightly to illuminate other areas in his life that were causing him stress. Mike was the type of client who might have found himself in a therapist's office if he was willing to overcome the stigma of "therapy." Here, in a now comfortable coaching partnership, and after experiencing a number of successes through our sessions together,

Mike was able to take an honest look at other areas of his life that might benefit from his honest evaluation. It soon became obvious to both of us that Mike was dealing with one of the most typical executive problems plaguing today's leader: work-life balance.

Mike's workload had increased dramatically, causing strain at work and at home. He was in the middle of a huge merger, completely involved in his role. He was working too many hours at the office, and when he went home, the work went with him. For the most part, his wife and his children were supportive, but his wife wasn't willing for Mike to be married to the company. We took a long look at this and even had some joint phone sessions with his wife, where I facilitated them to have the conversations they needed to have together. This process should not be confused with relationship coaching or counseling. This wasn't marriage counseling or therapy; I was not functioning as a therapist or counselor—I was a coach working with his client to ensure success in all areas of his life. The difference here, between marital therapy and relationship coaching, can sometimes be a fine line. Relationship coaching is a contextual paradigm where the couple does not have serious relationship problems that need intensive work, but can benefit from some mutual communication about desires, dreams, and visions for how they would like their relationship to be even better. Coaching is for the couples we often hoped would see us as therapists to get tune-ups for their relationship and an objective assessment of what's stopping their relationship from being the most loving and satisfying possible. And coaching is very effective and practical for busy couples who may not take the time for regular office visits. If I ever feel that more intensive work is needed, I, as the coach, can recommend marital counseling to the couple and make it part of my coaching life plan.

This particular area of discussion with Mike had an unexpected result. When I encouraged Mike to have a "courageous conversation" with his boss and explain the undue stress he often experienced, the company realized that Mike was indeed overworked. They had not known the extent of his workload, because he had not bothered to tell them. All this time he had been frantically scrambling to keep up, thinking that was expected of him. He was overassuming the demands of his work, which is another executive frailty. Coaching opened doors to alternatives. When he was able to clearly delineate his time and expectations, the company actually hired an additional contract employee to assist during this difficult time of the merger. I was able to validate Mike's needs, both to him and to his company. All this time Mike thought he was in trouble.

Mike was a classic case, typical of those who might be referred for executive coaching, even if self-referred. These high-level leaders tend to be pulled in many different directions, and it is almost guaranteed that their work-life balance is seriously out of alignment. Their management and communication skills are pinched, and their status with their teams is precarious at best. One of the greatest assets of coaching is that the client can learn to become a coach with his or her team. Command and control leadership does not work anymore, but the sincere encouragement of a leader as coach does. During the coaching process, Mike was able to observe how I worked, and its impact on his own work and life. He was able to see that we did it together, that he achieved a great deal more than he could have alone, and that he could do the same with his team. Mike learned that he could be a good listener, that he could ask powerful questions, that he could encourage rather than command others, and that he could be innovative.

ACCEPTABILITY OF COACHING TO MALE EXECUTIVES

It was not the intent of this article to single out men in high-level positions who are skeptical of executive coaching, but it is a very real condition that needs to be considered. Some of these men may very well benefit from seeing a therapist, but they may not really need therapy. They respond to and need a life coaching partner, and that is the joy in my work. I have found that coaching relationships are more joyful, less stressful than those in the therapy arena. As a therapist I was always very motivational and coach-like, never considering myself traditional or typical. However, the sign on the door set the tone. I was the doctor to my patients. The context of the counseling or therapy relationship, whether real or perceived, was usually hierarchical from the beginning. We were never partners for success, but always doctor and patient.

Most often people come into therapy with some level of perceived dysfunction, and that is always the looming issue. The steps to improvement are small, measured, and often grinding and tedious—maybe even painful. Steps taken during a coaching process are bigger, wider, more productive and more fulfilling—for both the client and the coach. Coaching is a creative partnership. It is a give-and-take relationship to explore new ground, to go where no therapist has gone before. The old questions that had to be delicately worded because they stepped on already wounded toes are now formed and received as the doorway to new horizons. The coach guides the agenda, but the client sees the vista and widens the door already opened.

After the agreed-upon term of six months, both the company and Mike evaluated the results of our coaching. I had joint meetings with Mike and his supervisor at the end of three months and again after six months. They were both pleased with the noticeable progress and Mike was able to identify specific areas of focus for the next several months. It was jointly determined by them to continue this contract to eleven months. Mike discovered tremendous skills he wasn't even aware of. He made discoveries he would never have dreamed of. He originally did not have any goals to "go to the top" or even any higher than where he was, but Mike was promoted, and the company saw excellent results. Not only was Mike doing his job better, he was also living his life better. Our coaching relationship lasted for several more months beyond the extended contract on an informal, irregular basis. Mike is happy. The company is happy.

And I am happy. It is a thrilling experience to enable someone to become, as the army puts it, "all that he can be." As a coach, I am privileged to witness greater life achievement in one client than I ever hoped for in a dozen therapy patients. Personally, I feel more valued. I am delighted when I get e-mails and voice-mails from clients between sessions. I hear about exciting changes, breakthroughs, and discoveries. I truly care for the people I coach, and I share the joy of their victories and achievements.

I will freely admit that being an experienced therapist has made me a better coach, but I also had the natural personality for a good coach to begin with. My years as a therapist merely enhanced my natural coaching instincts. I also know well that coaching is a profession that demands a few gray hairs well-earned in the game of life. Of course, twenty-year-olds, with the right set of skills and attitude, could coach, but they would have to coach other twenty-somethings! A good coach needs a lot of SLE – significant life experience.

Today, my background as a psychologist has married my inborn desire to coach, and I am doing what I love – enabling discovery instead of treating dysfunction. Discovery wins every time.

PRACTICAL INFORMATION

ADVICE FOR NEW EXECUTIVE COACHES

1. Executive coaching is where the whole movement began. It has been around in the corporate world for a long time, but today professionally trained coaches have given newfound popularity to this growing executive niche.
2. Executive coaching can be the most lucrative, but also the most demanding of coaching. Executives are "on the go" and need more flexibility in the coaching sessions and often want and need in-person time coupled with phone sessions
3. All coaching is life coaching. Be willing to go beyond just work performance issues. Coach the whole person behind the job title.

ADVICE FOR NEW THERAPIST-COACHES

1. Get formal coach training and then supplement this with some specific training in whatever specialty you want to pursue. It is important to have a general coach training as the operating system before specializing in executive coaching, corporate work, or coaching with business or professional clients.
2. Hire a successful coach who is also a therapist as your mentor.
3. Keep abreast of societal, business, and coaching trends. Read magazines like *Fortune, Fast Company, Business Week,* or *INC,* and more general publications such as *O, The Oprah Magazine, Time,* and *Newsweek.* Join the International Coach Federation (ICF), www.coachfederation.org, the professional voice for the coaching profession, which holds annual

national and international conventions, drawing draw big-name speakers and presenters and offering the opportunity to network with like-minded people.

MY FEES

I charge $250 per hour and usually make it a monthly retainer of $500 for two hours of coaching. We usually have three to four phone calls a month or maybe two one-hour calls. If in-person coaching is needed, that is billed separately unless it is part of a total package contract. In-person coaching is often figured at the same hourly rate or as part of a daily rate of $2000 per day, which takes into account travel and preparation. I require retainers paid in advance and a six-month minimum contract. If I have to travel, expenses are also billed.

WHAT I KNOW NOW

When I started executive coaching back in 1990, I was trying too hard to be an expert or more like a consultant and problem-solver. Today, I realize that my job as coach is to bring out the best in my clients, and help them learn how to get what they want and where they want by using the coaching conversations to speed up the process.

A BRIEF BIOGRAPHY

I am a clinical psychologist, who has always functioned more like a coach than a traditional therapist. I began executive coaching in 1990 as a supplement to my clinical practice and found it professionally stimulating and financially rewarding. In 1996, after some formal coach training, I closed my psychology practice completely and transitioned into full-time coaching by telephone with executives, professionals, and entrepreneurs. The joyfulness of coaching people to "design a life, not just get over a past" moved me into full-time coaching in 1996 after having a psychotherapy practice for 16 years.

My coaching business grew steadily until 1998, with international coaching clients, when I decided to train other therapists to transition into the growing profession of life coaching (of which executive coaching is one niche). In 1998, I founded Therapist U (now called the Institute for Life

Coach Training) to train mental health professionals in the art and science of coaching. I believe that therapists/counselors can become the very best coaches with some specific skill training, and marketing and business development. I have trained hundreds of therapists in the U.S., Canada, and Europe. I am also the coauthor of *Therapist as Life Coach: Transforming Your Practice.*

I am a Master Certified Coach, as granted by the International Coach Federation, and a charter member of the ICF. Most recently, I have had the privilege to work and train with Dave Ellis, author of *Falling Awake: Creating the Life of Your Dreams,* who is a masterful coach, mentor, and friend. In all my professional endeavors, I attempt to bring a whole-person approach to my work and present myself with integrity, a deep sense of caring, and a lightness of being.

In learning this profession in the past few years, I have been sure to hire the best as I embarked upon full-time coaching. My coaches have been Cheryl Richardson, Judy Feld, Jay Perry, John Seiffer, Phil Humbert, Lynn Grodzki, Dave Ellis, and Chuck Proudfit. In addition I have had informal relationships with certain coaches on special issues.

CONTACT INFORMATION

Patrick Williams, Ed.D.
2801 Wakonda Drive
Fort Collins, CO 80521
Phone: 970-224-9830
E-mail: doccoach@LifecoachTraining.com
Web site: www.LifecoachTraining.com

4

The Role of the Family-Business Coach

Kacie LaChapelle

Seeking council from a family-business coach represents a brave new world for most family business owners. While dramatic and alarming conflicts exist among family members struggling to work together, these high-achieving, fiercely independent entrepreneurs are wired to reject the notion of coaching as an unnecessary interference, and one for which they have little time or need. Although family-business coaching is a relatively new venue, family-controlled companies comprise 85–90 percent of North American businesses. Spanning all shapes and sizes, family-owned businesses include nearly a third of the Fortune 500.

When they work well, family companies have numerous competitive advantages and are frequently top performers in their respective industries. The very words *family business* create an association of a personal, inclusive, and caring kind of company. Hoping for a friendlier alternative to the forlorn corporate world, employees are drawn to this warmer, less formal environment. Many family-business owners are masters at engendering great loyalty from customers, and building long-lasting relationships. The legacy of a family-owned company rooted in solid values can become a hallmark of strength for the organization and a propelling force for generations to come.

Despite these potential strengths, however, the high mortality rate of family businesses is daunting. Only 30 percent of all first-generation family businesses are successfully passed to the second generation, and only 15 percent to the third. This lack of continuity is largely a result of family-related conflicts. Difficulties in managing the succession process are typically exacerbated by lack of planning and insufficient communication. Successors are ill-prepared for the challenges, decisions, and conflicts that emerge as control of the business shifts from one generation to the next. Complexities proliferate as family members' desires and expectations collide and concerns over power, control, money, and status erupt. In reality, 100 percent equality cannot be the chief concern of next-generation family-business owners. The soul of an enduring family business is trust and respect, along with true acceptance of the chosen successor and unwaivering accountability.

BEGINNING THE COACHING ENGAGEMENT

Typically, my involvement with a family-business client is the result of long-standing turmoil among the emerging generation of family owners or between senior and junior generations. During succession transitions where trust has eroded and emotions have escalated, I am usually contacted after frustration levels have already ascended beyond tolerable. I am considered "a last resort" by hurt and emotionally drained people trying to muster the energy to find a way "to make it work." The presenting complaints vary, depending on the family's history and communication patterns. In some cases, there are blatant arguments and threats of lawsuits. In others, the silence is deafening, as family members barely speak to one another, even regarding imperative business or personal concerns. Unclear business roles, responsibilities, and expectations, as well as uncooperative and unproductive work relationships are common. There are accusations and hurt feelings about perceived financial inequities or favoritism on the part of parents. These dilemmas, when fueled by lack of trust, result in no-win power struggles that thwart the family's ability to generate solutions and live by them. Spiraling mistrust leads to a cycle of grappling for power while refusing to assume professional accountability. When left unresolved, these problems will send even the most successful business crumbling to its knees.

Seated in the majestically adorned parlor of the Girard family estate, I begin, ever so gingerly, in the helping role. Jonathan Sr., the confident and charismatic 67-year-old chief executive officer of a third-generation retail business, is visibly anguished over his family's reaction to his decision to allow his eldest son, who he appointed president, to buy out his three other siblings. The session with Jonathan Sr. breeds an outpouring of truth-telling. With alarming suddenness, the hard shells of control, success, and confidence crack open, unveiling raw human emotion, vulnerability, and pain. The intensity of Jonathan Sr.'s revelations brings to mind a religious confession—a need to cleanse the soul from layers of grief. His voice quivering slightly, he recants the unfortunate culmination of events, and the resulting sting of his disappointed children. Although the buyout provided each of the three siblings, who have successful careers unrelated to the family company, nearly $2 million for the shares given to them by their father, they nevertheless blame him and their brother for pressuring them to sell. In divesting themselves from the family business, the siblings discovered that the money was not enough to console the unanticipated but poignant loss of identity they feel in no longer being connected to the family business. Jonathan Sr. continues: "I've really blown it, I've done the wrong thing for my children. They had counted on me to bring order to this thing and I don't know if they can ever forgive me for allowing Jon Jr. so much control. If anything, I should've sold to an outsider. Jon has always displayed the capability, and he's always shown a strong interest in the business; if only he could've treated his brother and sisters better and been more diplomatic."

As I make my voyage into the clandestine, privileged, and intricate world of family business, the nature and depth of the issues that are revealed to me inspire a sacred sense of responsibility that serves as my guide. Listening deeply, I try not to allow my own needs—to help, to offer something of value—to distract me from fully focusing on the issues at hand. Beyond the healing power of the bond of compassionate listening is the simple offering of the possibility of hope. Families, after all, are resilient systems with great capacities for forgiveness. But I am well aware that hope alone will not be enough to ease the weary souls of these family members who have hurt and been hurt, already for far too long.

At times, I am catapulted into the private, deeply anguished world created by talented, tenacious, sometimes brilliant, entrepreneurs, who pushing for relief want immediate answers. In the Johnson family, for example, defensiveness, anger, and mistrust ignited as siblings unreservedly wrestled one another for control, acceptance, and equality. As emotions skyrocketed during discussions with this family, I focused on finding an internal place of calmness and neutrality, so that I could be completely present, even while aware of minefields being triggered all around me. Steven, son of the founder of the business, S.S. Johnson Manufacturing, had worked under his father for 20 years. After Steven Sr. was killed in an automobile accident, vice-president Steven Jr. assumed the role of president in the $100 million a year business. Much to Steven's surprise, his four sisters, who inherited stock ownership, but did not work in the company, began to question their brother's motives and operational decisions. They insisted upon explanations for the high compensation he received, his need for the company helicopter, and even the means by which he acquired the multimillion-dollar estate where he resided. The youngest sister, Julie, boldly decided to join the business and take matters into her own hands. While Steven Jr. initially welcomed Julie, he was completely unaware that her motivation for employment in the company was to monitor his performance and that of other management. Without hesitation, Julie assumed an aggressive posture, commanding authority with employees and using her family name and ownership status to wield power and demand information. When Steven Jr. learned of these acts, he calmly but firmly asked Julie to work in her position without disturbing the structure of the organization. Julie's response was to resign and threaten legal action. In our meeting, Steven Jr. reflected: "I thought that my greatest challenge would be to create the best possible business in our competitive industry, but now I see that by far our greatest vulnerability is whether we can keep peace with the family shareholders." Inevitably, I am reminded of the magnitude of the challenges that overcome so many business families and even the coach who is trying to help.

THE DRAMA OF SUCCESSION

A family business tends to evolve more by default than by design, as a by-product of a tenacious, devoted entrepreneur who successfully crafted a business venture with the sustainability to outlive him (the founders in all my cases thus far have been males). Having invested so much of himself in growing the business, the entrepreneur prefers to perpetuate it rather than to see it sold. Even though he would like to see the business live on, his focus remains directed toward his comfort zone, the needs of the business itself, rather than the thorny process of dealing with the next generation's issues. Succumbing to the demands of business operations, while weary of the sensitivities and potentially conflicting agendas of family members, these entrepreneurs fall short in establishing the necessary foundation for the emerging generation of shareholders and business leaders. Expressing the sentiments of many of his contemporaries, one business founder noted: "We've got a business to run here, and no time to worry about these little spats between the kids. They need to work things out and settle in."

When leadership succession planning is not attended to, the family business is vulnerable to the next generation's disappointed expectations and unrealistic feelings of entitlement, which all too often lead to irreparable strains in family relations. The next generation may be unwilling to accept the assignment of a sibling in the role of new president, finding him or her to be a poor replacement for Dad or Mom. Sadly, as the warning signs of simmering discontentment are ignored, the next generation inherits a framework that is insufficient to support their emerging partnerships. The way in which the first-generation founder and succeeding generations respond to these and other important dilemmas is critical for what is to come.

DAD, THE ENTREPRENEUR

As large as they may grow and as successful as they may become, family businesses remain highly personal enterprises. Their founders are relentlessly devoted to, at times even affectionately labeled as obsessed with, the survival, care, and control of the business. Throughout the first generation and often well beyond, for better or for worse, the company evolves in the very likeness of its founder's personality, values, and idiosyncrasies. The identity of the founder is inextricably linked with the culture of the business, and although he's unlikely to admit it publicly, it's extremely hard for a founder to really believe that anyone could run the business as well as he can. A life without the business in its center would be a change that in his heart he might not truly want. Especially when the entrepreneur lacks other passions and plans, a personal crisis of sorts is associated with retirement. Instead of being relieved about the prospect of greater freedom, he may feel ambivalent about the idea of not being needed any longer to manage all of the burdens and hassles that long ago became second nature to him.

One of the stumbling blocks a senior-generation leader needs to reconcile is his attachment to controlling the business that he has spent his life building and being responsible for. Oh, a part of him definitely wants to, but the devil on his shoulder keeps whispering, "Don't do it. You're a fool. Are you gonna let the thing you've worked your whole life to build fall apart without you there—while you do what, play golf? Your kids are good kids, and yeah, they mean well, but no one can do it like you, old man." So, Dad usually goes into a very long and confusing stage often referred to as "semi-retirement." Much to the dismay of successors, this transition stage can go on for many years, even decades, where Dad plays a little bit more golf, becomes a snowbird, or otherwise occupies himself so that he is working "part-time" just 50 hours a week. But when there's a decision to be made, he's on the job. When he's back at work, Dad's somehow in the center of everything once again. The employees know who the real boss is. And the next-generation leaders have their hands tied, knowing they aren't really calling the shots (sometimes even when holding the title of president). Over time, their struggle for more power may become more aggressive, creating an unusually high degree of conflict with parents and siblings. Conversely, driven by the tendency to avoid confrontation altogether, some would-be successors withdraw from what seems to be a hopeless situation, resigning themselves to routine complacency. These kinds of transitions can go on for many, many years.

FAMILY MEMBER HEIRS

As the next generation of business family members comes of age, there are both privileges and perils that need to be reconciled. Carrying on a family name that is connected to a successful, prominent business may be a great source of pride. Sons and daughters of business owners inherit a presence in the community that can command recognition and provide a special identity. Growing up working in the business exposes them to many different kinds of jobs within the company. Many learn from a young age that being part of the action is the best way to be connected to Dad's world and to be more visible in his eyes. The family business offers an abundance of opportunities to rise to higher levels of authority, status, and income than might otherwise be possible. The other side of the coin is that Dad tends to be hard on his sons and daughters (especially his sons, and even more so, his oldest son). Even highly capable next-generation adults may be reduced to feeling like small children in his huge shadow. Gaining the acceptance of Dad and feeling good enough can be a life-long struggle for successors.

Having worked in the business for many years, as competent family members enter their thirties and forties, their need for autonomy and authority naturally rises. When work ethic, talent, and commitment have been adequately demonstrated, family members who aspire to leadership roles need to understand the opportunities that lie ahead, as well as what is expected of them. Ideally, company leadership will initiate the creation of a growth plan, outlining steps for advancement and increased responsibility for the family member to work toward. More typically, though, this type of planning is overlooked and developmental possibilities remain open-ended and vague.

When his grandmother died, Peter Jr. inherited more stock in the family's third-generation transportation company than his brother or sister. It became clear that he was the designated successor of the highly successful business started by his grandfather. But when his high-powered father appointed 29-year-old Peter Jr. president, the title was not accompanied by much actual authority. To his advantage, Peter Jr. by nature was a patient person, who decided to use the opportunity to learn and to develop greater credibility with the senior management team. The power to make important decisions came gradually, over the next decade. In the long interim, Peter Jr. had the tenacity to handle the pressure of trying to fill the tall shoes of his infamous father. Somehow, he learned to take things in stride and develop his own style. Ultimately, his approach to leadership, while different from his father's, served him well and proved more effective for the changing needs of the organization.

In contrast, 40-year-old Jim had served as vice-president of a $10 million third-generation manufacturing business, alongside his parents, for 15 years. Having grown confident in his abilities and knowledge of the business, Jim longed for more autonomy and felt that his efforts were all too often unfairly scrutinized by his parents. According to Jim, if things were not done exactly the way his parents wanted, they were not done right. Responding to his predicament with great frustration, Jim began expressing anger and sarcasm toward his parents on a regular basis. His growing resentment spilled into his relationships with others, leading his parents to question whether Jim had the leadership skills sufficient to run the business. These concerns gave them reason to clutch the reins more tightly, leading to explosive power struggles between them.

THE SUPPORTING CAST

Although the wives of most of my clients were not the founders of the family business and do not hold formal full-time positions in the company, the role of the matriarch in the family-business system is important and highly influential. Founders' wives, especially, have made many personal sacrifices, functioning largely as single parents to allow their husbands the freedom to devote their time and energy to building the business. Family-business wives, in general, play a crucial role as chief sounding board and informal advisor, often responding to the business concerns of their husbands with finesse and sound judgment. A great deal of strength and social wisdom can be provided by the matriarch. Her loving, emotionally bonding force can serve as a powerful glue to help hold the family together through thick and thin. When her social skills are highly developed, Mom tends to be a bearer of warmth to employees and a nurturer of important business contacts in the community.

The matriarch's role is not an easy one, however. All too often it is fraught with worry and frustration. Mom knows a lot about the problems of the business and the family, and even when information is not freely flowing to her, she is expert at reading between the lines and putting the pieces together. But at times, she feels powerless and frustrated that she cannot do more to help solve the problems. She despairs, especially when she watches her family members working so very hard and struggling with each other, instead of being able to enjoy the fruits of their labor. She invariably asks, "How can my family find a way just to appreciate what they have, to work together and be happy?"

On the other hand, Mom's desire to protect family members may back-fire if she is not conscious of the entire business system. Even with the best of intentions, the matriarch must be cautious in the kinds of interventions she attempts. Chain-of-command and authority issues are already ambigu-ous and fragile in many family businesses. Boundaries tend to be blurred as family members who are managers, or even just employees, may have higher status and authority than the nonfamily managers. It can be coun-terproductive and harmful to the integrity of the organization's structure if Mom attempts to rule in ways that undermine the scope of a family member's (or nonfamily member's) earned authority, circumventing the company management's chain of command.

Mom has the potential to serve the family business in the critical role of a "trust catalyst" (LaChapelle, K., & Barnes, L., *Family Business Review,* 1998, March), helping to build bridges of communication and renewed faith between family members. Family-business wives need to be acknowl-edged for their helpful ways and deeply valued by their families. The greater the support and respect they receive, the more they will be able to work their magic.

Spouses of the younger generation also have very important roles and need to be aware of the powerful impact they can have on family relations, for better or for worse. Depending on their responses to issues that arise, spouses either help to build family peace or add to the seeds of destruction. Since they are the ones who have to live with weary family-business members, when tensions are high in the business spouses are inundated with the frustrations and negativity of their partners. They are besieged with one-sided views about the inequities and hassles that their partners have endured. When spouses accept verbatim these exclusive perspectives, they can become resentful and angry toward family members. These bad feelings overflow into family gatherings and over time can even adversely effect the next generations' relationships. Regardless of how saintly and wonderful their husbands or wives are, spouses need to remember that the "realities" they hear about, more often than not, contain incomplete pictures and underrepresented versions of the positions of other parties.

A spouse can be of the greatest help by acting as a sounding board, striving to add an objective, balanced perspective. With a clear commitment to taking the high road, spouses can soothe and help remove some of the sting that their partners are feeling, while at the same time encourage good faith and direct communication between the involved parties.

GAINING PERSPECTIVE

The foundation for building family-business coaching relationships is established during individual interview sessions with family members and, whenever possible, nonfamily senior management. These confidential meetings allow the coach to gain background information, while providing a confidential forum for each individual to express concerns, hopes, and goals. Although this is a time for the coach to gather data, it is prudent to view this process also as an intervention, in and of itself. Particularly in high-tension situations, these meetings can easily be used to vent frustrations and try to gain the alliance of the coach. While it is helpful to convey support for each individual, there is a need to exercise caution when responding to client concerns. At this stage, statements made to any individual by the coach should be statements that the coach would be comfortable saying to the group at large. Attempts can be made to build bridges and create goodwill despite divergent perspectives of this dramatic cast of characters. Inquiring about previous attempts to improve interpersonal dynamics may be helpful, as well as sharing strategies and positive outcomes that have worked for others in similar situations. As interviews continue, pieces of the puzzle are added and the tapestry of family dynamics and roles begins to come into focus. From this perspective, the coach can begin to gain greater clarity and identify initial coaching strategies.

In addition to ongoing individual sessions, I lead group family member meetings. Agendas for these sessions are based on initial objectives and recommendations I create, along with input from family members. One example of a valuable focus for a family meeting may be to spend time articulating the family and business vision. These meetings provide a means for helping families to improve their ability to engage in productive meetings where issues are identified and effective problem-solving can take place. This practice of productive communication scheduled at regular intervals is the lifeline for effective family-business ownership. From a business perspective, professional business meetings that include other managers are also essential. Meetings can be quite challenging for families with a history of chronic conflict and unresolved power issues. In an environment of low trust, meetings will all too often spiral into destructive and hurtful bashing sessions.

From a facilitator's perspective, responding in such an emotionally charged environment begets a versatile approach. While the coach works to table individual family-member issues, goals, and agendas in a way that can lead to generating possible solutions, family harmony hangs in the balance. Emotional blocks and family conflicts derail noble attempts at objective analysis. While a therapist might attempt to delve into an exploration of feelings, the coach will work to redirect the focus toward potential solutions that can optimize the company's performance and enhance its leadership capacities. During the heat of intense emotional outbursts, however, the best of proposals are likely to fall on deaf ears. When people are feeling hurt and threatened, common responses tend to be to retreat or attack, rather than to assume responsibility for their own unproductive behaviors or role in a problem. In high-conflict cases, I wrestle with the juxtaposition of conveying the urgent need for a call to action—for individuals to assume responsibility for change—and trying to provide a source of relief and inspire people to keep the faith under very trying circumstances.

TRUST AND ACCOUNTABILITY

In my experience, creating trust with clients is based on both their belief in the professional competence of the coach, as well as the feeling that the coach is a genuinely caring individual who has concern for their well-being. Building trust is especially challenging with clients who have been living and working in the throes of a low-trust environment where emotional safety is deficient and there has been little recognition of efforts, contributions, or abilities. Asking individuals to assume responsibility for examining their own roles and understanding the impact of their behavior as part of a problematic dynamic is more difficult under these circumstances. The courage to consider possibilities for altering behaviors and reactions may develop over time and is more likely when there is a trusting coaching relationship. With a client/coach connection of understanding and affirmation, it is more likely that defenses will be lowered to permit discussions about personal accountability. Throughout the process, I present caring but direct feedback about my observations concerning the individual's role.

While traversing through the dilemmas of each individual family-business client, I search for ways to encourage a spirit of discovery, appreciation, and pride. Illumination of individual strengths and positive behavior is a good foundation to work from. Highlighting the special talents, contributions, and qualities of each person, along with areas that are working well within the family and the business, also provides an opportunity to continue building on these strengths. Clients who are prepared to take some responsibility for their role as part of a problem and to be open to expanding their competencies for contributing to and serving the business are the ones who become most appreciative of the coaching process. Their willingness to open the door makes these clients the most "coachable" and usually the most enjoyable to work with.

In spite of great efforts to develop collaborative and connected relationships with many different personalities in a given case, the reality is that a coach's role is not always enthusiastically valued or accepted by each and every member of a family-business engagement. Inevitably, there will be certain members of a family business who adopt a "thanks-anyway" attitude, indicating that they could somehow manage to get by without the coaching. Particularly during times when I am promoting more structure, clarity about individual roles, and mutual accountability, I have occasionally bumped up against an individual who has expressed resentment toward me or lack of interest in working with me. Such was the case with Martha, a young woman who had worked part-time in her family's furniture business from a young age. Although she was the youngest in her sibling group, with the least amount of experience or skill, Martha felt that because she inherited stock she should be involved in all business decisions. She portrayed an attitude of entitlement, insisting on being consulted in operational matters in departments that her siblings were managing. She also conveyed a lack of acceptance about having a sibling for a boss or in a higher position. Martha stated that regardless of experience and years in the business, salaries of family members should all be equal. When her demands were not agreed to, Martha became enraged and in most meetings cried and attacked everyone involved (me included) for mistreating her.

These individuals, usually but not always the youngest in birth order, have taken on the role of the family baby. Having been overindulged, they've learned to be masterful manipulators who know how to get what they want from their parents. Especially when rules and standards have been loose or nonexistent in the business, the "family-business baby" tends to be quite rebellious toward authority figures and difficult to coach. Feeling overlooked for too long, they quickly lose interest in the coaching process—unless they find the coach to be a vehicle for helping them to get things to turn their way. Directly or indirectly, they are likely to try to find a way out of participating. Responses to these challenging relationships vary. Initially, I might attempt to find new or less threatening ways to connect with the individual. Or, if I can trace a change in behavior to a certain meeting, incident, or time frame, I might choose to query the individual about my perception of his or her lack of interest or initiative. At other times, I elect to follow his or her lead for less involvement and wait and see what develops.

THE SURROGATE LEADERSHIP ROLE

There are many times when I realize that my role as family-business coach has grown to that of a leadership partner. I am stepping in as a co-leader, supplementing the needs and weaknesses of the business owners, and helping to fill leadership voids in the organization. This is a surrogate leadership role in the sense that I am not the real leader, but am serving for a finite period of time. Regardless of how promising or helpful this role might be to the business, surrogate leadership is activated only to the degree that the client is open to it and finds it valuable. The senior generation's success and reputation over the years may have elevated him to a legendary status, at least within his world. Sharing some of the control and power is not the norm. Predictably, the strong-willed-gladiator type does not find much enjoyment in receiving instruction or being told what to do. He exudes a certainty about most things, making it clear along the way that he has earned the right to do what he darn well pleases. Even though there has been due warning for the times that he will exempt himself from keeping his part of a recent agreement, or exercise his right to change his mind in midstream, I still find myself being naively surprised when it happens.

Needless to say, the strength and stubbornness of this type presents its fair share of challenges to an outsider in a helping role. Fortunately, by the time I am called in to work on a case, many of these gentlemen entrepreneurs are aging gracefully and are even willing to soften—at least a little bit. It also helps that he is greatly in need of some relief from the stress of many failed attempts at trying to get the family to be happy. At least at the outset of the coaching engagement, it is typically his view that we are trying to help others or fix problems outside of himself. In some instances, my presence seems to offer an unexpected novelty that he seems to enjoy. In the times that he is aging less gracefully and seems more intractable than ever, he is usually distancing himself from the headaches and the conflict enough to allow me to mobilize others in the direction of change. In the rare but poignant instances where he is very much there and not budging, nothing will happen unless he approves it. Then it is essential to discover the degree to which his internal vision truly includes the commitment to fostering a family business. If it does not, the efforts made are merely window dressing and there will be many mixed messages with few lasting changes.

On the whole, the family business owners with whom I work closely develop an appreciation for the value of the co-leadership role and are willing to share some of their power. The process begins with their support in allowing me to hold confidential meetings with their family members and other business managers. Further, encouraging those individuals to call upon me as needed is also a step in this direction. Developing these relationships lands the coach in a highly influential spot. The importance of using this influence with extreme care and integrity cannot be overemphasized. There is power in being an outsider who has been given permission to tell the truth to the business owners and leaders. Sharing what I have learned about people's perceptions of the organization and its leadership sometimes involves great courage. The client may see things very differently and may not feel that the data or perceptions I am bringing to light are true or even important. Conveying the perspective of employees involves presenting clear and direct feedback in a respectful and caring manner, while maintaining individual confidentiality. As the client relationship continues to grow it is easier to learn the kinds of approaches that work best in a given situation and to anticipate, to some degree, how a client is likely to respond to feedback.

In conveying perspectives of employees, family members, and others who are important to the success of an organization, I assist business owners and leaders in reflecting on their own philosophies and roles and the leadership practices that have emerged from these views. Generally, the entrepreneur's hands-on leadership approach that has built the business is no longer sufficient to manage a more mature organization with several hundred or more employees. Often the greatest strengths of the business founders and entrepreneurial types is in taking action rather than talking, listening, or teaching. The entrepreneurial management approach has focused on rewarding individual performance in lieu of coaching others and developing highly capable future leaders. Consequently, the business may be overly dependent upon the owner and unprepared to run effectively in his absence. The hands-on culture spills over into the succeeding generations. I partner with the entrepreneurial leaders to provide some of the mentoring and coaching that is missing in the organization. Helping to develop leadership attributes in others ultimately creates a more stable structure for the organization.

As the coaching relationship progresses, many clients find value in having a sounding board with whom they are comfortable discussing their leadership dilemmas, strategic matters, or critical business and family decisions. Such was the case with 29-year-old Tom who took over for his ailing 68-year-old father. Although Tom had an older brother also working in the business, it was understood that Tom's personality and skills were best suited to the administrative and leadership role and that he, rather than his older brother would become president. Tom was nonetheless lacking in both preparation and confidence when he was called upon, prematurely, to accept the enormous responsibility of leading the $20 million-a-year construction company. Adding pressure to an already difficult situation was the fact that the 75-year-old company had been struggling to break even for the preceding several years.

Throughout this lengthy transition process, I worked closely with Tom as he crafted his new leadership identity and took incremental steps in earning the respect and credibility of skeptical employees and concerned family members. Tom's high level of integrity, humility, exceptional character, and ability to ride vast waves of instability created the basis for the success that was to come. The transition was helped in this case by Tom Sr.'s willingness to step away from day-to-day responsibilities, enabling—even forcing—Tom Jr. to learn. Tom's father was willing to work with me and allow me to guide the process. I helped him to manage his own anxiety while encouraging him to provide his valuable counsel from behind the scenes in a much more subtle and less visible manner that he would normally have. Paradoxically, his courage to remove himself from the day-to-day operations gave his son room to truly assume responsibility and learn to do the job.

A Supportive Partnership

There are elements of a supportive partnership in an effective coaching relationship. While my credentials and experience qualify me to lend expertise, I refrain from presenting myself as the distinguished expert hired to tell people how to live their lives. Rather, my preferred role involves raising critical questions that help to illuminate insights and alternatives, perhaps inciting motivation for positive actions that can help produce greater success and self-confidence. Along the way, I also offer benchmarks from other business families to help expand my clients' perspectives, while encouraging them to take responsibility for utilizing this information to find their own best answers.

Looking ahead, there are two core philosophies that I feel are especially germane to running a family business successfully. First, a foundation for success is based on shareholders who are both devoted to and capable of nurturing a strong family bond with each other—based on trust, respect, and communication. Second, family members must be willing to commit to high standards of mutual accountability. Conversely, an attitude of entitlement or the philosophy that the business owes them whatever they desire because they have been working there or are shareholders is extremely destructive to any hope of building and enduring partnership.

The privilege of working with family-business owners and members has given me an appreciation and respect for the intricacies of their journeys and compassion for their challenges. I have also been witness to the extraordinary blessings they have the potential to enjoy. There are great opportunities to be capitalized on when the worlds of family and business can be gracefully united and solutions can be found for effectively managing their dilemmas. I have found it deeply rewarding as well as quite challenging to be of service to these creative, successful, and sometimes eccentric entrepreneurs as they navigate their way through the complexities of being a family in business. The moments I am most proud of as a family-business coach come from the client relationships where I am thought of as a trustworthy confidant who understands them well and truly cares.

PRACTICAL INFORMATION

ADVICE FOR NEW FAMILY-BUSINESS COACHES

1. In serving this client base, multidisciplinary experience and training are beneficial. For example, my background combines psychology, hands-on entrepreneurial business management, and organization development.

2. Despite the depth of knowledge and varied expertise necessary to perform effectively as a family-business coach, the family-business field is still just burgeoning and mentors and research are limited.

3. It can be a challenge to break into this market because it is new to most people and not well understood.

ADVICE FOR NEW THERAPIST-COACHES

1. It is helpful to be versatile in using both the approaches of facilitating (being nondirective) and making recommendations (being more directive). As I refer to it, the facilitative role focuses on listening and asking the right questions to help clients find their own best solutions. Conversely, making recommendations utilizes my objective perspective to tell the truth as I see it, and involves sharing my best ideas and suggestions, based on educated experience about practices that have been helpful to clients.

2. Have a clear distinction in your mind between the practice of therapy and that of coaching and communicate these definitions and the scope of your role to your clients.

3. Remember that ultimately the burden of change belongs to the client in whose hands lie the responsibility, choice, and motivation to meet his or her goals.

MY FEES

I charge a flat fee, typically ranging between $5,000 and $10,000 for an initial assessment that spans four to eight weeks. I then continue work on a quarterly retainer basis with fees derived from estimates of the amount of time I feel I will need to invest to effectively serve the client. The fee amount can be reviewed and adjusted when needed.

WHAT I KNOW NOW

The cases that I am hired to work on most often involve long-term chronic interpersonal problems and patterns that are very hard to break. These engagements, where family businesses are already in great disarray, are very difficult to turn around and sometimes there is more pain than reward.

A BRIEF BIOGRAPHY

I founded Family Business Dynamics in East Longmeadow Massachusetts in 1995. My client-businesses range in size from several million through multibillion dollars in annual revenues. The areas on which I concentrate are: leadership development, succession planning, family communication, and board facilitation.

I have a Ph.D. in organizational behavior, specializing in family-business management. My Master's degree is in community psychology with specialization in marriage and family studies. I hold licenses in marriage and family therapy and mental health counseling. I was in private practice between 1992 and 1995, providing individual and couples therapy, specializing in career development.

I am blessed, and on a bad day I might say cursed, to be both the daughter and wife of entrepreneurs. I've always considered myself an entrepreneur at heart (both through genes and environmental conditioning). My career began in the executive search firm founded by my first business teacher, my wonderful father, Harry Kalajian, between 1979 and 1987. I have also worked with my talented husband, Richard LaChapelle, in his real estate development and general contracting business over the years, sometimes in a consultative role, at other times in an unglamorous, hands-on capacity.

For several years I have been a Harvard Business School research associate, a facilitator of the Harvard Families in Business Executive Program, and author of numerous Harvard family-business case studies. Along the way, I was extremely fortunate to receive the guidance of several pioneers in the family-business field. Professor By Barnes of Harvard Business School worked closely with me as I attempted to make sense of the doctoral dissertation process. Based largely on By's inspiration, my dissertation came together around case-study work on the role of trust in family business. In the many projects we have subsequently worked on together, By has not only generously shared his wisdom but also has been a special friend whom I admire. Senior lecturer Dr. John Davis of Harvard Business School is a great contributor to the field and has been a true inspiration to watch and work with as he helps lead and learn from some of the largest and greatest family businesses internationally. I have also benefited from

John Ward's leadership in the family business field and from the counsel of Leon Danco, both pioneers in family business coaching.

CONTACT INFORMATION

Kacie LaChapelle, Ph.D.
Family Business Dynamics
PO Box 731
East Longmeadow, MA 01028
Phone: 413-525-9400
E-mail: Kaciefambus@cs.com

5

Coaching Professional Women to Speak Up
Linda D. Tillman

"I wear the prerequisite navy blue suit," Nan said. "And I never carry a purse. I'm always as nice as I can be to the head of my department. I really think I've done everything possible, but it just isn't working," she said with her voice rising at the end of each sentence.

"What isn't working?" I asked.

"I'm not getting promoted. The men in the department seem to have so much easier access to the higher positions. I can't seem to figure this out. That's why I called you."

As Nan and I talked in our first phone-coaching call, I learned that several years earlier she had entered the large corporation for which she worked. While men in similar positions had positive reviews and vertical moves in the company, she had not had a promotion in two years. She made a lateral move the year before and had felt frustrated ever since.

Nan is similar to most of the corporate women I coach. She is hitting the glass ceiling and is confused about why this is happening to her. Most of these women know how to "dress for success" but they are not as aware of how the culture has shaped them to blend into the background rather than stand out. After years of teaching assertiveness training in the community education program at Emory University and years of working with individual clients to speak up for themselves, coaching women in this predicament seemed like a natural next step for me.

"I'm sorry, but I've tried and tried to understand it," she said. "When I speak up in our meetings, I'll think that I've explained my idea really well.

But later a man in the group will say almost the same thing with just one or two words changed and everyone tells him it's a great plan. And of course, a few months later, he's a vice-president and I'm still an associate." Her voice sounded helpless and discouraged.

I could already hear some ways in which Nan could be more verbally assertive, but I wanted her to arrive at those conclusions with me so that we could make an action plan together to address the problem. As a therapist, I operate from a psychodynamic perspective. As a teacher, I provide more direction and engage in more cognitive work than in my therapy office. As a coach, my approach is somewhere between the two. I am not the teacher, but I try to provide my clients with the information they need to make decisions and action plans for themselves. I am not a therapist when I am coaching, but my personal goal for each client is similar to my goal for therapy clients: that he or she will gain the perspective and skills needed to achieve goals without my help.

THE BASIC ISSUES

"When are these meetings?" I asked Nan.

"Too often for my self-esteem!" she giggled. Then she added, "Every Monday morning."

I asked her to describe the room in which the meetings took place.

"It's a huge conference room," she said. "You know the kind—with a long table and those gigantic leather chairs."

"Where do you sit?" I asked.

"Oh, in whatever seat is empty. I'm trying so hard to do a great job these days that I work right up until the last minute, so when I get to the meeting most of the seats are taken."

Clearly, Nan needed to look at the nonverbal aspects of becoming more of a presence in her corporation. With most of the corporate women I coach, I find that the nonverbal has to be addressed before we begin to work on the verbal aspects of speaking up. In addition, focusing on the nonverbal is less threatening than working to change a person's way of speaking and is an easy way to make a connection and begin work with a client.

The room situation illustrates what many corporate women face. In our culture, women are trained unconsciously to yield to men. For example, in her book *The Frailty Myth,* Colette Dowling notes that when a man and woman walk toward each other on the sidewalk, inevitably the woman steps aside, if she is not conscious of what such a gesture conveys. By arriving at the last minute to the meeting table, Nan was in effect stepping aside to allow all the others at the meeting to take their place ahead of her.

I talked to Nan about tables and seating positions. Since the division head, Mr. Williams, sat at one end of the table and one of the dominant men sat at the other, we discussed the power statement these positions made. While the dominant man at the other end of the table did have some power by virtue of the position he chose, he, by opposing the division head's position, might feel inclined to argue with Mr. Williams.

If Nan could sit at an angle to the division head, she would be in a very assertive and still respectful position. Sitting off to one side conveys the respect for each person's choice to participate in the conversation. We decided that the ideal place for Nan to sit would be at the right hand of the division head. With this plan, he would notice her and she would be able to speak strongly without appearing confrontational.

"What will have to happen for you to get that seat?" I asked Nan.

"Obviously I'll have to get there early. I know it's essential for my advancement to be heard in the meeting. If where I sit is important, I can do that."

Often my first step with coaching clients is to get them to become keen observers of themselves. As we began to address Nan's nonverbal assertiveness, I wanted Nan to see what an impact it might make for her to sit in a different position. We also needed to think about the chairs.

Many chairs in corporate conference rooms are designed for the six-foot male. If a typical woman sits back in the type of large leather chair that Nan described, she looks as if she has been swallowed up. We lose power by seeming small and insignificant. I encouraged Nan to sit toward the front of her chair throughout the meeting and when she spoke, to lean forward. Nan had a notebook with her, as I had suggested before we started coaching, and she wrote her first goal in the notebook: "I want to speak up and be heard in the Monday meetings."

"Okay," I said. "Now let's write action steps to take to move toward this goal." I always talk about moving *toward* a goal, rather than *meeting* the goal. The coaching client then feels success in the progress toward the goal rather than the all-or-nothing approach of reaching the goal or failing to reach it.

"Well, I have two already," she said. "I'm going to take the place next to the division head and I'm not going to sit back in the chair."

We agreed that Nan would also begin observing the nonverbal aspects of the people at the meeting the following Monday. She would try to notice how the people who spoke up handle themselves physically. She intended to write her observations in her notebook so she could remember it all before our next coaching call the subsequent Thursday.

When I answered the telephone on Thursday, Nan's enthusiasm was apparent.

"Just the plan of claiming that seat made such a difference," she said. "I usually arrive at the meeting still thinking about the work I left at my desk. By getting there early enough to get the seat beside Mr. Williams, I was able to settle down and think about my plan for the meeting."

"Great!" I said. "You've already added something toward establishing your presence. It also sounds like you were more relaxed from the beginning."

"And who would believe that sitting next to the division head could have so much impact!" Nan said next.

She reported that when she spoke, Mr. Williams looked right at her. When he looked at anyone who was speaking further down the table, he seemed to make eye contact with all the faces of all of the people between him and the speaker. By sitting at his right hand, Nan gained his full attention if she spoke.

"It wasn't easy to sit forward in that chair for an hour," she said. "But I did notice that I felt more like I was a part of things throughout the meeting, even when I was just listening."

Before we moved into increasing her verbal skills in speaking up, Nan and I needed to address a few more nonverbal aspects of making one's presence felt. I asked Nan what she had observed about others in the room.

My plan was to encourage her by giving my positive support for her observations and to help her use what she had learned to build our next step.

"Well, I thought the men who spoke seemed to take up a lot of space when they talked. And it sure is easy to hear their deep voices." As often happens with coaching clients, Nan provided the perfect transition to our next level of work.

"I'm glad you paid attention to that, Nan, because we need to work on your voice. I've noticed that when you feel helpless about changing something, your voice rises at the end of the sentence," I said.

"Do you think it does?" she asked and then laughed at herself as her voice rose.

"Your voice is supposed to rise at the end of a question like yours just did, but if it rises at the end of a statement, you lose power. It's as if a helium balloon is tied to the end of your words and they float away."

We practiced with Nan saying, "Sir, my opinion is different from that." It was a struggle for her to bring her voice down. When I said the phrase for her with my voice rising at the end, she was able to hear how something meant as a statement can sound like a question with the lifted ending. I asked her to imagine a choir director, leading with hand motions to bring the words down at the end, and she improved in her delivery.

Suddenly she was quiet on the other end of the phone. "I was just writing it down in my notebook," she said. "Bring voice down at the end of sentences for more power."

"Great," I said, "and while we're talking about voices, let's think about the other comment you made about the men in the room—that they seemed to take up a lot of space when they talked." For some women, learning to appear to take up space when talking goes against the cultural grain. Many women keep themselves looking small, holding their arms close to their bodies and standing delicately, or lady-like as they say in the South.

As I was standing in the subway station in Atlanta yesterday, I looked around at the waiting people. All of the men were standing with two feet planted firmly on the ground. Some of the women stood so that the majority of their weight rested on one leg, with the other leg crossed at the ankle.

Others kept their feet close together with the two feet in an unsteady dance position. These women looked as if they could be knocked off balance quite easily.

I imagined that Nan probably had some physical movements that made her seem to take up less space in the world. Here is where face-to-face work has an advantage over telephone coaching. I would not get to observe Nan and we needed to determine a way in which she could get feedback about her own use of her physical presence.

"How did the men at the meeting seem to take up a lot of space?" I asked her.

"Well, they gestured a lot and when they did, they emphatically spread their arms wide. And all of them were loud and interrupted each other. There were a couple of other women at the meeting. When they spoke, they tended to use their arms in open gestures, although not as big as the men did, and they looked around the room as they said what they wanted to say."

This would be a challenge in our coaching work together. I asked Nan to brainstorm with me to see if we could find a way to get feedback for her nonverbal use of self. She thought she could ask her younger sister to watch her and give her feedback.

"Great idea," I said. "Now since we're brainstorming, let's see what else we can add to that." We discussed the way poker players learn when their opponents have a good hand by observing how they give themselves away nonverbally and unconsciously. Her job would be to see if she could find someone to report to her what her "tells" were. I encouraged her to ask her teenage daughter since my own daughters have always been keen observers of my nonverbal behavior. My oldest daughter quite recently told me that when I am worrying about something, she knows it because I will put my hand on my mouth, covering my chin. Family members are often quite capable of telling each other what they know about them from their nonverbal signals.

"I have a video camera," said Nan. "I can videotape myself having an imaginary conversation at the Monday meeting."

While that would not be as good as direct observation, she would get some feedback that way. I suggested that she continue to look for good models of nonverbal assertiveness on television news channels and in her corporation. She could also have pretend discussions in her mirror and see what she could learn about herself. She wanted to ask her secretary for feedback, but we threw out that idea because it might make Nan seem too vulnerable to the secretary at a time when Nan wants to seem more powerful.

I recommended that Nan write the possibilities for observation in her notebook as "Ideas to try" and convert them to action plan steps each time she took the opportunity to try one of them.

MOVING BEYOND THE INITIAL GOAL

Although working on a client's nonverbal skills is an essential aspect of coaching corporate women, I knew that, to stay responsive to her goals, in our next call Nan and I would have to move on to speaking up verbally. I have each client send me a focus form before each call. On Nan's focus form, she always wrote that at the end of the call she would like to have some skills to speak up more effectively. After the second call, I began to think about how I would coach her verbally and sandwich in a little more nonverbal as we went further in our work.

The next Thursday, Nan was bubbling with information about herself.

"I have learned a lot," she said, "especially from my sister." Her sister had told Nan that she often looked down when she was saying something important. Even if she had good eye contact, as soon as she began talking about something that she wasn't confident about, then Nan would look down.

"So I didn't wait for you," Nan said. "I wrote that down as an action step and for the rest of this week, I've been forcing myself to keep eye contact when I say something important. It's easier some places than others. I can do it with coworkers in my department or with my secretary, but I still can't hold my eye contact with Mr. Williams when I speak at the Monday meeting."

Great, I thought. She has the idea now and my work will be easier. She will come up with her own solutions much more quickly from here on out.

In addition, now that she is more tuned in to the nonverbal, we can move on to verbal assertiveness.

"I'm looking at your focus form," I said to her when we finished talking a little more about eye contact. "Sounds like you are ready to learn more about your verbal assertiveness." Nan had written on her focus form: "I am beginning to understand the importance of nonverbal actions. Now I'd like to learn to choose the right words."

"I'm sorry, was that okay to ask?" she said. "I hope it was all right to put that on the form."

"Nan, you've just used several words that I hoped we'd get a chance to pay attention to. For example, let's look at your apology. Was there something for which you needed to apologize?"

"My friends say that I apologize too much," Nan said. "Is this one of those times?"

"There are two parts of this apology issue," I said. "If you make a mistake, the appropriate thing to do is to apologize, but if you say 'I'm sorry' as a way to start a sentence, you may be heard as if you are apologizing for existing—which takes away from your power and impact."

I reviewed with Nan the approach that Deborah Tannen points out in *Talking Nine to Five*. Tannen notes that sometimes we strike a social balance in relationships through the use of apology. Nan might say to Susan, her secretary, "I'm sorry, I don't know what time we're meeting. Do you?" To keep the balance Susan would say, "Oh, I'm sorry, it's at 9 a.m." However, if Nan takes the risk of saying, "I'm sorry," and Susan does not return the apology, then Nan is in the one-down position. A person who is striving to be seen as more powerful and to gain more respect does not need to risk putting herself in a one-down position.

Nan and I agreed that she would keep a tally of the times she apologized when she had done nothing wrong. In addition, she would keep count of the times when she had to stop herself from apologizing unnecessarily. She would report her findings the next Thursday.

Time passes quickly in a 30-minute coaching call. I find that I operate with a much tighter focus than I do in a therapy session because I have one eye on the clock the entire time. I want my client to leave feeling good about progress made as well as having goals for the next time we get together. Nan had a few minutes left in this call and I wanted to maximize it.

"While we are paying attention to words, I want to encourage you to look at the way you qualify what you say."

"What do you mean by qualify?" she asked.

"Qualifiers are phrases like: 'I hope it's okay to say this, but' or 'I'm not sure you'll think this is a good idea, but' or 'You'll probably think this is ridiculous, but.' Earlier you said, 'I hope it is all right that I wrote it on the form.' Using qualifiers injects doubt into what you are saying. If you don't quite stand behind your idea yourself, why should the other person?"

"I know I do a lot of that," Nan said. "I think it is a way to open the door, but if I understand what you are saying, I am actually making the door a tiny pathway."

"Absolutely," I said.

"I'll add that to my action plan for this week, " Nan said. "I'll notice when I use qualifying statements."

Although Nan and I had set several action steps for her to take, I wanted the call to end on a note of success. I asked her before we hung up to tell me what pearl she was taking away from this call.

"I've never thought about the words we talked about today," she said. "This call has given me a whole new way to look at how I speak and what words I am using. I can't wait to try some of these changes."

For me the pearl was Nan's continued enthusiasm. Working with her was a joy because she was so motivated and wanted to learn so much about her style of presentation. I frequently tell clients what the pearl is for me as well. Maybe that's my way of balancing the relationship, but it also reinforces the huge efforts they are putting into working on themselves.

FOLLOWING A CLIENT'S PROGRESS

Over the next weeks, Nan and I worked not only on her qualifiers and apologies, but we also began developing a list of effective and powerful verbs to use. She began the list on her handheld organizer and added to it every day. She found verbs on the Internet, in meetings, listening to TV reporters. She challenged herself to try to use at least one of the impact-dealing verbs every day with someone higher up than she in the corporation. When she found a verb she really liked she e-mailed it to me.

I always offer coaching clients contact through e-mail between sessions. Contact by e-mail allows for a spontaneity that isn't available in therapy and keeps us both in touch with progress. Some clients never take advantage of the e-mail opportunity, but Nan usually e-mailed me at least once a week.

I wish that I could report that Nan was promoted to vice-president, but that hasn't happened yet. Nan and I have a telephone coaching session only once a month now and each call brings new victories for her in her progress to speak up more effectively. I fully expect that if any woman can become a vice-president in her corporation, she will.

She frequently speaks up at the Monday meetings and each time improves her delivery. She tells me that as she speaks she manages to maintain eye contact with Mr. Williams and with others in the room. Her goal for herself now is to present a proposal for a change that she thinks will influence the progress of her department. She is working on writing a plan for this presentation.

At her last performance review, she went in to the meeting with an assertive list of what she knew she had accomplished in the company. She presented this to her division head before he had time to tell her what she had or had not done. Although the glass ceiling prevailed and she did not get the promotion she thought she deserved, she did get a substantial raise.

The experience of working with Nan brings energy to my life every time we have a coaching call. I love the focus of the coaching relationship. Setting specific goals that can be measured as one progresses is fulfilling both for me as the coach and for my client who can see actual gains and changes in his or her life. Just as in working with therapy clients, each coaching client provides a unique experience. With Nan, as with others, I look forward to each opportunity to do this work and to encourage and cheer another young woman on to personal gain and the victory of promotion in the workplace.

PRACTICAL INFORMATION

ADVICE FOR NEW ASSERTIVENESS COACHES

1. Women have not been culturally trained to move forward in corporations, so there is a lot of territory to cover in coaching.
2. As Betty Harragan has pointed out in *Games Mother Never Taught You*, to coach in this area requires some familiarity with football and the military, not for the purpose of acting like a man might but for understanding where the male mentality may originate.
3. Women bring untapped strengths to corporations. This is a potent area for coaching. Women have the ability to connect well, have sensitivity to others, and can often handle multiple tasks at once. When coaching women in corporations, the work can focus on women maximizing these unique talents and skills that come more naturally to females.

ADVICE FOR NEW THERAPIST-COACHES

1. A coaching practice takes time to get started, especially if you have an existing therapy practice. Building a business can be a full-time job and most of us have to learn to balance working on a coaching practice while running a therapy practice and making time for our own life activities.
2. Be creative in how you make your presence as a coach known. Once I eoffered my coaching services as an auction item on eBay.
3. Get your name out as often and as positively as you can: for example, volunteer to host chats on Web sites that relate to your area; give speeches and workshops in your hometown; write articles for magazines and newsletters.

MY FEES

I base my coaching fee on a $200 hour. If the client wants to talk twice a month for 30 minutes, then the fee is $200 a month. If he or she wants to talk more often or to have a longer call, the fee is more, still calculated on the $200 hour. I have tried several hourly fees in an effort to find one that both meets my financial needs and keeps the client comfortable.

I'm still struggling with what to charge for groups. I seem to use a different fee each time I offer a for-pay telegroup and haven't yet settled on a firm group fee.

I often offer my services as a prize. For example, when I teach face-to-face classes in Atlanta, I hold a drawing at the end of class for a free hour of coaching. I also offer half-price coaching for one year after a client has completed a face-to-face class with me.

WHAT I KNOW NOW

The time it takes to get this type of business off the ground varies with each individual. Although I have a full-time psychotherapy practice, all of my children have left the nest, which gave me some evening hours in which to work on my coaching business. I also had an easier time than some of the colleagues with whom I trained because I felt comfortable with the computer.

The difference between coaching and psychotherapy is vague and still undefined even by APA. Coaching involves taking the risk of being on the cutting edge when boundary issues have not been clarified by the professional organizations

Although I love the coaching in many more ways than I have enjoyed my therapy practice in these days of managed care, I have felt some shame in my professional circles when I call myself a coach. When I was training, I kept my involvement with coaching a secret. I can almost feel the contempt reaction in my colleagues when I talk about my coaching business. I imagine the reaction is somewhat like it would be if a physician told his or her colleagues that he or she is training to become a chiropractor. I think the reason for my experience is twofold: (1) many coaches are not as well-trained in their field as therapists are in theirs, and (2) change often occurs slowly in communities where people have difficulty accepting something unfamiliar.

A BRIEF BIOGRAPHY

I am a psychologist, a coach, and a mother with three grown daughters. I have a Ph.D. in psychology from George Peabody College of Vanderbilt University (1980). I am licensed in the state of Georgia, where I have been in private practice since 1984.

My therapy career began with a job as assistant director/adjunct faculty member at the Emory University Counseling Center. I left Emory to take a part-time job at Georgia Regional Hospital so that I could begin to build a private practice in my off hours. There my job was to train the hospital staff in team building, connection with each other, and stress management. I also taught workshops on becoming a leader, speaking up to a supervisor, and increasing negotiation skills.

Although I have long since left hospital work behind, I continue to teach and work with people in many different contexts to make the best of difficult situations. In addition to my therapy practice, I regularly teach seminars in Atlanta corporations on planning, time management, assertiveness, communication skills, delegating, organizing, and relaxing under stress, among other topics. For the last 16 years, I have been teaching assertiveness training in Emory University's community education program. Every quarter I have a full class of people wanting to change their impact in their personal and business lives.

I have been coaching since 1999. After hearing Ben Dean of Mentor Coach Program (MCP) speak at an APA meeting, I couldn't wait to learn to be a coach. While training with Ben, I jumped right into the field by establishing two Web sites: www.speakupforyourself.com and www.fertility-coach.com. With encouragement from Ben's continuing class and a small support group consisting of wonderful coaches and friends, I have pushed forward, publishing monthly e-mail newsletters and offering monthly telegroups.

CONTACT INFORMATION

Linda D. Tillman, Ph.D.
2004 Cliff Valley Way
Atlanta, GA 30329
Phone: 404-728-0728
Fax: 404-634-7802
E-mail: linda@speakupforyourself.com; linda@fertilitycoach.com
Web sites: www.speakupforyourself.com; www.fertiiltycoach.com

6

The Hardiness Factor: Heightening Executive Productivity

Carole D. Stovall

Seven years ago while I was working as a therapist in private practice, a couple came to see me. The husband, Gary, was a senior vice-president at a Fortune 100 company, and his wife worked in a career that allowed her the flexibility needed to be home with their young children. They were a wonderful couple with a lovely family, but it became obvious that a large part of the family's difficulties had to do with Gary's Type A personality, his ongoing job stresses, and his job requirements. Over the next few months, I began narrowing the focus of the clinical work until we were at the point where it was obvious that the family would greatly benefit if Gary was better able to understand and modify his own work-related assumptions and behaviors. At this point, I began working with him individually. Because he was very intellectual, structured, and driven, I used the Meyers Briggs Type Inventory to help him learn more about himself and his personal style. Rather than rely solely on talk therapy, I began working with him to develop written assignments and exercises to move the process along. The goal was to meet in person on a regular basis, but because of his unpredictable work and travel schedule, he sometimes resorted to faxing me his written assignments and talking with me by phone.

Four months after starting the individual work with Gary, it was clear that he had made significant progress. According to his wife, he was more relaxed and less demanding at home. He reported compliments from his executive assistant about how he "listened better," was "less rushed" and "easier to work with." Most importantly, Gary felt less stressed, more productive, and happier due to the better relationships he was able to develop at home and with his executive team and staff. He even showed greater insight into the motivations and needs of the employees who reported to him.

I knew that our work together had gone well, but I was surprised when Gary told me that the strategic work we had done together was better than the work he had completed with an executive coach a year before. I then realized that the focus of our work and the structure that I had devised in order to help him was more like executive coaching than traditional psychotherapy. Once I had assessed that his situation was connected to problems of style, stress, and choices as opposed to a diagnosable *DSM-IV* classification, I had shifted our work away from a clinical approach. This reformulation allowed me to move from the role of therapist to that of coach/consultant/advisor.

Gary passed my name along as a coach to the human resource department in his corporation, who handled executive training and services. At the same time, I decided that I wanted to explore doing more executive coaching and began the skill-honing, retraining, and transformation process that would take me from therapist to coach.

Seven years ago there were very few training programs for people interested in learning how to be a coach, and there was little written about coaching. I began a piece-meal approach to learning all that I could about those areas that I thought were relevant to executive coaching—the behavior-change process (as discussed by the human potential movement and systems theorists), organizational development, and leadership models. I familiarized myself with assessment instruments for work environments. I read and studied business periodicals and journals, in order to better understand the important ideas and trends relevant to contemporary business practices. I focused on available case studies of successful businesses, large and small, and the executives and entrepreneurs credited with their success.

I talked to everyone that I possibly could to learn about their perspectives on executive coaching and organizational development—business leaders, friends who are industrial organizational psychologists, professors in business schools. Eventually, I developed a mentorship relationship with two highly-seasoned organizational development professors and practitioners. They furthered my development and knowledge base by introducing me to organizations like The National Training Lab that interface with the community from a sociological and psychological perspective. Most importantly, these mentors were willing to serve as my sounding boards as I thought through the process of my professional transformation. They understood that I loved my role and identity as a psychologist, yet wanted to expand by learning new ideas that could be integrated into my existing therapeutic schemata in order to create a broader systems view of human potential and change.

Executives began to hear about me as a coach and called for appointments. The flow of referrals signified that I was on track with the work that I was doing, but I realized that I was asking people to work with me in a coaching process that I had not personally experienced. In order for me to feel credible, I needed to do what I was asking executives to do. It was time to find my coach.

Like many therapists, I had received extensive clinical supervision and years of psychotherapy. What really helped me to understand that coaching was a different process from therapy was to actually work one-on-one with a coach. The coaching experience integrated the intellectual exercise of coaching—the "who, what, where, and how"—with the emotional—the "why"—of coaching. Getting coached allowed me to realize the positive power and depth of the coaching process. I began to clarify my personal values. I have always considered myself as someone who is very achievement-oriented, and I have succeeded at a number of things, but felt drawn to achieving more. What I had never done was to ask myself some of the straightforward, simple, and yet profound questions that my coach asked me: What is stopping you from getting what you want? How does this relate to your life purpose and the way you want to live? What do you do differently when you are speaking and acting from your heart versus from your head?

I was always so busy "doing" that I had never really stopped to consider the emotional "why" of what I was doing. I had never created a picture of my ideal life, much less explored the process necessary to create that ideal life. Coaching caused me to reorder my priorities, reevaluate what was and is most important for me personally and professionally, and put an emphasis on strategic ways to accomplish my personal work-life balance.

Through being coached, I became clearer about the specific skills and knowledge that I had to offer as a coach. As a trauma specialist, I was well aware of the effects of stress on productivity in the workplace. I knew that an executive's ability to manage and direct stress within the midst of a fast-paced and ever-changing corporate lifestyle would be of paramount importance to his or her productivity. The issue of psychological *hardiness* or stress resistance became my area of confidence.

I began by offering stress reduction workshops for corporations, which gave me opportunities to explain the concept of hardiness and show how it related to greater workplace productivity and life balance. The workshops gave me access to executives as well as to senior-level human resources decision-makers who were often responsible for hiring coaches within an organization.

Over time, I developed another coaching specialty in leadership development. What contributed to my uniqueness as a coach was my ability to help the "whole" executive explore the issue of hardiness, life balance, and productivity.

The initial materials that I send to new clients include my own lifestyle measure, which asks executives how much sleep they get, who their significant friendships are with, how much coffee and alcoholic beverages they consume, whether they have a practice of spirituality, how happy they are, what hobbies they have, what sources of stress bother them, and to identify any Type A personality characteristics that might exist or be problamatic. This lifestyle measure helps the executive focus on the issue of his or her hardiness, as it relates to his or her overall workplace performance.

LIFESTYLE MEASURES

James, the senior vice-president of a large company, wanted to find more efficient ways to supervise and motivate his staff. He felt that he was spending too much time responding to crises and managing people, and not enough time providing leadership and shaping the direction of his division. He perpetually felt bogged down and overextended. The assessment measures that I gave him included my lifestyle assessment, the Meyers Briggs, a social IQ scale, and several stress measures. I also agreed to reinterpret his 360-degree feedback report taken three months prior to my contract with him.

Our initial assessment feedback session lasted three hours. Using the assessments and the 360 report, we began to develop a list of goals so that he could achieve more direct and specific communication with his staff regarding strategic goals and role expectation. James was intrigued with the idea that lifestyle changes could produce immediate results at work. For example, I saw from the lifestyle measure that he reported getting only four to five hours of sleep a night. He rarely ate lunch, had stopped exercising, felt constantly tired, irritable, stressed, and overwhelmed. I asked him to increase his sleep time, begin eating lunch on a regular basis, take vitamins, and take five-minute walking breaks throughout the day. He added to my list of suggestions by proposing that he hire a personal trainer.

Once those changes were in place, we focused on core leadership development issues. I assisted him in reprioritizing the work he gave to his administrative assistant and suggested that he, along with his executive team, attend a one-day class on managing business and life priorities. After several coaching sessions James said he felt more balanced; he had a better perception of what needed to change inside him and outside him to maintain this balance. Rather than feeling constantly stressed, he could view issues that emerged as interesting "puzzles" to be solved. His wife and daughter felt delighted with his changes. Now he showed up to eat dinner more often and at dinner, feeling less distracted and pressured, he engaged happily in family conversation. And as he continued to understand the concept of hardiness, he mobilized himself to operate more productively on the job.

PERSONAL VALUES

The more I work as I coach, the more I have had to look at what it means to me personally to work within the corporate arena. On first glance, the values espoused in the stereotypes of corporate America are very different, often at odds with, values espoused by therapists and others within the human potential movement. As a witness and sometimes participant of social activism of the sixties where the enemy was identified as the military-industrial complex, I had concerns about working with corporate America.

I wrestled with my personal values to understand how they were similar or different to those within the corporate arena, focusing on the disparity between *stated* versus *expressed* values in other large organizational systems. Corporate America is like any other system. The values most often stated are that corporations exist to make a profit for their shareholders by providing goods and services that fulfill a public need. Most companies understand that in order to reach this objective, they need to address and respond to worker productivity issues. Well-run corporations do this by expressing the values of teamwork, leadership, and caring for their employees, promoting the creativity, innovation, and human potential of their staff. I believe that employee satisfaction directly effects productivity and the profit-and-loss bottom line of any company. Racism, sexism, or other types of degrading behavior stifle the stated values. It is within the best interests of corporations to create and support a healthy work environment.

As an executive coach, I help translate these values, to show the effect that actions of individuals have on the greater good of the organization and the collective bottom line. Holding to these core values allows my coaching to be powerful, useful, and consistent. These values are the same ones I embraced as a mental health professional.

Other therapists often ask me to compare my work as an executive coach to my work as a therapist. As a coach, I have more variety in my workday and need to be more flexible. I enter a dynamic, chaotic, and ever-changing workplace and I can't adhere to the rigid therapeutic containment boundaries necessary for psychotherapy. As a clinician, I was accustomed to not being "seen," to establishing a neutral veil; it was a challenge intellectually for me to operate as a coach in a more "present" mode. But in the ever-changing and fast-paced executive world, providing good feedback to people who sometimes feel like moving targets within a dynamic and political process is a critical skill. I have to be able to assess the competencies and limitations of the executives I work with and understand the culture of the company they work within.

THE DAILY PROCESS OF COACHING

I have some standard steps I take when working with an executive, particularly in the beginning. It is crucial to establish what the executive is looking for—what he or she hopes to accomplish: leadership development, team building, higher emotional IQ, hardiness. Many of the executives that I work with are self-referred, and come to coaching with a specific agenda or set of goals in mind. They consider coaching a process of development, without a concrete ending time. After all, Tiger Woods still has a coach. Some executives are referred through a human resources department or through an individual, usually a vice-president responsible for executive development. When a third party is part of the referral process, the dynamic changes. Usually the referral source has very solid ideas of what they would like to see the executive accomplish within a specified time frame. In this situation, the first order of business is to clarify the boundaries and expectations of all the parties.

The next step is assessment. The assessment instruments I use vary, depending on the needs of the executive. For leadership development, I use some sort of 360-degree feedback tool. In a 360-degree process, data is collected about the executive from his or her direct reports, and from peers and supervisor(s). The data is then compared to a self-assessment measure completed by the executive. This powerful process, which measures a number of leadership characteristics along with general characteristics such as stress resiliency, provides an excellent snapshot of how the executive sees him- or herself versus how he or she is seen by others. Other instruments I administer include the Meyers-Briggs Type Inventory, the California Personality Inventory, and those that measure social IQ, stress, organizational efficiency, team building, and communication skills. I have developed several lifestyle measures of my own. I stock approximately 10 to 12 different tests with various versions. I have personally taken every single assessment tool I use, which allows me to be more strategic in deciding which to administer.

Once the assessment and feedback process is completed, I work with the executive to strategically target areas where development would be useful. These goals are often folded into a written long-term plan and then broken down into sequential steps. As the process proceeds, a regular meeting time is set up for an hour every week or for one and a half hours every two weeks. At this point of coaching regularity is important, so meetings occur in any number of settings. For executives in my geographical area, we initially meet face-to-face in their office, my office, or over lunch. Coaching sessions also take place by phone from planes, trains, hotels, and automobiles. With this flexibility, I can coach executives across the United States.

As the coaching relationship proceeds, executives often shift their perception of my role and usefulness. Over time I frequently become both a coach and a sounding board for many of their professional and personal concerns. We discuss a range of organizational problems, including disciplinary issues, lay-offs, and firings. I coach executives to use their executive assistants more effectively, encourage team building, and discuss how to make their workplace less stressful. I have even given referrals to one executive who wanted to have her child academically tested.

Sometimes executives want me to bring my mental health training front and center, to help them understand people. Last year I assisted three CEOs in the selection of their corporate chief financial officers (CFO). In each case, the executives felt very comfortable with the professional and technical skills of the candidates. But they all wanted various feedbacks as to the soft skills—the people skills—these CFOs would bring into their corporate environment. Senior executives often value soft skills and understand their importance in the overall needs of the organization. Once an executive learns to trust me as a coach, my mental health skills (translated into practical language) are also highly regarded.

Considering how the scope of the work of a coach can change daily, a "typical" day does not exist, but here is my journal of a recent day.

Wednesday morning. I schedule three phone sessions with three different executives starting at 8:00 a.m. Since I can conduct these phone sessions from home, I am comfortable with an early start time. Each call lasts about an hour, so by 11:30 a.m. I am finished and begin returning my calls from the previous day and answering e-mails. The phone calls and e-mails are follow-ups from clients and status reports, such as: "The interview with the new sales director went very well. Want you to take a look at her resume and give me feedback" (usually ASAP).

Wednesday lunchtime. Most days I either schedule lunch with a new or perspective client, or read. Today I have a quick lunch and then spend time catching up on reading current issues of *Harvard Business Review, Fast Company Magazine,* and *Business Week.*

Wednesday afternoon. I reserve the afternoon hours for meetings or coaching sessions at my office, by phone, or occasionally at a client site. Today Alice, a new vice-president of her company, calls for a scheduled coaching session. Here is our conversation:

CAROLE: Hi Alice, how are you today?

ALICE: I am overwhelmed. Remember my concern about Tony, my employee? When I saw that Tony couldn't do the technical part of his job, I asked human resources to double-check his references and found out that he lied about having a degree. He will be fired, but the customer loves him. I am losing him and still haven't been able to replace three senior managerial positions or hire a new administrative assistant.

   The work group that I inherited is bucking me because I was brought in to reorder things in the department. They hate change.

   To add to this, my son Adam seems to be doing well in school after our move across the country from Colorado for me to take this job, but, he is also very clingy right now because I've been working so many late nights and weekends trying to get on top of all of the work.

   I've only been in this job four months, but is seems like a year with very few things going right. I don't even seem to have time to go to the movies with my husband. By the way, our house in Colorado still has not sold. I don't feel like I'm doing anything well. I'm not sleeping well at all.

CAROLE: You have a lot on your plate right now. Which of these issues do you think will resolve without you doing anything?

ALICE: Human resources will be notifying Tony of his dismissal in a few days and I have already transferred him off of the client account.

CAROLE: Good! Let's talk about the things that are left that need to be addressed. What is the one thing that bothers you the most?

ALICE: Just the stress of everything. I feel like I can't think straight—there is no time to make the kind of quality decisions that I usually make.

CAROLE: Okay. Let's go over how to get come control around the stress that you are feeling, to keep it from building up and feeling worse. [*At this point, I point out the physical stress reduction competence she needs— short exercise breaks, relaxing music during the day, eating lunch, drinking enough water, stretching, blocking time on her calendar for the important things that must get done, going to sleep at a regular time every evening, etc.*] I'd like you to choose the issue to resolve that would make the biggest difference in reducing your stress level.

ALICE: I need new staff. Right now, I am basically filling the role of three managers and an administrative assistant.

CAROLE: What is blocking your ability to get this done?

ALICE: I put Tony in a supervisory position and I am afraid of making another mistake.

CAROLE: Tony is gone. What did you learn about hiring supervisors that will be useful to you from here on out?

ALICE: To trust my gut more. Also, not to turn over the reins so completely without knowing the capabilities of the person better.

CAROLE: What do you think would happen if you looked at your fear of making a mistake as a signal that a puzzle needs to be solved instead of a sign of danger?

ALICE: [*Surprised at the question*] Puzzles are not frightening.

CAROLE: It also seems like you can anticipate some of the problems that might occur in terms of the new managers that you are in the process of interviewing.

ALICE: I absolutely learned a lot. I certainly have a better sense of what not to do.

CAROLE: But, you also did some things right, that you might want to repeat.

ALICE: Yes, when I saw the group was in trouble, I got involved up to my elbows. My involvement made a big difference, but I should have done it earlier.

CAROLE: Sounds like the old dilemma of when to be a manager versus when to be a leader.

ALICE: That can be confusing because I've never had this many responsibilities before.

CAROLE: The results of the 360-degree feedback should be helpful in separating out some of this. We'll have a better road map that will probably undercover some behaviors that you can focus on to help you get a better handle on your management versus leadership issues.

ALICE: I really look forward to being able to talk about this issue more.

CAROLE: Okay. When we talk again, let's see where you are in terms of physically managing the stress. Also, I have a question that I would like you to consider and answer for me next time we talk. I know there is a lot of stress you are facing, but if you were at your best, what different decisions would you be making right now?

No two days in my coaching practice are alike, since each day is full of variety, interesting people, and stimulating challenges. The change in my practice from therapist to coach has also transformed me: I am in an ongoing processes that requires lateral thinking, using old skills in new ways, and expanding myself in order to meet larger professional goals.

Family and friends have told me that I have changed since becoming an executive coach. They say I am more talkative, present, able to laugh, and relaxed. I agree. I still love holding onto a few hours a week of being a therapist by seeing therapy clients in my office, but I recognize that in my therapeutic role I can't be as free, genuine, and visible as when I am a coach. Just as my honed therapeutic skills have made me a better coach, so have my coaching skills made me a better therapist. The executive coaching process allows me to balance the listening and receptive aspects of myself with my initiating, dynamic, and active elements, increasing my own hardiness level. I look forward to seeing where this ongoing transformation will lead me.

PRACTICAL INFORMATION

ADVICE FOR NEW EXECUTIVE COACHES

1. Being an expert in human relations and complex change gives therapists a distinct advantage in executive coaching. However, business people do not want to work with a therapist. All concepts and ideas must be expressed using the language of the business environment.

2. Becoming an executive coach requires that you not only be accepting and comfortable with business issues, concepts, and people, but also that you continuously submerge yourself in the business world.
3. Being useful and serving as a sounding board is one of the most important tasks of being an executive coach. However, there is no room or tolerance for guessing. In a fast-paced environment with money on the line, you must know what you are doing and what you are talking about.

ADVICE FOR NEW THERAPIST-COACHES

1. In order to be a good coach, work with your own coach.
2. Plan a minimum of two years of intensive learning experiences before you can be an effective and a major contributor to an organization.
3. Competition in the field of executive coaching is increasing dramatically, so it is of the utmost importance to realize that results count sooner rather than later.

MY FEES

As an executive coach my role is to add monetary value to executives by helping to increase work and life efficiency and productivity. I charge executives $1500 per month for three to five one-hour sessions excluding e-mail and short checking-in conversations. The initial assessment is three to five thousand dollars and includes all instruments and extensive feedback.

A BRIEF BIOGRAPHY

I am a Ph.D., licensed psychologist, executive coach, and organization-effectiveness consultant. I am based in Washington, DC but work nationally as a psychologist, TV and print commentator, consultant, and coach to success-oriented, high-functioning achievers.

For the last seven years, I have worked as a coach with individuals and companies around the issues of leadership development, productivity, diversity, and change. My clients include a wide variety of legal, financial services, and technology companies.

Since 1984, I have been the owner of a clinical private practice, where I focus on the diagnosis and treatment of anxiety, depression, and trauma issues. I am a national training facilitator for the EMDR Institute in Palo Alto, California and am a former adjunct faculty and lecturer in psychology at George Washington University in Washington, DC. I earned my Ph.D. in counseling psychology at the University of Maryland where I was an American Psychological Association Fellowship recipient as well as a Congressional Fellow, U.S. House of Representatives.

CONTACT INFORMATION

Carole D. Stovall, Ph.D.
4501 Connecticut Avenue, NW, Suite 215
Washington, DC, 20008
Phone: 202-362-7594
E-mail: cs@DrStovall.com

Part II

Personal Coaching

7

Beyond Insight to Vision
Susan Shevlin

D r. Griffin touched my hand tenderly and quietly pronounced, "You have retinitis pigmentosa, and you will soon lose all your sight." Little did I know at 16 that this would be one of the most decisive days of my life and that my journey through blindness would lead me professionally to the field of rehabilitation and therapy and onto coaching. The doctor's words empowered me and allowed me to begin taking personal responsibility for my life. In that moment, I chose not to be a victim of my circumstances but to be a creator of my life. I transformed my physical blindness into insight. Today, I practice what I call "vision coaching."

In dealing with my blindness, I went through many shifts and changes during which I discovered my strengths and limitations. I had a drive for developing my strengths and minimizing my limitations. That passion later turned to a vision for assisting others to use and maximize their own strengths which in turn led me to the field of therapy and coaching. My passion turned into a professional vision or dream. This vision is an expression of who I am. The creation and fulfillment of such dreams is what I offer my coaching clients.

In his book *Conversations with God,* Neale Donald Walsch speaks of life being a creation: "Life is not a process of discovery, but a process of creation. You are not discovering yourself, but creating yourself anew. Seek, therefore, not to find out who you are, seek to determine who you want to be." I agree. I believe, however, that creation is a choice. On that dramatic day in the doctor's office, I made a choice to live a full life no matter what

I had to handle in the process of becoming blind and subsequently in living with blindness. By making such a choice, I was able to discover many things about myself, which empowered me to develop and unfold my passion. In the natural process of life, one can discover and learn a wealth of information, but without direction or a vision, the information accomplishes little or produces scattered and inconsistent results. When one chooses to focus, he or she begins the process of creation. Having a focus or vision calls forth creation. While therapy is primarily a process of discovery that may lead to creation, coaching is a process of creation in which one might make discoveries.

DISCOVERY AND CREATION

This process of both discovery and creation is possible and available for therapy and coaching clients. Therapy concentrates on the process of discovery. Coaching is a process of creation. During counseling sessions, I assist many clients in discovering emotional blocks and dysfunctional patterns of behavior in their lives. When clients begin to take responsibility for their blocks and patterns, they can begin to recreate their life. Coaching clients are already taking responsibility for themselves; they request coaching to create. To illustrate this, I offer Portia Nelson's "A Short Autobiography," written in a personal growth seminar:

CHAPTER ONE

I walk down a dark street. There is a deep hole in the sidewalk. I fall in. I am lost. I am helpless. It isn't my fault. It takes forever to find my way out.

CHAPTER TWO

I walk down the same street. There is a deep hole in the sidewalk. I pretend I don't see it. I fall in it again. I can't believe I am in the same place. But it isn't my fault. It still takes a long time to get out.

CHAPTER THREE

I walk down the same street. There is a deep hole in the side-

walk. I see it is there. I still fall in. It is a habit. My eyes are open.
I know where I am. It is my fault. I get out immediately.

CHAPTER FOUR

I walk down the same street. There is a deep hole in the sidewalk. I walk around it.

CHAPTER FIVE

I walk down another street.

In his audiocassette series *The Secrets to Manifesting Your Destiny,*
Wayne Dyer discusses this autobiography because it so aptly demonstrates
the bumps or "holes" that we encounter and discover as we travel through
our lives. Often, as a coach, I give it to clients to read as they are running
into challenges on their journey. Like Portia Nelson, counseling and coaching clients are on a journey. They have a destiny. When Portia Nelson sees
the "hole" and takes responsibility for where she is going, her destiny
changes, and she is more able to direct it. Taking responsibility is the first
step in creation. Making a choice to take responsibility marks the transition or the distinction between therapy and coaching. Portia Nelson might
have used a counselor during the first two chapters of her life. During the
third chapter, she was ready for coaching.

When I heard the words that notified me of my impending blindness, I
took responsibility for my blindness and designed a vision for my future
life. Once I accepted what was so, I created a journey for myself. Although
I ran into many obstacles along that path, my vision kept me going and
allowed me to handle the roadblocks. The roadblocks, the holes, and the
bumps were, and still are, my teachers. When I embrace the lessons they
teach, my vision sharpens. As a counselor, I shine the light on my clients'
blocks. As a coach, I partner with them to create their vision and develop
ways to empower and fulfill their dreams or visions; this often involves
shining a light on blind spots.

One of the bumps in the journey for me was the physical and emotional
adjustment to both blindness and life circumstances. Studying and practicing as a counselor gave me the supportive emotional information and
environment I needed. As I provide this for my clients, they uncover the
patterns of the emotional world in which they live. Such insights are com-

parable to the day I faced my physical blindness. Like Dr. Griffin, a therapist works with a client to uncover his or her blindness. Where Dr. Griffin
exposed a physical block, the therapist assists the client in revealing the
emotional blocks. Although I did not personally go through a course of
therapy to handle the emotional adjustment to blindness, I did go through
a rehabilitation program, which taught me new ways to operate. Like the
new ways of functioning I learned in my rehabilitation, my counseling
clients are emotionally rehabilitated by learning a new way of thinking
about their circumstances and handling their emotions. The following
composite case study, which began with counseling, illustrates the differences and similarities between therapy and coaching.

"I have just been discharged from the hospital, and I am so depressed,"
Patricia blurted to me on the telephone. Patricia was expressing an emotional crisis, and I immediately made a counseling appointment for her to
see me.

Patricia was 35 years old and had recently separated from her husband.
She reported feeling very lonely and depressed. Her mother and father
were both dead. Her mother had committed suicide, and her father, who
had died six months prior to our appointment, had been an alcoholic.
Patricia had a Master's degree in business and worked as a hospital administrator. She was having difficulty focusing and had missed nearly a month
of work. She had been in the hospital for her depression for five days.

As a counselor, I worked with Patricia for over a year. We discussed and
uncovered many of her hidden or unconscious feelings. Patricia was
extremely angry at her mother for leaving her alone to cope with her
father. She was also angry with her husband for smothering her. She
blamed him for the fact that she had no friends or support system. She
blamed herself and her mother for her father's alcoholism. "If only I had
been a better daughter, he wouldn't have been drinking so much, and
maybe he wouldn't have died," she repeated session after session.

As she expressed her feelings, often with many tears, I started to explore
with Patricia the distinction between blame and responsibility. Patricia
noticed that she was blaming herself over circumstances in which she had
no control. She was also blaming her mother for her mental illness and
excusing her father for his alcoholism. As she saw the patterns of her own

perceptions, these same perceptions began to shift. Patricia began to create a new story about her circumstances. With this new story, or creation, Patricia generated acceptance and compassion for both her mother's and father's circumstances. Compassion was a new emotion, and it began to replace her anger. She then began to feel compassion for herself. In our final counseling session, we had a ceremony of forgiveness, in which Patricia forgave her parents and herself and let go of the past anger, which had been controlling her.

During counseling, Patricia was able to express and examine her emotions. In generating compassion instead of anger, Patricia began to take responsibility for her emotions. First Patricia had to discover and accept the feelings she was having. These feelings were the past-based emotional environment in which she lived. By shifting her interpretation of the situation, she changed her emotional environment, and was then able to see a new possibility for herself.

I believe my blindness was an asset to me as a counselor. I often share with clients that moment when Dr. Griffin told me I would lose my sight. I describe the feeling of freedom that comes with acceptance and recognition: "The truth will set you free." Because I had developed an attitude of acceptance, it gave clients the room to accept and freely express their emotions. Without visual cues, I developed a keen ear for listening and sensing the unconscious motivation beneath the words. My life also served as an example of what is possible. I had accepted the circumstances and created a successful life. When my clients came to my office, which was in my home, they saw an ordered environment, which had been managed by a person without sight. My clients observed a model for handling circumstances. They saw that I approached or saw situations in a different way. While a client might complain about an emotional situation, they observed me, without complaining, as I led an extraordinary and healthy life, which contributed to their healing. When I would bump into some unexpected physical obstacle in my office or not notice that a light bulb had burned out, they watched me note the location of the obstacle or replace the bulb without any attention to my blindness. By modeling behavior, I encouraged my clients to stop complaining about their feelings and develop new ways of thinking and acting. When I lost my sight, I developed new ways of perceiving. This demonstrated a way for them to heal, and they understood the need to design more useful and powerful perceptions. Like Patricia, the more creative a client could be, the faster they healed.

By knowing and seeing a different possibility or opportunity for my clients, as a counselor I provided a healing environment for these clients. I could see what they couldn't. Walsch writes about this kind of empowering insight: "Let's say that people tend to see in themselves what we see in them. The grander our vision, the grander their willingness to access and display the part of them we have already shown them."

During the process of counseling, Patricia healed her emotions, changed her emotional environment, and was then able to consider and take actions to shift her circumstances. Toward the end of our time together for counseling, Patricia took a new position in a hospital in another state. She was physically and emotionally moving to a new environment in which to continue growing. Simultaneously, I was beginning the transition from a counseling practice to a coaching practice. When Patricia inquired about ways in which we could continue our work together, I suggested that she might want to consider a coaching relationship.

Patricia had moved quite a distance from my office, so we began to conduct coaching sessions by telephone. We spoke weekly for about 45 minutes. Being blind and used to listening without visual cues, this worked for me. I believe it also helped Patricia to distinguish coaching from the previous counseling. The box of tissues was not sitting in front of her, and she did not have the familiar cues to trigger an old emotional response. This allowed me to partner with Patricia in taking positive actions, rather than in uncovering and dealing with emotional feelings. She was sitting in her new home or in a new office.

ASSESSING RESERVES

Patricia had cleaned up her emotional environment and was ready to design her new life. The first thing I did as a coach was to administer "The Clean Sweep" assessment, a written tool developed by Coach University to determine specific areas in a person's life that might be out of order. Because of the distance, Patricia and I communicated by e-mail as well as by telephone. I sent this program to her through e-mail, and she returned it quickly. It revealed several areas that she might want to improve as she built a new life.

Although Patricia had a strong emotional foundation after counseling, the assessment showed weaknesses in managing her finances and developing supportive relationships. I knew from my own life experiences, training as a coach, and experiences of other clients that creating reserves in any area was important in building a life foundation. The assessment exposed parts of the foundation that were lacking or needed reinforcements.

With my guidance, Patricia wrote and followed a daily program to increase her reserves in the financial and relationship area. For example, as a response to a fieldwork assignment to develop new habits, she began to balance her checkbook daily. This action kept her eyes on her money and made her constantly aware of her expenditures. Although a seemingly simple action, it is commonly accepted that what we focus on is what we manifest. She made a budget and took steps daily to put the budget into practice. In terms of relationships, she included in her daily habits the practice of doing something nice for someone each day. This turned her attention to other people around her. This action might be sending a birthday card to a coworker or saying hello to a stranger. Patricia also began to explore new social activities. She found a church and joined a study group.

While Patricia was handling her finances and completing her divorce, we were discussing a vision for her life. She started exploring important questions. Where do you want to be in ten years? If you were to die, what would you want others to say about you? What characteristics do you admire in others? Through this inquiry, which we were engaged in for several weeks, Patricia revealed her appreciation for learning and for the intricate dealings in the business world. She was defining the direction she wanted to head in her life.

FIELDWORK TO ADVANCE PERSONAL VISION

I regularly give coaching clients homework, which will move them along the road toward their goals. This fieldwork is only a request, and my clients have no obligation to accept such suggestions. But by taking such action, clients can move more quickly. One week, I requested that Patricia write a vision statement for her life. With her background in business, she immediately understood the value of this assignment. I stressed that she should concentrate on who she wanted to be, not what she wanted to do. Patricia wrote, "I am financially free and solvent and give away the blessings and resources for such financial opportunity and freedom to others."

With this written vision statement, Patricia and I were able to work together and establish other fieldwork assignments that advanced the expression and fulfillment of her vision. One week, she chose to talk to various financial planners. She then hired one to work with her on personal financial investments. Having previously done the fieldwork of balancing her checkbook as a daily practice, Patricia knew the value of regularly keeping track of her investments. Rather than give total responsibility for her finances to her financial planner, she was able to partner with him. This new type of partnering relationship was a direct result of coaching. Coaching requires partnership, where each person, client and coach, is responsible. This partnership transferred to her other relationships, and Patricia's effectiveness in the area of relationships also increased.

Because of the partnership nature of a coaching relationship, I was also able to grow through my relationship with Patricia. One way I know that a coaching relationship is succeeding is to observe whether it is contributing to my personal vision: "My life is creative, inspiring, spiritual, thoughtful, and filled with beauty. I participate in all aspects of my life with grace, excellence, and integrity. I am a powerful contribution, inspiring others to a thoughtful and creative life."

In my counseling relationships, I contributed to my clients, and my growth was independent of their movement. In coaching, I find that I am growing with my clients. They tend to be one step ahead of me or one step behind.

Today Patricia is teaching business courses at a major university, as well as consulting with several hospital administrators. She has many friends and travels all over the world with them. She is dating and establishing healthy relationships. I am still coaching Patricia. We speak twice a month by telephone. I occasionally e-mail her with information about a project or with an encouraging story. I still give her homework or fieldwork, which she uses to take action on her intentions. We created a partnership to fulfill Patricia's vision.

Patricia is a perfect example of a client who transitioned from a therapy client to a coaching client. When I first heard Patricia's voice on the telephone, I knew she needed emotional healing. As she expressed and examined her feelings, she began to lay a foundation to reconstruct her interpretation of her circumstances. With a stronger and more secure emotional foundation, Patricia was able to explore other areas of her life. At that point she shifted her relationship with me. I became Patricia's coach. Patricia had discovered the power of choice. We became partners in designing Patricia's life and in creating an environment in which she could fulfill her dreams.

As a coach, I often say to my clients, "There are no accidents." It was no accident that I was shifting my practice from therapy to coaching as Patricia was healing and available for coaching. As a therapist, I had assumed the role of an expert. Indeed, I had studied psychology and I was quite aware of the emotional environment in which human beings live. As a coach, I shifted the role of expert to partner. Although I studied and developed techniques for coaching, I trusted Patricia's vision and served as her guide and a sounding board. As a therapist, I was required to see. As a coach, I was to be the guide in opening Patricia's eyes. In counseling I saw the solutions; in coaching Patricia saw and created the vision, and we partnered on fulfilling the dreams.

Coaching is a creative process. I like to say that in coaching, we do what works, rather than following a formula. When Patricia moved, we began our sessions on the telephone and used e-mail to exchange information and resources. I now do much of my coaching by telephone and deliver resources through e-mail. While I am developing an international practice with such aids, I still have many local clients who prefer to meet in person. I anticipate that someday all my clients will appreciate the convenience of interacting by telephone and e-mail. Counseling sessions tended to occur weekly for a very structured hour. In doing what works, I structure my coaching time to fit the needs of my clients. Sessions usually are 30–40 minutes, and they may occur only two or three times a month. With counseling clients, I took responsibility for the direction of the session. In partnership with my client, I design conversations, fieldwork, and exercises to fit and forward the individual client's style and goals. A coaching client is equally responsible for the outcome of the session.

While Patricia was my first official coaching client, in reality I had been using coaching techniques and methods with many of my counseling clients for several years prior to Patricia's transition. I had attended many personal growth and educational seminars that trained me and demonstrated coaching techniques. I also did part-time training and coaching for one of these organizations. I attracted counseling clients who were responsive to such techniques. These clients were looking to handle specific adjustment issues and to move forward in their life. When I saw the rapid results produced by these coaching techniques, I enrolled in Coach University for specific training that allowed me to more fully and effectively practice as a coach. Many of my former counseling clients have now become coaching clients. Like my relationship with Patricia, I have more of a partnership with these clients. The individuals who are now in coaching have more of a focus and direction for their life. They have or are developing a healthier lifestyle. With my focus on a client's vision, I am now drawing business and corporate clients too. My coaching practice consists of clients who want to establish their vision or who want to more extensively express that vision.

As a coach, I encourage clients to design a vision for themselves. Knowing what they want their life to look like or to be about gives them direction and allows them to make choices, which support the fulfillment of that vision. Initially, my own vision was to be successful, not to be a victim of my blindness. In order to fulfill and empower my vision, I had to be trained to operate without sight. I knew that I would be as effective as my training. I needed a strong foundation on which to build my vision. Likewise, coaching clients refuse to be victims and need this same strong foundation to build and fill their vision. A coach assists in creating the vision and is a resource for implementing the steps toward meeting the goals. The coach cheers the client on as he runs down the appropriate street to his dreams.

I, too, am living my dreams, a life that had me evolve into a coach. Being a coach represents peace and the fulfilling of a vision. I journeyed through many stages and have returned to the same places again and again. During this time, I lost and found my vision over and over. Each time, I chose to expand my vision and to do the work and receive the experience, which in turn empowered the vision. Therapy, in the form of emotional healing, was a part of that work and experience. I chose to both professionally work as a therapist to facilitate emotional healing for others and to heal my own emotional dysfunction. Today, when I see such dysfunction interfering with the expression of a client's dreams, I may suggest therapy as a part of the structure to accomplish client's goals. Emotional disease can limit and cloud the creation and impede the work of building a foundation for the dreams to emerge. Living your dreams requires an alignment of vision with a firm personal foundation or structure. I, too, nourish my emotional well-being to continue living my dreams. For me, coaching is an empowering partnership with clients to create consciously a vision, to work to have structures that contribute and nourish the vision, and to live in peace and connection with the universe.

My powerful coaching partnerships allow me to experience an integrated life with that connection and peace. While still physically blind, I am living with a powerful vision, and through vision coaching I am able to assist others in opening their eyes and in creating effective insights, dreams, and actions.

PRACTICAL INFORMATION

ADVICE FOR NEW VISION COACHES

There are three processes to vision coaching. The first, which is essential to working with the other two aspects, involves having clients express or design a vision, purpose, or goals. The second includes assessing the strengths and weaknesses of clients' present structure and assisting them to build a supportive foundation for fulfilling their goals. The third part is to maintain the structures and to continue to nourish clients' creativity and growth.

ADVICE FOR NEW THERAPIST-COACHES

1. Get a coach.
2. Find a coach-training program and participate fully.
3. Implement coaching techniques in your own life and with clients; get started!

MY FEES

I charge by the month for coaching. My fees are $200 per month for two one-hour sessions and $300 for four 45-minute sessions. I accept calls and e-mails between sessions and often send out resources that support the client's development.

WHAT I KNOW NOW

I wish I had investigated coach training and had gotten involved with a program earlier, rather than tackling it independently. I also wish I had recognized the value of having an appropriate coach as a partner.

A BRIEF BIOGRAPHY

I feel as though I have always been a coach. This profession has been a natural match and a perfect evolution from the field of therapy. As a child, I was always interested in learning and developing myself. Although blind, I observed human behavior and could see opportunities for others.

I graduated from Wells College with a BA in psychology and a minor in philosophy and religion. These courses led me into the field of rehabilitation and therapy, and I received my M.Ed. in counseling from the University of Iowa in 1972. I later developed a private practice in counseling.

With my desire to continue growing, I participated in many educational seminars. I volunteered and worked as a part-time project manager for Landmark Education, one such seminar program. My association with Landmark gave me coaching experience, and I began to use coaching techniques in my counseling practice. Seeing the progress and results of this way of interacting, I naturally evolved my counseling practice into a coaching practice.

I increased my coaching skills and credibility by enrolling in Coach University. I contracted with a mentor coach, who is my partner in designing a very full private coaching practice. I continue to nurture myself by using the resources of my clients, other coaches, my family and friends, and nature. For me, being connected to these resources has helped me grow both as a coach and as a contributing human being. My vision continues to expand.

CONTACT INFORMATION

Susan Shevlin
Vision Coaching
1135 B Salem Drive
Charlotte, NC 28209
Phone: 704-334-2625
E-mail: sshevlin@bellsouth.net

8

Using Lightness and Humor to Coach Highly Creative People

Roz Van Meter

At the end of each day, Donna felt like she'd been pulled through a knothole backwards. The large urban school district where she worked was embroiled in public scandal, fiery resignations, dramatic midnight dismissals, threats of lawsuits and countersuits, and nightly exposés on area television.

A bright, highly educated, gracious woman, Donna wanted no part of all the conflict and melodrama. She needed to figure out how to maneuver through the minefield without getting blown up. Knowing that the political intrigues and upheavals in the district would eventually settle out, she was determined to hang on until then. Meantime, she and I were engaged in a coaching relationship; even as we were devising serious strategies, I made sure we laughed a lot. *[Our shared laughter accomplished two things. It allowed her to relax and feel braver, and it helped us bond. These bracketed comments are my way of pointing out coaching techniques to therapists who are on the path to becoming personal coaches.]*

Once I told her the writer's definition of a literary critic: A critic is one who walks onto the battlefield after the war is over and shoots the survivors. "Not me!" she said. "I'm coming out of this intact."

We had already had a dress rehearsal for all this political upheaval. Several months earlier, we had brainstormed strategies for handling various machinations she thought she might encounter at a family reunion. She wanted to assess where to engage and where to disengage, and learn to stretch her comfort level. We did some role-plays—as she put it, "So I'd know what I was doing." Based on her success at the reunion, we decided our winning formula was V + P = M: visualizing plus practice equals mastery. *[Donna's real task was to become more direct and assertive, to begin setting clear boundaries. By rehearsing her family reunion, she gained confidence that could be generalized to interactions in many settings, not just the family or the workplace.]*

Next I showed her how to establish a mental force-field against the turmoil at work; how to see other people's diatribes as statements about them, not about her; how to detach from the craziness until it subsided, management was replaced, and the general paranoia settled out; and how to take good care of herself while staying visible and continuing to be effective. We role-played her gentle but firm confrontation with an intimidating subordinate, who ended up becoming one of her staunchest supporters. We rehearsed a speech she gave to reassure an audience of anxious employees, and she ended up wowing them. *[She was excellent at taking care of others. Now she was learning to use those same skills for self-care.]*

Gradually Donna became almost bullet-proof, a serene little craft hovering over the action but not personalizing it, listening with empathy but not hooking into the factions. All sides came to understand that she was neutral and eventually stopped trying to enlist her.

The Power of E-coaching

The following e-mail exchange occurred during the process of building Donna's personal strength and self-assurance. Never doubt the power of e-coaching. It is a different kind of conversation that is sometimes more effective than talking. I usually coach almost exclusively by telephone, with occasional short e-mails between appointments. However, I allowed Donna's long and eloquent e-mails to be a significant part of her coaching. Below is a transcript of some of our e-mail exchanges. She explains how writing helps her sort through her feelings and cognitions, reflecting and editing to clarify for herself, as well as for me, just what is going on with her. If you are a user of e-mail, you will understand that the portions marked by double carats << are her comments. My remarks, sent as an e-mail response, are marked by an arrow → symbol.

Subj: Communicating Calmly and Powerfully

→ Hi! Several things you just wrote really resonated with me. You wrote:

<< What I have to do is to write. I'm getting better at verbal responses but my real strength is in my writing. It's as if my brain has a direct link to my fingers and my keyboard.

→ Me too. I know exactly what you mean. *[I reinforced another commonality we shared.]*

<< I can say things that are harder for me to say out loud, face-to-face, and then look at the words and reflect and make sure that what I'm saying is exactly what I want to say.

→ Writing helps you organize your thoughts. Gives you a chance to say it succinctly, grown-up-ly, rationally, convincingly. Lets you delete what is irrelevant, redundant, poorly timed. When you ultimately do talk, your ideas and attitudes have become calm, powerful, more persuasive. You are neither a victim nor a control freak, but simply a colleague with valuable observations and ideas

<< My boss is such a hands-on micromanager that I find myself becoming paralyzed. Afraid to make decisions because they will be nitpicked and made wrong. Evidently this week she heard that concern from me and from at least one other staff member whom she respects. She says she is rethinking her management style. She is so much like my father. Explode and not listen. Very little encouragement, only criticism. So this is probably my lesson—to get over these last vestiges of power he had over me.

→ Keep in mind that she is anxious. *[Note that I choose not to go back into her past, as I might if she were a therapy client. Instead, we are working on the here-and-now and the future.]* She's got an Inner Critic too, and she's scared that any deviation from her preconceived path will land her in quicksand. If you get that, you can be calmly supportive of her, empathetic with her anxiety, and able to repeat back to her, calmly, what you hear her saying to be sure you got it all. That act alone will calm her down. *[Note how many times* calm *is used in this paragraph as encouragement and as an embedded suggestion.]*

<< One thing I've realized is that when she does compliment me, I discount it, because I know that in the next e-mail, sentence, or encounter, there will be something that is cause for criticism.

→ Get over it. When she compliments you, acknowledge it with a thanks. What you reinforce is what you'll get more of, including appreciation. So what if the next transaction is critical? Don't contaminate one with the other.

<< I do not believe people grow from showing them their warts. I believe people grow from showing them their strengths. I will bend over backwards for people who believe in me. I feel defeated by those who point out my shortcomings.

→ So that's your management style, and good for you. But it's not hers. You can accept that fact instead of criticizing her (in your heart) because she doesn't do it your way. (Sound familiar?) She is not going to change hugely, but she has already changed somewhat in your direction. Good for you both!

Remember, the meaning of critical is "to critique." When Roger Ebert says a movie is one of his top ten of the year, he's making a critical statement. Your boss isn't tactful about how she critiques, but if you mentally remove the prickly casing it comes in, you may find that the fruit inside is useful. And even if it isn't, it was an attempt on her part, successful or not, to get something to work better or to try to avoid problems.

<< And, of course, it's not all black and white. The woman is a genius (so was my father). Philosophically, I am very close to her beliefs about education. *[Donna has already begun to look at all sides of her situation, to move away from her sense of helplessness.]*

→ So maybe you could tell her how much it means to you to work with a talented woman who shares your values, how gratifying it is to be working passionately to change a dysfunctional system. You might not make it the whole hundred miles, but it's good to be moving down the right road. In spite of detours and roadblocks, you're both on the same path. It's inspiring not to be working for someone who is just as resolutely heading down an evil or venal path. You can tell her these things, or some version of them, because they are your truth. Not all of it, not the personality frustrations, but an important part. *[This is a classic reframe.]*

<< I am also inspired by the deeply committed people I am getting to know. With the right leadership, there should be no way that we can't turn things around. There are too many good people in the organization. And that's what keeps me going.

I keep looking at things from a systems perspective. Every meeting I run, every work session I call, I focus people on systems. I do not allow any blaming. I use my quality tools to do constructive, structured brainstorming about problems. *[I don't remember what she meant by "quality tools," whether these were strategies I gave her or part of her preexisting skill set. It doesn't really matter. They obviously were useful to her.]*

When people can all get on the same side of the problem and look at the mountain, it gets beyond personalities—it gets to problem solving, changing systems. Some of it seems so easy and logical. But people have been so polarized (and so put down) for so long that they want to defend what they've been doing. So, that's a long, long way to say I love what I'm doing. I feel like I'm making a difference. I'm getting some very positive feedback. And at the same time, my boss is making life miserable. But, it's my problem, right?

→ Yep. It's your problem, because it's your reaction. You can choose to change your interpretation, and thus your feelings. And as you respond to her in a collegial way, she will respect you more. *[I can now get tougher with her, because she has taken her power and responsibility back. Sometimes I do this too soon with prospective clients during an initial interview, and they decline to hire me. I have decided that's okay, because I only enjoy working with people who may be vulnerable but aren't quakingly fragile, and I only coach people I enjoy. I walk the coaching talk of creating my ideal life.]*

<< It is me who has to teach her how to treat me. I have to do a better job of communicating to her, keeping her informed, but in an assertive way. There is no way she is going to survive unless she begins to trust some of us. There are way too many things going on for her to micromanage everything.

→ That's a lovely, supportive point of view. I love that approach.

<< I appreciate your being there. I can feel your encouragement and your love even without constant communication. Thank you.

→ You are entirely welcome. Love, Roz

P.S. You know, as I look back on what I just wrote to you, I think about other clients from all over the country, and how universal our paths really are. All of them, in one way or another, are working to detach from the manipulations that go on within the systems. I mention this because I know you are working to be a coach within your job. As you go forward in your coach training, you'll find that most of us aren't so different from each other, really. We all are doing the best we can, and the important thing is to just keep making our best get better!

When the dust settled and the firing and hiring subsided, Donna ended up with exactly the job she had always wanted: consulting with teachers to develop better strategies to help the students learn, not just make passing grades. She says, "People keep telling teachers how to do things instead of listening to where they are. I see coaching as an extension of what I'm doing with the teachers—helping people set their own goals and go with their strengths." She will make a fine coach. I am proud to be her mentor.

HELPING A CLIENT ORGANIZE HER LIFE

My process with Kathy, another coaching client, was more typical of my coaching approach; our e-mails were shorter, our goals more behavioral, and our process done mostly by phone. She was less introspective than Donna, more focused on demonstrable outcome over which she had control, and motivated by action steps with immediate payoffs.

A freelance writer, Kathy had been given an assignment by a senior editor at a magazine to write an article entitled, "To Get A Life, I Got A Life Coach." Several years earlier Kathy had written about finally getting diagnosed with attention-deficit disorder, and what a difference medication had made in her life. Now, although she was no longer agitated and short-fused, she still slogged daily through an accumulation of clutter, distraction, and unfinished projects. Not only was she spinning too many plates like a Cirque du Soleil performer, she also still carried the burden of ADD.

ADD wasn't all she was toting. She was working on a novel and a book of poetry, writing freelance articles for magazines, keeping a large house, and looking after two teenaged sons and her husband, Tom, an airline pilot. Kathy felt overwhelmed, a feeling familiar to millions who have too many roles and not enough time.

Our core goal was to get her organized and calm enough to proceed strategically with her home and writing projects, while nurturing her own natural exuberance. Up front I told her that many right-brain creative people have at least some degree of ADD, that her childhood day-dreaming and story-weaving were gifts from her beautiful right brain. *[In this way I reframed her out-to-lunch tendencies as being part of her own particular creativity, which is absolutely true.]*

We soon learned that we are both fans of Anne Lamott, author of the writer's guide *Bird by Bird* I reminded Kathy of Lamott's assignment to write only what you can see in a one-inch frame. Using that same concept, Kathy started by decluttering her kitchen counter, a small area she could finish in a few minutes. I proposed that she use my three-piles strategy: pile one for keepers, pile two for dumpers, and pile three for undecideds, to be triaged later.

I suggested that she put the keepers in lovely wicker baskets. This became her favorite strategy, and Kathy found more beautiful wicker baskets that I would have dreamed possible—oval, rectangular, square, in many sizes and shades of willow and wicker.

Soon after we began coaching, I asked Kathy about her muse. Muse? She hadn't really thought about that. *[Often I use phrases such as "inner wisdom" or "muse" to represent an inspiring and supportive alter ego.]*

I suggested that a lovely muse lives inside her and really ought to have a name. My voice got dreamy as I said, "You know how you were telling me about standing in your swimming pool up to your waist, reading a book? In my imagination you looked up from your book and began to gaze at the fence where your neighbor's honeysuckle keeps coming back, even though he cuts it down every year. I don't know if you just looked at the honeysuckle, or maybe noticed the lacy shadow it throws, or maybe thought about its indomitable spirit, how it keeps coming back and will not be denied."

Kathy was silent for half a minute, then said, "Honeysuckle! That's her name!" Of course, I knew who she meant. I also knew she had made some new connections in her brain, new portals of possibility. *[Even over the phone, my lower, slower voice had induced a light trance to reach her unconscious. I come from a long line of Texas storytellers and was using stories to change perception and embed suggestions long before neurolinguistic programming, but I didn't tell colleagues because I feared they'd think me unprofessional. Now that Ericksonian hypnosis is a common therapeutic tool, I feel vindicated. Besides, it's fun and it works.]*

The next day she called to tell me that actually her muse's name was Sarah. Lovely name, I said.

A day later she called and said triumphantly, "Sarah Honeysuckle!" She ordered a brass plate engraved with the name and displayed it prominently on her desk. Who was that, her boys asked? She told them about her muse, who by this time was clearly cohabiting her office and her spirit. The boys and Tom, who treasure her flights of fancy, were happy to welcome Sarah.

Kathy had already cleared off her kitchen counter and desk and bought lovely wicker baskets. She must have cornered the market on those baskets; ultimately she owned dozens and used them elegantly all through her house.

However, after Sarah Honeysuckle came on the scene, Kathy decided the office needed more than lovely baskets. Sarah deserved not just a pretty office, but one that was also deep-down organized. I asked, "What is your worst pack-rat challenge?" She said, "All the old drafts and treatments of dozens of articles, several drafts of novels—paper, paper, paper." Then I asked if she had those same drafts saved onto her hard drive. Yes. And backed up? No, but she would do that tonight, create two back-up disks and take one of them to her safety deposit box tomorrow. By this time her enthusiasm was crackling over the phone.

The next day she sent an excited e-mail about her new paper shredder. Why did she need a shredder? Because she didn't want that paper ever to come back! She laughed at the image of discarded paper sneaking back into the house, but I support whatever works, and that paper shredder became her six-gun as she mowed down her excess paper. The very first day she filled several large garbage sacks and put them out for recycling. *[I teased her about her paper shredder: "Kathy, I can't believe you did that!" with conspiratorial admiration in my voice. It was an indirect "attagirl" aimed at her unconscious rebellion against ordinariness. Her triumph was evident at this determined but offbeat and creative approach to decluttering.]*

Two weeks later her delighted husband surprised her with a new, heavy-duty paper shredder. Kathy was as thrilled as if it had been a roomful of roses. She wrote, "This one is a lot nicer and cross-cuts! First thing Mon morning, after I get the boys on the bus, I plan to get on my exercise bike, then I'll hit the office and feed my new paper shredder with all those four- and five-year-old insurance papers and the zillion copies of my novel that I don't need. Carting off another load of trash. You'd be proud. This is just the tip of the iceberg, baby!!!"

I gave her plenty of permission and encouragement about the post-it notes that still bristled on her bulletin board and the edge of her computer. "They are babysitting your brainchildren," I told her, "keeping them safe until you can get back to them. Meantime, you can f-o-c-u-s on the project at hand, which at this moment is the magazine article." *[Using metaphors and analogies is an integral part of my style. I even teach it to other coaches. It is particularly effective with creative people.]*

Understanding her aesthetic, I suggested that other important projects might be kept in Christmas gift bags with 3x5 cards stapled to their sides, naming each. That way, she can clip an article, tear off an entire newspaper page, or print out a web page, drop it into the bag, and stay current without becoming distracted from job #1.

In our conversations I discovered that unlike her other writing, which flows effortlessly at first, Kathy was stuck in places on her novel. I reminded her that Anne Lamott teaches her writing students about "the shitty first draft." It is imperative, Lamott says, because it's the only way to get started. Every writer she knows writes a shitty first draft, Lamott says, except just one, and she suspects that person doesn't have a very rich inner life. Kathy and I laughed at the quip yet realized Lamott's wisdom, and how often people get paralyzed with what I call premature perfectionism. Ultimately you want to put out the best possible product, but at first you need to just let 'er rip. *[In coaching as in therapy, humor is my greatest ally, more than experience or skills or strategies, because humor connects me to my client's core self. Once I mesh with the client's sense of humor, especially when its character is similar to my own, the relationship clicks into place like a docking shuttle. If the humor is occasionally outrageous, the bond gets even deeper. We are true colleagues and coconspirators, enjoying our partnership in a new, mischievous, delightful way.]*

Using Life-coping Tools

During our phone sessions I gave Kathy my two best life-coping tools. First, I had her install an imaginary pause button in her left palm. This is an easy assignment for creatives. I taught Kathy to press her pause button any time she felt overwhelmed, resentful, or bewildered, so she could freeze-frame the situation and consider a good response rather than a knee-jerk reaction. *[When I'm coaching literal-minded linear thinkers I tell them to hallucinate the button just for fun, and so far no one has failed to install and enjoy it.]*

The second tool is my one-to-ten big-deal scale. I explained that any scale is useful only if it's calibrated, and that on this scale a ten is nuclear holocaust. Then what's a one? Nothing, actually, because if an event is that inconsequential, you won't be asking yourself, "How big a deal is this?"

We discussed how frustrating it can be when one spouse considers something a nine and the other thinks it shouldn't even move the needle. Kathy and her husband got quite accomplished at recalibrating their respective big-deal scales to stay objective and also to honor the other person's scale. I was providing subtle relationship coaching. Our agendas included increasing her sense of confidence in handling tasks that were traditionally Tom's bailiwick. He was as delighted as she was at her emerging independence.

I soon had an opportunity to demonstrate the use of the big deal scale. Here is an excerpt from one of my e-mails to her:

→ Hi, Kathy!

Had an adventure today. I went downstairs here at the office, turned on the ignition, and my battery EXPLODED!! with a very loud bang and some impressive smoke. Bystanders gathered quickly; they thought someone had shot a gun.

So that's my drama du jour. How big is it on a scale of 1 to 10? Less than a 2. Of course, if I'd been in traffic on the freeway at 5:00 in 103 degree weather, it would have felt like a plus-7. Even so, I've got AAA membership and a cell phone and lots of friends, so even if Robert had not been available, I'd have been able to bring it down the old scale to a 3.5.

Now, as I sit here in my air-conditioned office writing to you while my knight in chinos fixes my chariot, I feel both competent and cherished. Nice way to feel.

Hope you are the same. Roz

The very next morning Kathy got in her car and found she had a dead battery! She laughed out loud at the coincidence, then proceeded to handle it herself. She quickly came to know that she was much more capable than she'd realized, that she didn't have to twist her hankie and wait for her husband to come home. She figured out why her computer was acting weird, got assertive about telling her kids to clean up their rooms, and said no thanks to a writing assignment that wasn't a good fit.

As her self-confidence grew, her relationship with Tom became more lateral, more adult-to-adult. She was able to stay calm with her boys, more authoritative when appropriate. They had always had fun together, but now their fun wasn't tinged with tension.

Here is Kathy's first outcome e-mail. Note her stream-of-consciousness writing. She does this in all her rough drafts, getting her spontaneous thoughts down first. In a piece for publication she will edit and re-edit later, but even then she first captures her spontaneous impressions. No premature perfectionism cramps her style. *[One of my most important coaching tools is my outcome report. I find that both the coach and the client benefit hugely from this completed circuit. As in all communication, it is the feedback loop that validates and furthers the transaction.]*

<< Outcome sheet from first coaching session with Roz:

Lots of validation that how I am is okay. All we're doing is shining it up, although I think I'm really rewriting my self story to come out the way I want it to. Now we can improve on the strategies I am already using. Noticed the delicate resiliency and determined perseverance of the honeysuckle. Named my muse/wisewoman Honeysuckle.

Began to understand the support of having a person who understands you completely, is totally on your side, yet also objective and candid—who stretches you to be more completely You.

Even though Roz has been doing personal coaching for over 20 years, she still has her own coach for those same reasons. Principles Roz gave me to ask myself: Is it currently true? Does it fit? Is it in my own best interest?

Learned how people take care of others and themselves: NURTURE AND PROTECT. Honeysuckle is there to help me do both. >>

Here is an excerpt from another e-mail I sent her:

→ Hi, Kathy.

I'm up late. I love late-at-night times. Just read your e-mail and have several comments that I don't want to wait till our next session to say.

First: You didn't say you think in fits and starts, you said, SPITS and FURTS, and I love it. Nutty and hilarious, but somehow sounds profound.

As for your sounding like an airhead, that's not my take. Rather, I hear you as a brilliantly creative person who gets excited about thoughts and chases random ones that dart across the mental path. You and I do the same thing, yet I think affectionately of my "rabbit chasing" and actually see it as an asset, bringing color and texture to my thought process, sparking new ideas (okay, tangents, but so what?). *[Again, I show her our commonality. Creatives pop out ideas like a popcorn machine. Many are worth recording for possible future use. The challenge is not to allow them to sidetrack the current project.]*

It's all in the perception. The trick is not to treat yourself scornfully, yet still remain responsible. That's why I am particularly impressed by your aha! that you were being petulant and childish when you got outraged that your husband wasn't listening to you RIGHT NOW (accompanied by a stamp of your tiny foot). Great insight!

You have a lot of character, Kathy. I love character above all things—well, along with intelligence and humor, which you've also got an abundance of. I enjoy you so much. *[My clients know I'm deeply and genuinely fond of them, so they recognize my admiring comments as authentic, not just clinical reinforcement.]*

Sorry about your dead battery, but tickled pink that you invoked the big deal scale. Good for you! Every time you use it, it becomes more automatic. Sometimes you'll use it retroactively—"That thing that happened this morning wasn't such a big deal." Then you'll learn to do it in the moment, as you did with your battery. Eventually you'll learn to use it preemptively—that is, catch yourself catastrophizing about some imagined future problem, and laugh.

'Night.

Roz

As part of my ongoing goal to help Kathy take good care of herself and hold herself in high esteem, I later e-mailed this to her:

→ You are more than a writer, you are a human being—a person, a beautiful spirit and lovely human being—and you need to take care of yourself, as you would a baby. Sometimes that means put the baby down for a nap, take the baby out for an airing, or the baby's got too many clothes on, or let the baby just splash in the backyard pool. And it always means protect the baby from toxic materials, situations, or people.

Remember the importance of just being at rest, letting the well fill back up. Not only will your writing well fill up, your soul will too. Roz.

With Donna and Kathy I was able to take more liberties, be more confrontive and more openly loving than with therapy clients. We still correspond. They are both friends of my heart. *[I have never been very adept at keeping the so-called therapeutic distance with clients. Coaching allows me to reap the fruits of a fond relationship, as well as help clients succeed in their aspirations.]*

Each client brings a unique delightfulness. I think fondly of the young couples who need better communication skills quickly; the people in transition who truly want to improve their lives but don't know where to start; the procrastinators who joke that they would have hired a coach sooner but kept putting it off; the singles who need to learn how to date smart, instead of choosing the same wrong partners (in different guises) over and over. There is nothing "virtual" about these telephone and e-mail relationships. They are real and deeply rewarding. My clients enrich my life as much as I enrich theirs. For me, coaching is the most powerful helping profession in the world.

PRACTICAL INFORMATION

ADVICE FOR NEW CREATIVITY COACHES

1. Right-brain creatives need to think out loud and run with their thoughts because they shoot out ideas like sparks from a sparkler. If your coaching style is linear, do yourself a favor and refer the creatives to someone who matches their style of idea generation.
2. The best way I can serve creatives is to take notes as they whirl and soar, and later reflect their brain-sparks back to them. This is important, because they may go into an altered state and literally become bemused.
3. Toward the end of a coaching call, the client and I decide which ideas to relegate to the future, and which ones to pursue immediately. Only then do we add structure and accountability. After we have agreed on the next best steps to take, I ask him or her to put a timetable on each one, building in time for diversions. If a client thinks it will take 45 minutes to create the outline of an article, I suggest blocking an hour. Committing to blocks of time seems to work well for many creatives. I suggest the use of a timer. "Work for 45 minutes, then when the dinger dings, take a break. Of course, if you're on a roll and don't want to stop, keep going, but don't burn yourself out."

ADVICE FOR NEW THERAPIST-COACHES

1. When I launched my coaching business, I completed three things in quick succession—put out an announcement mailing, launched a Web site, and hired a coach (actually, two coaches for the first few months). That is my advice to emerging coaches. Hire a coach! Getting coached allowed me to apprentice with a knowledgeable veteran, jump-started my visibility, and helped me attract half a dozen clients almost immediately. I was off and running.

2. My first aim is to have fun and be a first-rate change-agent coach. My second is to have a hassle-free life, so I only accept clients who have access to e-mail. I don't want to bother with sending out materials by "snail mail," so I send my welcome packet and all subsequent materials electronically. There may be coaches who do not have e-mail, but I don't know them. Members of the International Coach Federation receive its announcements, newsletters, and correspondence via e-mail.

3. Mine is an international Internet business. Many clients find me through my Web sites, and I recently became a regular guest on an Internet radio talk show, answering "call-in" e-mail questions. E-mail also allows me to send my part of a conversation to people in Norway, Germany, Australia, at a time they may be sleeping. Within a few hours, their response shows up. I am selective about my clients. For every one I accept there are a couple I decline and refer elsewhere. I only want to work with motivated, bright people who are questing, flexible, and willing to stretch.

MY FEES

My client contracts are for one month at a time. I require no minimum and respect a client who wants to suspend for a month or two, for financial or scheduling reasons. So far those people have always resumed. Except for a half-hour free brainstorming call to see if we'll be a good fit, I have charged my coaching clients full fare from the beginning. In my case, that's $350 or $450 for three or four calls a month, plus generous e-mails.

I make some exceptions. For example, a young local professional asked for just one two-hour lunch meeting per month (his treat), plus frequent e-mails, for $250. It was an interesting and creative idea and is working out beautifully. I've enjoyed some excellent lunches, and he has moved up into a new job approaching six figures, reconnected to his family, and boosted his self-image dramatically.

WHAT I KNOW NOW

For several years I discounted myself for not having a coaching niche. The conventional question "Who is your ideal client?" didn't work for me. My ideal client was whoever I enjoyed at the moment, and I tend to enjoy almost everyone. Having a niche can be a wonderful thing if it's a natural one, based on your experience and expertise. Marketing is easier if you have a target group to reach. However, I have learned that it's not mandatory. Many clients come by word of mouth, and since people of like sensibilities find each other, over the years I have attracted the people I most enjoy, who most like and learn from me.

For me, similarities of style, humor, and energy level are more important than similarity of profession. I coach writers, physicians, educators, emerging coaches, business owners, single parents, married couples, middle-aged people in transition, and college students.

With a lot of life experience behind me, I have learned to take good care of myself. One important aspect of that self-care is a fine-tuned internal warning system. If I get the feeling that a prospective client is not a good fit for me, I refer the person to someone else. That's no reflection on either of us. If it's not a good fit, trying to sandpaper yourself or the other person won't make it a fit. It just skins you up.

A BRIEF BIOGRAPHY

I rejected managed care over ten years ago, preferring to work half the hours for the same income, as well as to reclaim my autonomy. I've always been a bottom-line, results-oriented therapist, so coaching was a natural transition for me. I also continue to maintain my counseling practice, because I still enjoy it hugely.

I am a licensed professional counselor and a licensed marriage and family therapist, with 24 years in private practice, specializing in communication in business and intimate relationships. In addition, I am certified as a sex therapist by the American Association of Sex Educators, Counselors, and Therapists. I am also a Professional Certified Coach. I have been coaching for about four years. I have written two books: *Life Savor: How To Turn On Delight* and *Passion! Reclaiming the Fire In Your Heart.*

I'm starting to think about where I'd like to live in my "retirement" years. As a therapist I have been office-bound for over 20 years. As a coach, however, geography is irrelevant. I can live anywhere that has electricity and a phone line for my laptop. I can't see ever retiring from coaching. It's fun, gives me immediate gratification, and affords relationships with insightful, eager clients.

CONTACT INFORMATION

Roz Van Meter
8588 Northwest Plaza Drive, Suite 302
Dallas, TX 75225
Phone: 214-361-0500
E-mail: roz@coachroz.com
Web sites: www.coachroz.com; www.The-Wizard-Of-Roz.com

9

A Spiritual Approach to Coaching

Debbie Call

I'd like to be able to say that my transition from therapist to coach was smooth and successful. It wasn't. It took some adjusting to shift from being expert in the therapy field to starting over as student/novice coach in my new career; to shift from the nonprofit world to the world of profit; to learn a new craft and run a business. But I have found comfort in the words of Max De Pree, author of *Leadership Is an Art:* "In the end, it is important to remember that we cannot become what we need to be by remaining where we are."

Little did I know when I decided to change careers and become a coach that I would be undergoing one of the biggest transformations in my own life. There were many highs and lows in this transition. There were the initial months I spent in blissful sabbatical, engaging in the luxury of self-discovery and discerning new career directions. There was the thrill of embarking on a new career in coaching, stretching myself intellectually with fresh, innovative ideas. There was the joy of coaching clients and getting paid for doing work I love. The lows came upon the heels of depleted savings leading to crises in confidence: "Can I really make it financially?" Living on one income (spouse's), when used to two, created financial hardships. As I inflicted more pressure upon myself to produce, I experienced less joy.

Looking back, I see the silver lining in the personal challenges and fears that had developed. They were the impetus prompting me to the next level of growth. I found myself searching for a way to live and work more holistically, and to expand my old notions of success. Like a detective, I was searching for that missing piece. How could I create a sustainable business without feeling like I was pushing a boulder up a hill? How could I honor all of who I was and stop holding back?

Striving hard to "make something happen" became a joyless way to reach success. Although this strategy had worked for me in the past, it now took up a lot of my energy and felt like a struggle. Most clients coming to me faced a similar dilemma. I wondered how I could learn to get out of my own way and help others to do the same. After two years of coaching clients, I knew deep down there had to be another way.

With the perfection of synchronicity, the universe threw me a rope and I grabbed it. A coaching colleague encouraged me to join her in entering a new advanced program for coaches, called "Coaching From Spirit," developed by Sharon Wilson. This program teaches coaches how to use a five-step coaching process based on spiritual, metaphysical, and energetic methods to help clients unlearn negativity and trust their inner guidance. For me, this program felt like coming home. Finally, there was an approach where intuition, heart, and spirit could be integrated with linear thinking.

During the following year of this transformational training, I began my own process of "inner alignment." I learned how to tap into my "inner coach" for guidance, release self-sabotaging energies, create new constructive belief systems, and begin to attract what I desired in my external world. Getting into the flow of positive energy far surpassed my old notion of "making something happen." I finally understood that creating change on the outside happens more quickly when the change begins from within.

As I trained in this process, I began to realize that Coaching from Spirit was less a series of techniques and more an expanded way of being, which set it apart from other coaching methods. I needed to first internalize the spiritual concepts and processes for myself, so that I could hold the energy of that possibility for my clients. My spiritual approach to coaching is a conscious partnering with a higher power, what I call Spirit, the source of highest love. As I tap into this inner guidance, I can better assist my clients to tap into the wisdom and knowledge of their own inner coach, and to understand the intuitional information that comes through this type of guided process. By experiencing these practical tools in my life, I create a place of safety, trust, and confidence for my clients to do the same. This is the basis of my coaching with others.

By using a spiritual approach, every area of my life has grown beyond my expectations—including miracles in my relationships with my children, a stronger marriage, ever-increasing business income, awesome clients, an abundance of opportunities, financial reserves, more solid self-confidence, and a profound deep trust in life. Reliance on a spiritual approach gives me the knowledge that I am always surrounded by guidance and help, although much of it is experienced in subtle, unseen ways. I carry this sense that anything is possible into my coaching sessions and use it to help clients see with new eyes. When we work together, I hold a vision for them that they are already whole, perfect, and complete. I don't get hooked into their old, limited life dramas or stories; instead, I coach them to create new stories for their lives.

Some of the metaphysical concepts and processes that I introduce to clients are also written about in best-selling books. Gary Zukav, author of *The Seat of the Soul* and *Soul Stories,* stresses the importance of routinely listening to and acting upon intuition. In *Soul Stories,* he talks about the presence of "non-physical teachers" who are available to provide guidance and clarity to everyone. He adds that this information from "non-physical teachers" comes through a voice, picture, or physical sensation.

THE PRACTICALITIES OF WORKING WITH CLIENTS

In practical terms, how does this translate into working with clients? Joan, a successful training and leadership consultant to corporate organizations, a professional speaker, and college faculty instructor, describes herself as a life-long learner and has been on a "spiritual path" for years. Joan grew up in an abusive, unloving, alcoholic family. Several years of intensive therapy as an adult healed much of the childhood trauma she endured. She courageously moved from survivor mode to actively choosing healthy relationships.

CENTERING

At the time of our coaching relationship, Joan wanted to advance her personal development and take her career to the next level. Several months into the coaching, she came to the session with an overwhelming sense of being unloved, triggered by a childhood memory. To compound this, physical pain accompanied the feelings.

I began our session, as I do with all my clients, with a brief centering exercise that we do together. I lead the exercise by asking my client to take a few deep breaths while I do the same, as a way to slow down our bodies and quiet our internal mental chatter. It brings us into the present moment and allows a space to open up for both of us to connect with inner guidance.

Joan articulated the session's focus as the emotional trigger described above. Some discussion followed and I asked her to tap into her own inner coach by first imagining that she was surrounded with a white light. I suggested she then imagine a place in her mind where she felt very safe and peaceful. (It may be a place in nature or somewhere a client has gone to on a favorite vacation, for example.). I asked Joan to imagine an outdoor theater screen and to ask when these feelings had first emerged in her life. She immediately saw pictures on the screen of herself as a young child, but then the pictures regressed in time to infancy and to a prenatal state, as she saw herself as unloved while still in her mother's womb.

Meanwhile, my inner guidance was active, too, suggesting quietly that I use a "rescripting" tool. This tool makes sense when a client is experiencing a sabotaging pattern or fear that has early childhood roots. Much of Joan's present-day energy was siphoned off by this childhood belief of being unloved. In her current life, she allowed it to keep her from taking risks professionally.

RESCRIPTING

Rescripting means rewriting a painful incident. It is *not* reliving or reexperiencing the incident. It is seeing the experience from a different perspective, one that is positive and more spiritually based. In this instance, I wanted Joan to connect with the higher self of everyone involved in her childhood. My clients have a choice of rewriting the experience themselves, or to have my help rescripting, which Joan asked me to do.

Inner guidance can come through in several ways for either the coach or the client: as a "mental download" of words, or through pictures or body sensations. My inner coach gave me information about another way to see this drama in the form of images and words, which I conveyed to Joan. Instead of seeing only an alcoholic, abusive father and dependent, ineffective mother, Joan saw the higher selves of her two parents in the hospital room where she was born. She heard their words of joy and love at the moment of her birth, their delight to be gifted with this daughter. As the words continued to flow over her, Joan felt indescribably loving energy from the higher selves of her parents. She said she was "swimming in a sea of unconditional love, honor, and reverence." Joan felt chills all over her body and could sense the unseen presence of this loving energy in the room with her right now. We asked Spirit and other divine helpers to transform her cells by removing all fear, and replacing that with the loving energy she was now experiencing. In effect, we were getting divine assistance to energetically "rewire" Joan.

"Divine" is defined by the client's belief system. There is no religiosity involved in my approach to coaching. For some it may mean God, Universal Love, Holy Spirit, Higher Guidance, Inner Coach, intuition, Spirit, mentor, or any other name connoting oneness with Higher Self or Highest Being. Likewise, depending upon the client, I can use these phrases interchangeably. The words we use are not important. One client told me he did not believe in God. However he did believe that he could build his business more effectively by learning how to, in his words, "attract what I want via the power of the universe." That was his definition of Spirit.

Joan saw this session as a major turning point in her life. It allowed her to shift from feeling like a victim of her past experiences to feeling that she was filled with a nurturing, loving energy. She could use this energy to maintain self-respect. Her physical pain subsided and she experienced a new lightness in her manner and a sense of expansiveness. Joan feels safe being honest and it's easier to allow others to get close. She sees herself "moving with purposeful energy" to take her professional work to the next level. For instance, she has accepted more challenging and self-disclosing speaking engagements, and has had excellent audience response.

Rescripting is such a powerful energetic tool that it may need to be used only once with a client. This is because the core fear or block that gets rescripted is often foundational in nature. By releasing the energetic connection to a foundational fear, subsequent fears built upon the core fear are dismantled as well. While I think that cognitive and/or behavioral approaches of therapy and traditional coaching work well for many issues, I find that core fears and beliefs are often stored energetically, like a blueprint, in our body's physical cells. They require energetic release for complete resolution. Core fears may not originate from any specific trauma or abuse, but they can still act in limiting and sabotaging ways. I notice that a core fear usually emerges when a client is ready to make a big shift.

For example, I used this tool to deal with my increasing fear of public speaking when the stakes became higher (more "important" companies were inviting me in). The fear of public speaking was connected to not feeling good enough, which took root when I was three years old. The rescripting tool worked well: One week later I was able to give a new talk to a financial group. Since that time in 1998, I've had many opportunities to do public speaking. As my script continues to evolve, I've discovered a more courageous voice that allows my character to shine through. Audience feedback on my presentations is encouraging, usually ranging from excellent to outstanding. Not bad results for one rescripting session!

WRITING A SACRED CONTRACT

Few of my coaching clients have a history of abuse or neglect, as Joan did. What they do share is a strong sense that it's time to make a change. Frequently they begin the coaching partnership feeling excitement at what they want to create and doubt about how to proceed. Introducing the "sacred contract" at this time can be especially beneficial and practical. This tool helps the client enter into an energetic process of creating. This process includes releasing negativity, positively claiming what is desired, partnering with and asking for divine assistance, and expressing gratitude. Paul identified several goals he desired to accomplish, but he didn't believe he *deserved* to reach them. I asked him to choose the most desirable goal and to write a sacred contract around it. Paul sat in front of his computer and wrote down every negative thought, belief, and feeling he had about this goal. This is the releasing part, which allows conflicting energy in the form of thoughts, old beliefs, and feelings to surface up. Paul wrote, "This exercise is loony" and "I've never had an easy time getting anything I want and this is no different." This part of the tool may be fairly long, depending upon the goal. Paul experienced a sense of physical lightness after unburdening himself on paper. The releasing also created an open space for him to claim what he specifically wanted. The claiming section is a series of statements framed in positive, concrete terms. Paul wrote everything he desired regarding his professional goal of finding meaningful, satisfying work that paid well. Rather than claiming things in a negative format, such as, "I don't want a controlling boss," I coached him to state the kind of boss he did want. "I want a boss who is fair and lets me do my job with autonomy."

Once all the elements of claiming were spelled out, Paul wrote down what he wanted assistance with from the divine. "I want assistance with being patient. I want assistance believing that I can accomplish things with greater ease." The sacred contract ends on an expression of gratitude for what one has in life now, and a conscious partnering with God, the universe, or Spirit to bring this contract to resolution, while at the same time releasing attachment to how this will occur. He read the contract daily, focusing especially on what he wanted to claim. If he found certain old beliefs and feelings resistantly hanging on, he was encouraged to repeat the releasing exercise. He was also instructed to look for evidence that what he claimed was actually showing up in his daily life. As he began to see evidence that aspects of his contract were being fulfilled, he felt more trusting and confident of the process.

OTHER TOOLS

There are other tools that complement the sacred contract, such as creating new belief statements and understanding how to effectively use the "law of attraction," a concept of being able to attract events, opportunities, and people into our lives based on changing our internal beliefs, personal actions, and feelings about ourselves. One of my clients was attracting some new clients and repelling other clients during the same time period; as we explored what might be causing this turn of events, she began to think it had to do with her internal conflicts, specifically those regarding money. With coaching, she created the following new belief statement: "I am doing work I love and am abundantly prosperous and I pass that prosperity along." I told her it was important that she use her own words and that the belief statement resonate in her body, as a way of feeling congruent; her body became the barometer of truth. If reading her belief statement didn't resonate, I asked her to do more tweaking to get to that place of "aha!" She felt excited about this belief statement, and within a brief period of time she attracted a corporate contract.

I believe that the law of attraction operates in our lives all the time, whether we understand how it works or not. Most of us focus on what can go wrong, and what we don't want. But viewing life from the perspective of the law of attraction, whatever we focus on, with thought and *feeling,* we attract. Our challenge is to focus our energy on what we *want,* not on what we don't want. Focusing on what we want reconditions our mind to stay very clear on our goals, even when present reality doesn't reflect them. One client decided to transition from consulting back to running a company. He mentally created the perfect professional CEO position, noting down lots of details. While his current reality reflected no job prospects, diminishing cash reserves, and concern about paying the mortgage, he still continued to focus daily on what he wanted. He did indeed attract his ideal CEO position, just as he had imagined it. Another client called, upset with a significant glitch toward reaching a goal. After explaining the law of attraction, I helped him to imagine a ladder, to see if he could move from the bottom rung to the next rung by choosing a thought that would be slightly less negative than the one he was currently thinking. During the coaching session he was able to climb up two or three rungs. This was progress, I explained to him, it's usually not possible to move from a negative state to a completely positive state in one leap. To help him stay focused, to move closer to his goal, he needed to create interim positive statements that were or could be true. At the end of this session, he identified some initial action steps to take. We stayed in contact by e-mail for the next day or two so that he could continue "climbing" higher on the ladder. His action steps were completed within a week and he was overjoyed and relieved to have moved through this difficulty to reach what he wanted. As he became more familiar with this concept and practiced it, he realized he could use it everyday. I also suggested that he read Lynn Grabhorn's book, *Excuse Me, Your Life is Waiting,* and visit the Web site, www.abraham-hicks.com, for audiotapes to help him stay on track.

Of course, I have my share of clients who make wonderful progress for a while and then hit the brick wall and appear to forget everything they learned. I hold a developmental view of growth and do not see it moving in a straight line. There is a lot of back-and-forth motion involved as we move toward optimum growth. We grow by "levels." Sometimes the next "wall" or block is simply the next level to move to. When clients break free from old fears and limiting patterns, they often experience a sense of euphoria. As the euphoria diminishes, it's important to introduce linear coaching tools to assist clients to act and behave in ways that serve them positively in the outside world. For instance, one client's release work involved significant internal changes. Others around him—colleagues, friends, family—noticed how much happier he seemed. He found himself attracting plum projects at work and gaining respect and admiration from colleagues. Now he needed linear coaching skills. We addressed his need to ramp up his team leadership skills, learn how to get the best from his people, how to run tight meetings, and how to coach his team and staff. In this way, I can combine a spiritual approach to coaching with linear coaching tools to help my clients create holistic change and success.

I learned a number of tools in the Coaching from Spirit program, but the tools themselves were not the essence of the approach. Blending inner guidance with outer action steps is what creates new realties. Clients learn to use intuitional wisdom and higher guidance to release energetic blocks and fears. The inner guidance directs external action steps that are in alignment with their best selves. Head and heart, working in sync with each other, release fears and blocks, free up positive energy, and attract what is desired. Success on the outer plane of physical reality is directly influenced by what is first created on the inner plane. Using this approach works quickly and deeply, and has lasting change.

When I first began using these expanded tools with clients in 1998, I divided my clients into two groups: those whom I deemed open to the use of metaphysical tools, and those whom I deemed needed traditional coaching tools. My own limiting beliefs created these unnecessary separations. I believed some clients would consider me too "out there," or that a client first had to be on a spiritual path to take advantage of these tools. After several months of working under these self-imposed limitations, I felt frustrated. I wasn't giving either set of clients the full range of what I had to offer. I was still holding back, still playing small.

I progressed toward integrating the use of metaphysical and linear coaching tools with all of my clients. No more artificial client groupings. It finally sunk in that I was a guide and my job was to offer the full repertoire of tools. In turn I honor the client by allowing him or her to decide if he or she wishes to use them. I find little resistance to the tools, and that may be because I use these tools in my own life, which imparts a sense of trust and safety for my clients.

My approach to coaching brings a sense of lightness, peace, and joy to clients in the early sessions. John came to our third session with heaviness about his upcoming sabbatical from work. Responsible and hardworking, he wondered if he deserved this break and how others might react. I asked John to choose a book from my library simply through intuition, one of a motivational or personal development nature. While John held the closed book in his hand, we asked for Spirit to guide him to find the passage with the most relevant message. John opened the book randomly and read a passage. This process is known as bibliomancy. After reading the message to himself, John did some centering, went to his favorite inner place, and met his inner guide. Then he began to laugh, and laughed hard for 10 minutes! He told me later that several playful inner guides showed up to take him on an imagined romp doing fun and silly things. They told him to slow down, be lighter, let go of the need to impress others. John ended the session in a different state from how he began. I also enjoyed his animated energy!

As a coach it is exhilarating to be a partner and witness to the transformation of others. There is a graceful sense of reciprocity in the coaching relationship. Clients may come for the experience, wisdom, or guidance I offer, and in return I am inspired by their courage as they begin a journey to create something new in their lives. I learn much from them, and they in turn affirm my gifts. Regardless of the presenting goal, the coaching clients I attract usually have a hunger, a sense that something is missing. I believe this is a universal yearning to return to our innate wholeness, a desire for full self-expression.

Who I am as a coach is my real gift, the tool that I offer to others. I don't need to be perfect, just authentic. My transparency and willingness to be real often brings courage to others. As Harry Beckwith says in his book, *Selling the Invisible,* "Prospects do not buy how good you are at what you do. They buy how good you are at who you are."

PRACTICAL INFORMATION

ADVICE FOR NEW SPIRIT COACHES

1. There is widespread hunger among the general public to create meaning in life. Others simply want to live saner lives. Both needs create a willingness to invest money in coaching. The demand for personal coaching extends to spirit coaching as well, due to the mainstreaming of spirit through numerous popular book authors and talk-show host Oprah Winfrey. I found that talking openly about this process with potential clients piqued their curiosity and was often a selling factor.

2. Coaching from Spirit offers transformational processes and tools that work quickly, with anybody who is open to change, with very practical applications and results in every aspect of life. Simply by adjusting the language I use, I put my clients at ease so that I can incorporate these tools, when appropriate, in our work together. I attract clients from many industries, especially hi-tech ones. Their goals may be diverse, ranging from changing careers, developing a more fulfilling life, increasing professional effectiveness, or starting up/growing a business. The common denominator seems to be a desire to draw upon intuition and other forms of inner guidance to create change. I look for clients who would enjoy being coached in these holistic ways-who connect with what I have to offer.

3. Coaching from Spirit appeals to coaches who understand that this is an expanded way of being. Coaches who coach from sprit first internalize the concepts and processes for themselves. In experiencing their own

transformational shifts, coaches can hold the energy of that possibility for clients. It's an energetic version of "walking your talk." Complete information on the advanced training program of Coaching from Spirit can be fund at www.coachingfromspirit.com.

ADVICE FOR NEW THERAPIST-COACHES

1. Be willing to invest in your own personal development—to be the best *you*. What you do with clients is secondary to who you are when you are with them.
2. Be careful not to position yourself to appeal to everyone. In doing so you appeal to no one. Go out on a limb and say who you really are and how you work. You will be rewarded with those clients who are a perfect fit for you.
3. Trust what you know. Trust who you are. Be willing to step out and be yourself. Don't be a cookie-cutter coach.

MY FEES

My fees for telephone coaching range from $350 for two hours a month to $500 for three hours. Rates include fax and e-mail support, and "in-between" phone calls as needed. I rarely do face-to-face coaching; however, if requested, that fee is higher than for telephone coaching, and is determined by travel costs, length of contract, etc.

WHAT I KNOW NOW

It takes financial reserves to make the transition from one career to another. If I had had more financial reserves when I started out, I wouldn't have put so much pressure on myself to produce.

A BRIEF BIOGRAPHY

I was a licensed independent clinical social worker (MSW/LISW, ACSW) for 20 years, where I conducted individual, family, and group therapy for non-profit community agencies. I developed new programs, supervised MSW graduate students, marketed clinical programs, and was published in two professional journals.

I am a graduate of Coach University, a Professional Certified Coach, a Certified Spiritual Life Coach, and a Certified Facilitator for the Coaching Clinic, a coaching skill-building workshop for managers and leaders. I am a member of International Coach Federation (ICF) and past chapter host for Greater Cincinnati Area Chapter of the ICF. In addition to running my own practice, I am the Coaching Division Manager for the Making a Life Coaching Company, www.makingalife.com. I write a free monthly e-zine, "In the Spirit of Success," which can be subscribed to at my Web site, www.movingspirit.com.

No one ever succeeds alone. I have a full cast who have helped me along various points of this journey. These people include my own personal coaches, my "buddy" (colleague) coaches, my husband, for his consistent support when I doubted myself, and Sharon Wilson, who introduced me to Coaching from Spirit. Most of all, I rely on Spirit, my own source of guidance.

CONTACT INFORMATION

Debbie Call, MSW, PCC
Phone: 513-821-5669
Fax: 513-821-6066
E-mail: Debbie@movingspirit.com
Web site: www.movingspirit.com

Part III

Peak-Performance Coaching

10

Uncommon-Sense Coaching
Carol Sommer

"**N**ow, don't hold anything back. I need to see just how nervous you can get," I reminded Maria as we entered the meeting room. How ironic that this otherwise successful executive, holding a vice-president position in a prominent consulting firm, would shrivel to pure helplessness when addressing a group of more than six people.

This was intended to be the meeting where I, the coach, proudly watched my client perform after conquering her paralyzing stage fright. But the coaching effort hadn't progressed as hoped. Sure, Maria had made some progress. She was actually getting up to face an audience; when she did poorly, she was brave enough to get up and try again. But it wasn't good enough for either of us. She was still shaking, stumbling over her words, and cracking her voice. We had exhausted all of the logical strategies: confidence building, visualization, relaxation, and affirmation. Maria had even joined a Toastmasters club, something I encourage clients who are anxious about public speaking to do, as it gives them an ongoing practice ground. The other club members were very supportive, doing much of what I had been doing as a coach. (Toastmasters International provides a forum, generally in the form of a weekly meeting, for members to practice and receive feedback on their communication and leadership skills.)

Getting through to Maria required a completely different approach. Somehow, I needed to make a 180-degree turn away from what was obviously not working. Altering my stance, I advised: "The more I think about what's going on with you, the more I feel I am missing something. I don't believe either of us fully understands the critical dynamics of your nervousness. We need to look at that more closely. I need to see the nervousness in action to determine exactly how it manifests. So, I would like to meet you at the next Toastmasters event when you are giving a speech. It will be extremely important that you maintain at least the same degree of nervousness you've been experiencing. You should even try to exaggerate those behaviors you've described, so I can see precisely what is going on. Prepare in your usual way; I know that doing your homework and being prepared has never been an issue for you. When it's your turn to speak, I want you to open by telling the audience exactly what is going on, that you are using this speaking opportunity to observe your nervousness more carefully, and they can help by letting you know what they observe as well. Since you have confided your nervousness to them before, this request should not appear unusual."

Up until then, Maria had felt terrible pressure to perform well, relax, and appear calm. Maria had been caught in her own trap of trying to force herself to relax, something that cannot be forced to happen. She, along with well-meaning others, had been trying very hard to make something happen that could only occur spontaneously, that is, relaxing. It's no surprise that she couldn't make it happen. When she tried to be nervous, she was caught in the same kind of paradox. This intervention lifted the pressure by actually prescribing the problem to occur. She couldn't pull that off either. Instead, she was calm, relaxed, and confident, and she gave a wonderful speech. The next move was critical. Showing undue pleasure and pronouncing her "cured" could easily produce the pressure to continue confident performances, putting her right back where she started. Instead, I took a slightly different approach.

"Well, that was certainly encouraging, yet you and I know better than to expect overnight miracles. When you give your next speech, you must try even harder to display those old symptoms so we can be sure we understand what they are about." But Maria continued to enjoy success and the old nervousness receded from her experience. She could not bring the nervousness on. With enough winning performances, she eventually overrode her habit of being nervous.

The brief strategic approach to resolving problems and promoting change is one I relied on heavily as a therapist and find equally useful as a coach. It proves particularly valuable with clients who have already exhausted the common-sense tactics affecting change, and with those who have been working at change for a long time and getting nowhere. The brief strategic model grew out of the work of Milton H. Erickson and Gregory Bateson. It operates under the premise that regardless of their "root cause," problems are behavioral; and when a problem persists, it is the very effort to resolve it that prevents it from going away. The client's, or client's significant others', repeated attempts to resolve the issue are precisely what reinforce and often even exacerbate the situation.

During a workshop in 1986, John Weakland, one of the model's founders, aptly described it this way, "Life is just one damn thing after another; it only becomes pathological when it's the same damn thing over and over." Weakland and his colleagues contended that problems result from the mishandling of everyday difficulties. Thus, having precisely defined the change the client wants to make, the brief strategic model looks next for the approach the client has repeatedly used in an attempt to make that change. Successful intervention consists of getting the client and/or significant other to abandon that approach. Whereas the client's goal is to make a change or resolve a problem, the coach's immediate goal is to get the client to give up her "attempted solution." Most coaches generally avoid talking about problems, focusing instead on goals—moving toward something we want rather than away from something we don't want. In coaching language, then, we might translate the brief strategic model as: "When someone has been unsuccessful in achieving a goal in spite of repeated honest attempts to achieve it, it is likely that the strategy he or she is using is the very thing standing in the way."

People who need coaching aren't much different from those who need therapy, in that most bring some form of their own resistance that is getting in the way of the changes they want to make. They know what they need to do to get what they want, but they don't do it. They seek out a coach to tell them to do what they already know how to do.

I love working with performers; they are creative and bright, driven to succeed, not to mention extremely talented. But they often persist in standing in their own way. By the time they knock on my door for coaching, they have exhausted several therapists and perhaps a few coaches too.

These folks don't respond well to common-sense coaching, but they *do* respond well to an uncommon-sense approach. The tools and frames of reference I find valuable for use within the coach setting include brief strategic therapy, solution-focused therapy, Ericksonian hypnosis, and neurolinguistic programming.

I officially began to label my work with certain clients as coaching rather than therapy when a client commented that she was embarrassed to tell her coworkers she was seeing a therapist to help overcome her fear of speaking up in meetings. I suggested she tell them she was working with a coach, since that described the work we were doing together. After that, I began screening my therapy intake calls more closely, filtering out the clients who could benefit just as much or more from coaching. In the process of making this shift, I noticed that more than half the clients in my therapy practice aspired to improve their performance in some area. Those I enjoyed working with the most were the baseball players and their coaches, other athletes, actors, dancers, writers, speakers, and singers. I now define myself as a performance coach, helping people make the most of their talents. Although I can't sing, dance, or even hit a baseball, I do understand the inner distractions that get in the way of those who can.

PARADOX AND PERFORMANCE

In an effort to overcome her speaking anxiety, Maria presented what brief strategic therapists call a "be spontaneous" paradox. She did this by saying, "I am trying very hard to make something occur that really can only occur spontaneously." Another common paradox clients present is the "never ready" paradox, attempting to master a feared event by postponing it. My client Lisa heaved a huge sigh of relief when I told her she should not even think about auditioning for the musical she so desperately wanted to be part of. She had been studying, practicing, and preparing for the "big league" for over two years. Yet, each time an audition opportunity presented itself, she backed out at the last minute, deciding she wasn't ready. Lisa had been acting, singing, and dancing practically all her life. She performed in hundreds of school and small-town events, receiving nothing but accolades from her family, friends, coaches, and audiences. Everyone in her life offered encouragement; there was no question she was a "star." Still, amid all this positive reassurance, Lisa feared she wasn't good enough. Another important audition was coming up soon and, although she wanted more than anything to participate, she had no reason to trust her confidence on this one either.

Lisa could enumerate dozens of reasons she wanted to overcome this obstacle. It would make her every dream come true. A career in the theater was what she'd always wanted. Also, she believed, at least rationally, that she did have the talent. Common-sense reassurance from me was certainly doomed to fail. Instead, I proceeded in this uncommon direction: "It certainly doesn't appear to be an issue of talent, given all you've accomplished thus far. And you certainly seem to have a clear sense of what you want to accomplish in the future. I'm wondering, though, just how thoroughly you have thought this through. Could there be some disadvantages to winning an audition and getting into big-time theater? I'm not suggesting there necessarily have to be some, but sometimes a protective part of you can hold you back until you've worked all that out for yourself. This might be a good thing, this fear of not being good enough." I asked Lisa if she would be willing to pass up this next audition as an opportunity to learn some important aspects of her own motivations. This posed no great sacrifice, since she fully expected herself to pass it up anyway.

"You should prepare for this audition the same as you would any other, that is, learn the music, know the lines, and practice the routines, even though you won't actually be auditioning. Go to the audition just to observe, and as you watch the other contenders perform, I'd like you to focus all of your attention on possible disadvantages for you if you were actually up there on stage and eventually picked for the musical. It is very important that you stay focused on this. Please don't allow your mind to wander. In fact, should your mind even begin to meander to the joys of performing and being in theater, you must bring it right back immediately to focus on disadvantages."

After the audition, Lisa reported that she had done what I asked. However, she had a difficult time staying focused because she had become absorbed in the music and kept thinking about how much fun it would be to be up there performing herself. She said she almost went up and auditioned "just for the heck of it" to see what it would be like. She did manage to come up with a couple of disadvantages, but they were fairly lame ones, which she knew she could deal with.

There was another chance to audition two weeks later and Lisa wondered if this time she should go for it. I cautioned her about moving too fast and suggested she at least allow herself one more opportunity to work through the pros and cons of pursuing in this direction. I asked her to approach the next audition just as she had previously, but with one allowance. If per chance she was tempted once again to actually audition, she should try to contain herself. However, if she couldn't do that, then it would be okay to just audition. It certainly wouldn't hurt to get the experience; and, if by some fate of the gods she actually got the part, she could always decline it.

Lisa did go to the next audition. She did participate. She did get the part. And she accepted it joyously.

Restraining Lisa from doing something she was afraid to do anyway served to relax the pressure to succeed. Lisa was caught up in an endless program of preparing to face something she was afraid to face, while at the same time delaying facing it. People often become paralyzed by the pressure to succeed—pressure they impose upon themselves, pressure others impose upon them, or both. The usual and most logical approach to this dilemma is to offer encouragement and reassurance. This was true in Lisa's case. By reframing her fear as something useful, such as a force helping her to fully appreciate the other side of success, the stigma of being afraid was significantly reduced. It's like saying, "You have this problem, but it could be a good thing, so don't try to get rid of it too hastily."

I routinely employ a version of soft restraint with clients in the very early stages of coaching. This message helps interrupt their cycle of trying too hard and their sense of urgency. The adage "If you want to get somewhere fast, go slow" applies in coaching as well as anywhere else. Once I identify with my clients where they've been stuck, I specifically ask them *not* to make any changes between now and our next session. Coupled with a simple assignment to observe or reflect on something relevant to their issues, this *go slow* message helps them approach things more objectively and reduces the pressure to perform. I took the go-slow strategy a step further with Lisa by suggesting potential disadvantages of change. To counter her presenting paradox, I imposed another one by exposing her to what she feared while not letting her engage in anything fearful.

The next example illustrates a similar strategy used in a somewhat different way. Here I coached the client to use the restraining tactic herself to help improve a relationship.

As a communication expert, Sandra was in high demand facilitating interpersonal skills seminars and workshops all over the world. Yet she was at a total loss when it came to fostering open communication in her own most important relationship—her marriage. Sandra was outgoing and gregarious, and expressing her feelings came naturally to her. But Paul, although an excellent social conversationalist, clammed up and refused to engage in any conversation with her on an intimate level. Even getting an occasional "I love you" from him was out of the question. Since Sandra was the only customer for change in this case, I decided to do relationship coaching with her alone. In essence, I agreed to coach her to coach her husband. As Sandra was psychologically quite savvy, I felt comfortable coaching her in this manner.

Sandra's goal was to have intimate, personal communication with Paul. Until now, she had been unsuccessful in getting him to open up and express any intimate feelings about their relationship as well as some difficult career and family issues he was dealing with. Sandra would know she was making progress if she could simply hear Paul say, "I love you, too" in response to an "I love you" from her. Both Sandra and I were satisfied that Paul's actual love was not in question.

What had Sandra attempted so far? She made herself available. She invited Paul to open up. She listened actively, she empathized, she encouraged, she reasoned, and possibly even begged and nagged to some degree. She "walked her talk" by modeling open, honest communication and assertively expressing her own feelings and needs. The catch: It was getting no results at home. In fact, Paul seemed to be clamming up even more.

I complimented and validated Sandra's efforts, adding: "This might be the perfect approach for someone else, say, someone who complains that her partner never talks to her intimately, never says 'I love you'; but she wouldn't dare ask him to because then it wouldn't be spontaneous and sincere (she'd always know she had to ask him for it). In that case, maybe all he needs is to know what she wants. But, you have certainly been very clear and up-front about that.

"When we look at the pattern of interaction and see that nothing changes, logic tells us we need to do something else. Not just anything else, but a complete turnaround: the opposite of what you've been doing. Apply an opposing force. The opposite of actively encouraging someone to behave in a certain way is to actively restrain him from doing it. It might at first sound like reverse psychology, but it's actually very different. You'll maintain credibility by acting with benevolence and from a somewhat one-down position and by framing your approach in the most logical terms. It must make perfect sense for you to suddenly do such an about-face.

"The script might go something like this (in your own words, of course):

> Paul, I have been doing an awful lot of thinking and soul search-ing over what's been happening between us. I've also spent some time with a coach. I just felt I needed some guidance on this. And I've finally come to realize that I have been very unfair to you. I am really sorry. Please, don't feel you have to say any-thing; I just need to get this off my chest.
>
> It's always been easy for me to talk—hell, I do it for a living! I can dump my feelings all over the place, but it's unfair to assume it should be that easy for everyone else. We're all wired differ-ently—not rightly or wrongly, just differently. I've been practi-cally forcing you to talk about things that are very, very personal, and not only is that unfair, but it might even be dangerous. You must have good reason to keep certain thoughts and feelings to yourself, and to try to divulge them prematurely could open up something neither of us is ready to deal with. I should never have been pushing you the way I was. I am so sorry.
>
> We have a lot of history together—the kids, (etc.), and that's all been very special. Yes, I admit, it is important for me to hear the words "I love you" and I would certainly love to feel needed

and be able to be of some support to you as you struggle with challenges at work and with your family. But those are my needs, not necessarily yours. I have to realize that people express their feelings and get their needs met in different ways. And I am going to try to be more attuned to that.

"This intentionally vague ending leaves room for a lot of interpretation on his part. Don't explain anything. If you have to, pretend you're just running at the mouth again, which he knows you're good at.

"At this point show some small gesture of affection and appreciation that he listened, then casually remember something else you have to do, and go do it as soon as you can gracefully disappear. If, God forbid, he should start to open up, restrain him:

Hey, you don't have to say anything. I've pressured you enough. I just needed to get this off my chest.

"Anytime later, should he begin to show signs of opening up, continue to restrain:

Now, wait, Paul—are you sure this is a good idea?

"Eventually, if he persists (begs), let him talk. Show appreciation, but don't go overboard."

I gave Sandra this rationale for what I was asking her to do: "Paul has been uncomfortable opening up; yet he feels pressure to do so. The more pressure he feels to do something that's out of his comfort zone, the scarier it is and the more he will resist. Most likely he wishes he could be as open as you are and feels inadequate; he just can't admit it. When he sees how easy it is for you, he feels even more inadequate. Your encouraging approach may be adding even more pressure, thus creating a vicious cycle. You are clearly in the dominant position (one-up), because you are the one requesting a change. Since what you want him to do is easy for you, you are 'right' and he is 'wrong.' This adds even more pressure. What I am asking you to do now will help lift that pressure by actually encouraging Paul *not* to change (yet). When the pressure is lifted, it will be easier for him to open up. And it will be his idea, when he is ready."

Enjoying Being One-Down

This one-down position also affords the coach a good deal of leverage, particularly with clients who have shown a pattern of resisting change.

Bill, a New York City attorney, announced that he had been to the best coaches, and he named a list of prominent helpers whom he had either fired or who had fired him. He wasn't any closer to taking that bar exam now than he was when he first sought help.

"Those folks you just mentioned sit high on my list of capable coaches and therapists. Whatever makes you think *I* could do anything more for you?" was my comeback. Since the very nature of the coach-client relationship naturally places the coach in a one-up position, taking a one-down stance creates a useful paradox which helps distinguish *this* relationship from previous ones. Rather than compliment Bill for finally arriving at the right door, I let him convince me why and how our relationship might be more effective than those he had engaged in previously. I needed to hear that *he* was going to do something different this time around.

One-down is a useful strategy to teach to clients who are caught in the paradoxical loop of what the brief strategic group calls "trying to reach accord through opposition," or trying to get someone to agree with you by disagreeing with them. This evolves into a never-ending and escalating cycle in which at least one party demands the respect and deference they believe is their due. We'll see how that can play out in the next example.

Ellen, a single mom, knew she was entangled in a no-win tug-of-war with her 17-year-old son, Tom, when she sought coaching to improve her parenting. Ellen's goal was for Tom to succeed in school, that is, maintain at least a B average, and comply with school requirements. Ellen dreaded the frequent telephone calls and routine monthly notices from teachers complaining that Tom was cutting classes and failing to turn in assignments. When asked how she had tried to help Tom succeed, she responded that she continually reminded him to do his homework, and talked to him about how important it was for him to study and get good grades so he could go to college and have a successful career. Her approaches all contained variations of the same theme: explaining and reasoning, which escalated into nagging, which escalated into screaming, which escalated into punishing and withdrawing privileges, and on and on. With each step, Tom tuned her out more, produced less schoolwork, and withdrew himself from home. Ellen knew she was getting nowhere, yet like most people, she believed she should try even harder. What kind of a parent would she be if she simply ignored her child's school difficulties? People will hang on to their methods of problem solving for dear life, either because they are tried-and-true logical methods handed down through the generations, or for fear that giving them up will cause the situation to worsen. Clearly, Tom's situation was progressively deteriorating by *not* letting go of the method.

In many ways Tom had already demonstrated he was intelligent, motivated, and capable of achieving just about anything he made up his mind to do. A technological whiz, he worked hard and responsibly at his part-time job to afford the luxuries he coveted, such as a car, stereo, and sophisticated computer setup. Ellen could see that the harder she tried to help Tom perform in school, the less he responded. She also knew Tom was very independent and able to take care of himself. He had shown himself consistently to be a self-starter in areas in which he wanted to achieve something.

I complimented Ellen on her dedication and persistence in helping her son: "Not all parents would have the tenacity to persevere and see nothing in return." I suggested she appeared to be doing all the work and carrying all the concern for Tom's future, leaving him with no responsibility himself. Perhaps she might be doing him a disservice in taking over responsibility he was fully capable of assuming. With this, she agreed to try an experiment. It is useful to frame such an intervention as an "experiment" to gather more information or to just see what might happen. Clients are generally more open to trying a short-term experiment than radically changing their behaviors. They will be much less critical of the outcome, since they are not evaluating whether the new behavior worked.

Ellen had just received another notice from the school regarding Tom's poor performance. Normally, this occasion was sure to trigger another of her futile lectures on the value of education. The experiment consisted of two parts. First, I asked Ellen to do the following, just once, and observe carefully so she could report back to me how Tom reacted.

With the school's notice in hand, she was to sit down next to Tom and say:

> Look Tom, I've been doing a lot of thinking about this school sit-
> uation. I've even been working with a coach on this, and one of
> the things she's made me realize is that I have been pushing you
> way too hard. And I am really sorry. I guess every parent wants
> to believe her child is a superstar, will get a college degree, and
> have a really wonderful career. I know you are really smart and
> have what it takes to do that, but I guess I just have to realize
> that college isn't for everyone. And I'm sorry for being so hard
> on you. All I am going to ask is that you do me one big favor:
> Please just keep the school off my back. If you could put forth
> just enough effort so they won't call me all the time and send
> these notices out, I'll be satisfied and grateful. I just don't know
> how to deal with them anymore.

I instructed Ellen to deliver the speech with all the humility, benevolence, and sincerity she could muster, and to avoid getting caught up in
explaining or defending her new position. She was then to drop the subject
and not to speak of anything related to school again.

The second part of her experiment required that she seize one or two
opportunities to glorify professions she knew Tom would find distasteful.
For example, while standing at the window watching the disposal crew pick
up garbage in sub-zero weather, she might say in passing:

> You know, that's not such a bad deal, garbage collecting—no-
> brainer, steady work, benefits, and I'll bet they find a lot of trea-
> sures they take home for themselves.

It has been encouraging to watch Tom's story unfold. As a result of
Ellen's change of strategy, Tom has done an about-face. Their relationship
continues to improve as he demonstrates more responsible behavior.

In the book, *Tactics of Change: Doing Therapy Briefly,* Richard Fisch,
John Weakland, and Lynn Segal devote the final chapter to defining their

therapy model as one suitable for solving human problems in general. Those in question need not even qualify for therapy. Ellen Amatea followed their lead with her book, *Strategic Intervention for School Behavior Problems.* Ten years later, management consultant Lucy Gill, applied the model to the business world in her book, *How to Work with Just about Anyone: A 3-Step Solution for Getting Difficult People to Change.* I extend the brief strategic model into the coaching arena in my work. This chapter addresses the ways in which people get stuck in repetitive, unsuccessful attempts to change. It illustrates some common patterns of problem-maintaining behavior that clients present, and presents examples of strategies for interrupting those vicious cycles. Lest you think *this* coach never considers any approach that makes sense, please be assured she does actually consider those *first.* Only when the client presents a persistent pattern of employing sensible strategies without success do I shift to a more paradoxical approach. The flexibility of having both common- and uncommonsense tools in my bag has afforded me success with more of my clients.

It is important to emphasize that before employing any paradoxical strategy, one must be very careful to design it around the specific efforts the client has been attempting and what you know about the client and her situation. "Paradox" is a term attributed too loosely or casually to any intervention that strikes one as novel, ironic, or contrary to common sense. Too often paradoxical interventions have been lifted out of context and applied to any situation that seems similar to one in which it was used before. When used carelessly, the intervention is not likely to succeed; in fact, it may even backfire, causing the situation to worsen. And, of course, you will need to frame and present the intervention in a way that makes it sound like the most logical approach toward the intended goal. Otherwise, your client will have no part of it.

Practical Information

Advice for New Peak-Performance Coaches

1. Start working with a performance coach yourself. What better way to break into the coaching field than to work with someone who has

already done it? Not only will you be working with a qualified professional committed to helping you to be successful, but you will also have the advantage of experiencing a performance coach in action and observing how coaching sessions are conducted. Your coach can also be a rich source of inside information about launching a coaching practice.

2. Resist the urge to teach, instruct, or train. Performance coaching is a process of helping a person unlock her own potential and maximize her performance. The most effective coaches know how to help their clients erase or minimize the internal obstacles to performance, rather then teach them specific skills of the trade. It may be especially tempting to shift into instructor mode when you, the coach, happen to perform well in the very area the client is seeking to improve performance. The "outer" performance can flow naturally from the performer, once she learns to manage the "inner" one. The coach must focus on the latter.

3. Listen to your performer-client and find out exactly what she wants. Then work on whatever she is most committed to working on at the moment. You don't need to fix her whole life. There was something prominent in the performer's mind when she decided to work with a coach, and that is where her motivation lies. People are clever; they catch on. Mastering one aspect of their lives invariably has a rippling effect and begins to affect others. Imagine several logs floating downstream. It only takes one log to get stuck and jam the entire flow. If we can jiggle that one log and free it up, the rest will fall into place by themselves and continue the flow. We don't need to adjust all of them.

ADVICE FOR NEW THERAPIST-COACHES

1. Define yourself as a coach. What's your niche? You'll want to spend some time reflecting on who you really want to coach and what market you want to target. Where will you have the most energy and passion to put forth your best coaching effort? Who are the people you'd enjoy working with the most? Who could most benefit from your services? Who would most likely be attracted to your background, style, and interests?

2. Join a professional coaching organization. Organizations such as International Coach Federation offer no end of valuable information

about the field of coaching, where to acquire training, and how to find a coach. Annual conferences and local chapter meetings provide wonderful opportunities to learn and to network. I have found other coaches to be very open and willing to share their ideas and experiences.

3. Consider all your therapeutic tools as viable options for coaching. I almost made the mistake of leaving the brief strategic therapy model behind when I transitioned from therapy to coaching, for fear its paradoxical nature might come across as too much "on the fringe" for my coaching clients. Some of us tend to trap ourselves into thinking a therapist claims more license to employ seemingly unusual tactics than does the coach, and that "psycho-babble" is acceptable in therapy, but not in coaching. Actually, therapists might do well to eliminate psychological jargon with their clients and relate to them in a more conversational, plain-English manner. The success of any intervention, whether for therapy or coaching, relies heavily on the presentation. For any intervention to succeed, it needs only be appropriate for what you intend to accomplish with your client and presented in a way that makes sense to that client, given her particular situation and belief system. Becoming a coach has actually helped me become a better therapist.

MY FEES

I offer an initial 30-minute telephone conversation at no charge to give both the client and me the chance to find out if we are suited to work with one another. I then ask the client to commit to a minimum of four sessions to be completed within three months at a fee of $500. These 45-minute sessions are usually conducted by telephone, although some local clients prefer face-to-face visits. Following this initial phase of coaching, clients often elect to continue working on a per-session basis at a fee of $125 per session. I welcome brief e-mail transactions between sessions at no extra fee. While this arrangement has worked well with most clients, I remain open to negotiate with those with different needs and circumstances.

WHAT I KNOW NOW

Had I known I didn't need to be an expert or highly skilled in areas around which I coached, I'd have entered the field much sooner. Since I had been doing a lot of consulting and training, both of which were often, and erroneously, called "coaching," it was important for me to learn the distinction between consulting and coaching. Whereas a consultant is expected to be the expert in the content area around which she consults, the same is not necessarily true for a coach. In coaching, the *client* is the expert or at least knows what steps are needed to acquire that expertise. I see the coach's role as that of *facilitator*. Facilitating is quite different from leading, training, instructing, or advising, all of which imply content expertise. As a facilitator, a coach manages the *process* by which the client moves toward her goal. Certainly, a coach ought to have some working knowledge in client's content area to in order communicate intelligibly and gauge whether client is on track. When I don't feel I have enough working knowledge, I will simply ask the client to clue me in: "Teach me about what you do. Help me understand enough about it to assist you with the process of getting where you want to go." In the end, however, the client remains in charge of the content. What a relief for me!

A Brief Biography

I have a Master's degree in counseling psychology and a licensed clinical professional counselor (LCPC) license. I also hold master practitioner and trainer certifications in neurolinguistic programming, as well as hypnosis certification and approved consultant status with American Society of Clinical Hypnosis. My formal training in coaching began with the Institute for Life Coach Training (formerly Therapist U). I am the author of *Conversational Hypnosis: A Manual of Indirect Suggestion* and the director of Sommer Solutions, Inc.

Coming from a career in computer science, I officially launched myself as a therapist in 1984. After working briefly on contract with a family service agency, I continued in private practice. Private practice for me included conducting one-on-one psychotherapy sessions, teaching college psychology, and training other clinicians in brief strategic approaches, hypnotherapy, and neurolinguistic programming.

Much of my formal coaching experience has come out of the corporate environment, working extensively with Fortune 500 companies. Since 1985, I have coached, consulted, trained, and facilitated individuals, groups, and teams. In this role, I have helped clients build relationships and interpersonal skills (communication, listening, speaking, and writing), boost self-confidence, overcome performance and creativity blocks, increase self-understanding (often using the MBTI and similar assessments), manage time and stress, and balance life and career.

CONTACT INFORMATION

Carol Sommer, M.S., L.C.P.C.
5242 Grand Avenue
Downers Grove, IL 60515
Phone: 630-852-1799
E-mail: sommerc@sommersolutions.com
Web site: www.sommersolutions.com

11

Coaching Amateur Athletes: From Frozen to Fearless

Wendy Allen

Sometimes the phone can act like a mirror. I saw my past accurately reflected in Sylvie's tearful phone message.

"Please call me," she implored. "I need to know if you can help me. I broke my arm riding my horse about a month ago. And now I need help even thinking about getting back on. But I really want to. Please call me at home."

"I really want to!" is the resounding call of the amateur horseback rider. "Wanting" signals amateur status: the athlete may be riding competitively, but is not at a professional level. Professional riders have such a grasp on their talent, skill, and mental game that they don't just *want* things to happen, they *make* things happen for themselves in the arena. Unlike professionals, adult amateurs bring their emotional, physical, and mental baggage to their riding. It always gets in their way of showcasing their talent and their attunement to their horses. They often have archeology to do: peeling away layers and layers of unfinished baggage in order to get to the talent underneath. This is where I step in as a peak-performance coach. Although I have coached many types of athletes to improve their functioning, as an amateur rider myself I have a special affinity for coaching other riders.

Just as I suspected, my sense of Sylvie's plight was correct. She was a 35-year-old amateur learning the sport for the first time. This is not unusual these days. More and more adults (middle-aged) are saddling up to fulfill a childhood dream. Usually these men and women have finished raising children and have their own money to pay for riding lessons. I have seen the 37-and-over classes get larger and larger at riding competitions with serious riders—riders who train hard, own their horses, and delight in winning a blue ribbon, just as the young riders do.

Sylvie owned a sweet but little-trained horse whom she loved. One day while they were walking up a hill, a flock of birds spooked the horse and he turned and ran. Sylvie panicked and broke a cardinal rule of horseriding. She bailed (jumped off) and broke her arm. The horse stopped as soon as he came upon a patch of grass and calmly grazed while she lay in agony.

"I panicked," she said. "And I forgot to turn him sharply in a small circle until he calmed down. I'm so embarrassed."

She was off riding for eight full weeks and had three more to go. "I heal slowly compared to the young riders at my barn. They're back on in two weeks. I feel like a semi-truck ran over me."

Sylvie managed a small laugh. "I could quit riding now and everyone would understand. What am I doing in my advanced age anyway? But I don't want to quit. I really don't. I want to get back on and continue my training. I'm very scared. I keep going over and over it. Every time I imagine it I get scared all over again. It's like I'm obsessed with the accident. I *hate* this. I *really want to* but I'm scared."

Her words were so familiar and compelling to me, that I decided it would be fun to work with her. There have been times when I've been 30 years older than some of the competitors in my riding classes. Whenever I've broken something, which every jumper does, I've had to struggle with the abrupt termination of doing something I love as well as the struggle to reconcile my heart and mind with getting back on.

Most of the athletes I coach see me in person. Sylvie came to my office the next week. She looked remarkably young and fit, but sounded almost desperate. I asked her to tell me the rest of her story.

She had started the sport a year ago with no previous experience. She had gone to a jumping competition to see her niece and had gotten hooked. "I want to do that!" she had said to herself. And yet, her only experience on a horse was pony rides and one aborted lesson as a teenager—she was so frightened that she left early and never came back. So, with her husband's surprised and proud encouragement, she began to take lessons at the local stables. She learned the basics of horsemanship and went on trail rides. "I was always scared," she told me. "I know it sounds crazy, but I also liked it. Although I got emotional, I still kept going back."

When the stables folded, the entire staff moved to another location with sprawling hills and two fenced-in arenas. She continued to learn the basics of English riding. She worked on her balance in the walk, trot, and canter. In fact, this was all she did for months on end and, like most beginning riders, she loved the challenge of molding her body into the new and exacting sitting positions on the saddle. She tried hard to keep her hands still, her heels down, and her legs strong.

"I loved the work and the discipline of it," she told me. "I went out all the time. I realized that just doing those three basic gaits was a lot harder than it looked, especially for my 35-year-old body. I ended each day with aches and pains so I began to work out with weights and stretches."

Her work with her trainer was sporadic. It was thrilling when her trainer was attentive to her, but terribly frustrating when her trainer was distracted or failed to show up. "I don't think I have a lot of natural ability," Sylvie told me. "But I love riding and I'm willing to work very hard. My trainer is not an easy person to train with; she has some personal problems and I get very angry at her, but never show it. I want to remain in her good graces because I respect how she teaches me."

Not getting along with one's trainer is a common complaint among amateur riders. Horse lessons at this level don't provide a good income for the trainer, who is usually in love with the horses but terrible at making a profit. Consequently, a trainer often has to struggle to stay in business and this serious stress can make them less accessible and consistent to their students. I questioned her more about her relationship to her trainer.

"I really love her. She can be magic with the horses. She takes in horses nobody wants and works with them. I can't find any other word but magic to describe what she does. She can be so much fun but she can also be flaky. I'm not one of her favorite students, mostly because I'm older. But I can live with that."

What she couldn't live with was the thought of getting back on her horse. As compelled and driven as she seemed to be, she was also frightened, teary, and angry about the accident. Shock from the event stayed with her and, as a psychologist used to working with trauma, it seemed to me that the traumatic material was causing some cognitive distortion. She seemed to have a very black/white perspective of what the fall *meant.*

As a therapist *and* a coach, I often view a client from two perspectives. My therapeutic assessment was that Sylvie was suffering from posttraumatic stress disorder (PTSD), the freezing effects of trauma on the brain. The "fight or flight" to stay on the horse or bail taps into primitive responses in the limbic or reptilian part of the brain. When trauma happens, the unresolved material remains fresh and easily triggered. It is only processed by one side of the brain's frontal lobe, giving rise to a cognitive skew in the perception of the victim. This perceptual imbalance led her to feel ashamed and unsettled. She was full of self-doubt as well as paralyzing fear. Every time she imagined herself getting back on the horse she retriggered the limbic material and reexperienced the trauma as if it had happened just the day before. No amount of verbal reassurances or supportive activities can help a person get rid of unresolved trauma.

As a coach, I knew that her fall was causing symptoms, but that her reaction was not a psychosis or a pathology. I wanted to frame her situation in a way that would help her both to understand what was happening to her and normalize her response to it, so she could be ready to take action to get back on the horse. I explained that she was going through a reaction to an ordeal that was quite prevalent with many war veterans or victims of terrible accidents. Her case, I felt, was quite moderate and could probably be easily remedied. Just telling her this seemed to bring some immediate relief.

"It's nice to know I'm not crazy," she said with a shaky laugh. "If a Vietnam vet can get over his problems, than I can get over this." With this goal in mind, Sylvie agreed to make a series of three appointments with me.

The next two, I explained, would specifically address her fear. "I'm not a trainer," I explained to her. "I know that sometimes a trainer can be the best therapist, coach, and ally an athlete could ever have. But I am in the unique position of learning about and addressing the big picture of everything you are and everything you bring into the sport—all the mental, emotional, psychological, and physiological stuff and how that all adds up to what it means to be Sylvie on a horse. This is something a trainer almost never has the time or skills to do."

SETTING GOALS

Athletes respond very well to goals, so we set three for the upcoming sessions. First, we would address and diffuse as much of the upsetting mindset as possible. Second, we would install a cognitive-behavioral link to support new skill integration and application. And third, we would look at her riding through the lens of an amateur but competitive athlete, to see how she could best make certain training decisions.

"I feel like I'm being heard seriously for the first time. Your approach lets me feel that I am taking care of everything I can. That's a wonderful relief," Sylvie enthused at the close of our session. "I know I'll never be a professional rider but I want to compete and compete hard, so much. You're the first person who seems to understand that."

I *did* understand. The journey of the middle-aged amateur is full of highs and lows. Yet, in my experience, adult amateurs bring so much heart to their sport that I find them a joy to work with.

Our national obsession with fitness and sports has increased dramatically in the last decade. This reflects a collective awareness of the parts of our lives that are increasingly out of control. Job insecurity, finances, crime, traffic, and global disturbances are laid at our feet through daily experience or the media and can make us feel helpless. The disciplined and stress-relieving lifestyle of the athlete has made becoming athletic more desirable.

Much of the popular media offers stories about overcoming odds and certainly the stories that focus on those who, despite everything, achieve athletic victory seem to be truly compelling to us. The media-savvy networks who cover the Olympics now try to profile every amateur athlete they can who has had to overcome any kind of obstacle. The viewing public responds very well to these heartfelt stories.

I believe, and have learned from my clients, that these stories are compelling because they lift us out of our obstacle-packed days filled with the myriad worries and stressors that come with living a regular life. I have begun to understand why the ancient Greeks, so full of creativity and inspiration in their daily lives grudgingly grew to admire the fierce discipline and regimental behaviors of their fellow rivals, the Spartans.

"I'm basically the same," Sylvie told me at the start of our next session. "Maybe a little bit worse. Or better. I don't know," she said resignedly. "Now whenever I go out to the barn and see my horse I feel flashes of anger at him. Like he was out to get me that day! Isn't that silly? He's not a mean horse like some are. But now I'm beginning to take it all very personally!"

If I was listening as a psychotherapist, I would ask her to explore her anger. But in my role as a sports coach I help clients to ignore most emotions and, instead, become thinking machines. I want my clients to discover their inner resources, transform their fears to action, and become powerful, aggressive competitors who can get the job done.

I often have my clients watch amateur ice skating competitions on TV, to see the skaters struggle with this task while on the ice. "Emotions have no place on the ice," is a motto skating coaches often extoll. The same sentiment applies to amateur jumpers. Paradoxically, when skaters (and all kinds of competitors) get the job done, without fragmenting when they make mistakes, they usually end up enjoying themselves.

TOOLS AND TECHNIQUES

I use an eclectic grouping of techniques to help clients put aside feelings to think more clearly and become stronger at their sport. First, I combine elements of eye movement desensitization and reprocessing (EMDR), neurolinguistic programming (NLP), shamanic healing, and Buddhist meditation into a technique I call "fire breath." The client is guided to choose a "power animal" that can become her aggressive and powerful self. She uses her breathing to accomplish this transformation and install this skill. I have all my clients practice the fire breath technique as they wait for their competition to begin. Sometimes when they lose their concentration during their event, I coach them to use fire breath to stay in the present.

Next, using light therapy and elements of thought field therapy (TFT) techniques I teach my clients some guided imagery to bring themselves into a calm, present, and centered place in order to combat anticipatory anxiety. This technique combined with fire breath can transform nervousness into excitement.

Third, we practice the sensation and skill of becoming a "thinking machine" by compartmentalizing fear as well as other emotions. I have my clients practice this through many future tense exercises in the office as well as in the arena. This is an acquired and installed skill that takes a lot of practice. My goal is to have a rider link his or her intensive level of concentration to the rhythm of the horse's strides in order to become lulled into a very present and exquisitely responsive "zone," attuned to the horse, themselves, and distances between the jumps. This zone should be all-encompassing. A runner will link this to his or her footfalls. A tennis player will link this to the rhythm of the ball going back and forth. In sports there is a lot of talk about what the zone is and how to achieve it. I believe it is a particular cognitive-affectual-behavior alignment. All of these techniques plus the added element of adrenaline consistently puts an athlete into their unique zone.

Finally, I usually ask many questions and come up with advice to help improve my client's relationship to her trainer, her training process, and her psychological and physiological fitness. This reflects a *holistic* approach that I bring to sports coaching, one that combines my experience as a therapist and a coach.

Of course, the coaching I was giving Sylvie needed to be complemented with lots of riding and lessons. Sports coaching does not supplant rigorous athletic training. My approach is based on learning theory and is tailored to the unique learning patterns of each client. The combination of lessons, time in the saddle alone, and the work they do with me gives them a way to link their emotional and cognitive learning to a kinesthetic modality.

My interest in coaching developed after I read James Hillman's book, *100 Years of Psychotherapy and the World's Getting Worse.* I began to think about the ways my work with my therapy clients could become more proactive. I wanted my clients to be able to take the benefits of good mental health and expand it into decisive, goal-oriented ways of approach along a broader spectrum of daily life and institutions. I wanted to help them to take their relational gains and apply them to systemic challenges.

I had previous training in NLP and used that to develop coaching strategies. In addition, I had conducted Ph.D. research about the "anchoring" necessary to bring each client into affective, cognitive, and behavioral alignment to be able to respond (instead of react) to outside stressors. I began to apply this tool to clients who needed to break through inner and external obstacles to achieve goals. I learned about the process of *equifinality,* meaning that the whole is greater than the sum of its parts. For example, when a client enters into a relationship with a system, change comes about through the dynamic of *constructed* paradox: a *second-order* shift takes place and unbalances the situation. The system and the client change in order to adapt to a new balance. Therapists have learned about this kind of change from family systems work.

But sometimes a client enters into a change-making dynamic with a system that offers an *inherent* paradox, and then a *third-order* shift takes place, bringing every element of the system to the next level, which I call an example of *evolution.* As a sports coach, I am interested in not just helping my clients change; I also want to assist them to evolve.

"My trainer says I should visualize getting back on my horse and walking up and down the hill. The problem is, I get scared and my mind starts coming up with worse things that could happen to spook him—an earthquake, a tree limb crashing down—you know, crazy things like that!"

I explained to her that I saw this as a natural progression of her fears. The longer her fear was left untreated, the more likely she would link it with irrational thoughts. This is a normal defense mechanism in reaction to fear, but she needed some help to quickly stop this pattern.

I decided to offer Sylvie EMDR, a powerful and increasingly popular tool for treating fear. It is currently the most successfully researched trauma treatment used across a broad population of survivors from Hurricane Floyd to the Oklahoma bombing. EMDR now has many other innovative applications. It has evolved from its inception in 1987 by Francine Shapiro to become a comprehensive therapeutic approach that can help clients rapidly eliminate a wide range of negative emotional states, as well as catalyze personal discovery and growth.

I have made EMDR an important part of my coaching strategies and combine several EMDR protocols to address specific needs. For Sylvie, I would use a standard EMDR protocol for trauma diffusion combined with one for peak performance. This is a powerful antidote for the injured competitor.

EMDR sessions are scheduled to last for 90 minutes. I explained to her that the process might bring up some surprising or unexpected thoughts or feelings but that we would quickly calm them to a lower scale of intensity.

Using the EMDR protocol I guided Sylvie's eyes back and forth, asking her to track my hand with her eyes at varying speeds. This action unlocks the frozen material from the limbic section of the brain. Sylvie would relive the fall, but in a quick and safe way, because the information would be evenly reprocessed through both frontal lobes.

Within a few minutes, she would become desensitized to the fall and be able to look at it in a new way. The new perceptual distance would create a resourceful control for her. As the memory of the fall resolved and faded away, I would then assist her to build a new belief system about what happened, reinforcing it through the use of the eye movements. From experience, I knew she would leave the session relaxed, empowered, and altered, able to put her new beliefs and feelings into better-aligned perceptions and more resourceful behaviors.

Following is an extract from her first EMDR session, with my silent thinking about the process as it unfolded in brackets:

Sylvie: The horse spun around and ran down the hill with me. I bailed. I thought at that moment, "I am completely helpless." [*She identifies her negative belief quickly and links it to her impulsive behavior as she replayed the memory. She feels panic and helplessness along with bodily sensations of no air in her lungs. I am going to continue repeating a series of eye movements, and expect that her fear will be reexperienced right now, and she may evidence heavy breaths, tears, or dilated pupils.*]

Sylvie: I can't stop him! I have to get off! [*She breathes quick shallow breaths and is quite flushed.*] All I can see is the ground rushing up at me! Then I hit it face down! [*She begins to cry. During the next set of eye movements, which take only a few seconds, her breathing calms considerably. She is through the worst of the remembering. She begins to report a slowing down of the memory in her mind as if she were on the back of her horse and the ride is happening in real time, but in slow motion. A sign of progress: She begins to observe the movie as well as reexperience it. She recalls minute details of the event, but this does not retrigger the fearful feelings and sensations. Her observing ego is emerging and strengthening as the limbic material begins to fade. At this point I begin to change directions: I ask her to identify some inner resources. She continues to calm down. My intention is to make the innate obvious and then help her reclaim or reprogram it. I call this resource installation.]*

COACH: Is it true you can picture this and take slower breaths?

SYLVIE: Yes.

COACH: Slow your breath down as you re-imagine the picture of the event. Is it true you can think about what is happening while you remember the ride?

SYLVIE: Yes.

COACH: Tell me what you are thinking as you go through it. [*She recites the story of the accident with her eyes moving back and forth, full of minute details that lets me know there is a release of frozen information from the brain. She is now able to link her experience to a thoughtful accounting—a good sign of resolution. She reports that the experience begins to fade until it is a vague memory, distant and unemotional.*]

SYLVIE: All I see now is the patch of dirt where I landed. It's empty. All the trees around it are green and the hills behind it are beautiful. The sun is shining just where I landed. [*She begins to laugh—a common reaction when a client has reached resolution.*] It looks so peaceful now. Nothing bad could happen there anymore!

At that point I installed a positive cognition that emerged from Sylvie during the reprocessing of the event. I like that Sylvie had actually given thought to how and where to jump off; in doing so, she has almost completed a successful and difficult vaulting maneuver! We installed all these positive elements so that she would be able to leave our session believing she had done the best she could, at the time, with what she had.

Her embarrassment, shame, and helplessness were extinguished. Her fear abated. We finished with what I call "future tense." We went back into the memory of the event and corrected all the mistakes she made, as if a trainer had been there and calling out directions to her. We worked repeatedly on the instructions to lean back on the horse with a firm rein, a response that does not feel logical or natural but must become instinctive for every successful rider.

The point of these installations was to create a cognitive pathway that can store and then retrieve these resources when needed. A similar event will trigger these resources for Sylvie and make the difference between a fight or flight reaction as opposed to a clear-thinking response.

Sylvie came smiling into our next session. "I got back on my horse and walked him up and down the hill," she proudly announced. "Then we trotted up and down. Even with my cast on! I practiced everything we went through in our session, even turning him in tight circles. I figure if I train myself to think this way, maybe I can do this if it ever happens again."

This was good news, yet we still had more to cover. A bridge needed to be crossed to take Sylvia from rider to fierce competitor. I decided to use a three-step process: one, I needed to teach her a tool I use to transform her innate fear into aggression, which is a valuable emotion for athletes; two, I wanted to teach her a good relaxation technique she could use while she was waiting to enter the arena; and three, I needed to help her learn another tool to help her compartmentalize her emotions, that is, to put fear into a far corner of her experience while she "got the job done" on the horse during her rides.

In addition to helping her learn these tools, at the end of this session I suggested some practical matters, such as whether or not she might consider moving to another, more professional barn, one in which all the students compete, where the horses are well-trained, and the trainer is fully committed to each student.

"It will be very hard to leave my barn," she told me. "I feel so attached. I'd be afraid to train with all those great people." She eventually did move up to a show barn after a long period of uneven training. She competes regularly. She loves to win and trains even harder when she doesn't. I respect her goals to compete and win blue ribbons, even though I know she faces some obstacles to reach them. She is moving up through circuit competitions to go to A-level shows.

I still see Sylvie periodically. She comes in for three-session series when she needs them. Her base anxiety level has dramatically decreased while her skill and challenge levels continue to increase. My coaching tools adapt to her specific needs. She is now a bona fide amateur athlete and an effective competitor. She has been a circuit champion for the last two years.

"I'm acting just like the kind of person I've always wanted to be," she told me recently. "I'm braver. I can think clearly while the air is rushing past me. Whenever I run into a scary moment at work or in my life, all I have to remember is how I can look down a line of jumps and know I'll end up at the other end. And sometimes I'll end up at the other end and have done it very well, and I'll have won the blue ribbon!"

PRACTICAL INFORMATION

ADVICE FOR NEW PEAK-PERFORMANCE COACHES

1. In coaching, peak is used as both a noun and a verb. It is both an act of *doing,* as well as an elevated *place* fixed in personal imagery.
2. A peak-performance program is inherently holistic for both you and your client. It must address the body and mind, both cognitive and kinesthetic responses. This is your chance to combine and blend all your theory, skill, and experience into a rich and robust program.
3. You must have your own experience in peak-performance. If you are not a competitor or a performer then this is your chance to develop those skills and face your own fears, setbacks, and victories in the public arena.

ADVICE FOR NEW THERAPIST-COACHES

1. Be a role model. You must have your own personal area of expertise—an area of achievement that includes the basic fundamentals of coach-

ing. Your own achievements are the role models and the proof to be plumbed for your clients.

2. Charge high-enough fees to challenge both you and your client. Therapists facilitate change. Coaches make promises. Don't promise anything you can't deliver. Make sure all your promises are realistic and reasonable, yet challenge you to do your best work.

3. It's in the details. The best coaching advice is practical and based on a series of small steps and victories for your client. The more practical the goals, the more your client will be inspired to reach, stretch, and achieve.

MY FEES

I charge $125 an hour in my office for a peak performance session. EMDR sessions are $175 for 90 minutes. Off-site sessions are $200 an hour with a two-hour minimum. I am also a business coach for therapists in private practice who want to become more successful in their practices. I charge $250 per month for business coaching sessions by phone.

WHAT I KNOW NOW

1. No issue or vision is too small or too big for coaching. A coach must be prepared to set up practical strategies to help her client be effective in the smallest personal arena or in a globalized system. I once used my peak-performance coaching skills with a pregnant client who was terrified of going through labor and childbirth. I also coached a client who wanted to leave his philosophical stamp on the world stage through politics. We set up a localized strategy that linked up with a globalized vision.

2. A system is a system is a system. All systems have the same inherent properties that keep them stuck and help them to change. All people have the same inherent qualities that help them to change and learn, assimilate, and accommodate. This makes the possibilities almost endless for helping a client reach her goals. Coaching should be exciting, creative, and resourceful for the client and the coach.

3. A client needs to be positioned to reach both micro- and macro-congruent goals. What a client contributes to one goal is exactly what he or she

needs to live, breathe, and act upon to achieve all other goals. A set of goals and strategies should absolutely reflect who the client is and can be. A coach needs to builds a strategy of personal inquiry that facilitates this knowing so that it underscores all other efforts.

A BRIEF BIOGRAPHY

I am a Ph.D. and have been a therapist for 20 years. My coaching clients find me through word-of-mouth. I have found the addition of coaching services in my practice to be easy and well-received. My coaching clients call me with an interest in peak performance.

My coaching is influenced by my Ph.D. research on how to facilitate change in a variety of systems using third-order paradox. I also have had the good fortune to work with a brilliant horse trainer, Leslie Pinkerton, whose techniques I deconstructed, then liberally adapted into many good coaching ideas. I have heuristically interviewed my fellow competitors to understand their perceptions of how they learn and win in a high-stimuli activity.

I studied with Michael Harner and learned powerful, extreme, and absolute methods of transformation in shamanic work that opened up a whole new area of study for me. I have studied extensively in the burgeoning field of sports psychology. I also benefited from reading techniques of coaching in Lynn Grodzki's book, *Building Your Ideal Private Practice.* I consider this required reading for all coaches.

CONTACT INFORMATION

Wendy Allen, Ph.D.
27 E. Victoria, Suite L
Santa Barbara, CA 93101
Phone: 805-962-2212
E-mail: weallen@earthlink.net

12

Coaching Professional Athletes: Alignment 101

Audrey Penn

It was simple. If I could guarantee them dates with "foxy chicks," they would give my personal brand of alignment coaching a chance. I agreed. In an auditorium the size of an airplane hanger, I, a 21-year-old ballet-jazz dancer, weighing in at 104 pounds, stood in front of a pro-football team and taught them the Bump, the Mashed Potato, and the Shimmy. In the process of introducing rhythm as an integral part of alignment coaching, these awesome athletes were soon fully warmed up, well-stretched, and aware of how their bodies move on the playing field. As to my promise, the players left the auditorium dancing the dances of which dream dates are made.

Rhythm and alignment are everything in sport. If an athlete's timing is off by half a second, it could mean the loss of a game, or the loss of a life. Part of my job as an alignment coach is to help establish the rhythm of a sport and the rhythmic movements used in that sport. The most important part of my job, however, is aligning the athlete, or training him or her* to "find center"—not just physically, but mentally, emotionally, and psychologically as well. To achieve these goals, I use a combination of biomechanical (or physical) alignment, "mapping" for visual and psychological alignment, and "gyroscoping" for electrical and heart alignment. I begin by creating a series of stretching, lengthening, and strengthening exercises that define and articulate the athlete's under-muscle as well as defining the

---

*For the remainder of this chapter, I will use the masculine terminology purely for the sake of making a more readable document. It does not imply that males need this training, while females do not. Both benefit tremendously from it.

rhythm and movement of his sport. Under-muscle refers to the slower developing tendons and ligaments that are needed to support the top muscle created by the sport. Under-muscle is also used as a bracing system for the vulnerable "joist" areas where ligaments and cartilage are more often at risk. The joist area extends beyond the joint system of the body. It includes the pulley system of the top and under-muscle both above and below the joint that steady and support the joint. For instance, the calf and thigh are treated with the knee joint, strengthening the entire joist system the way an engineer would treat the joist areas of a span bridge.

It has been 30 years since I struck that bargain with the football players, yet my method for winning over athletes has remained the same: music and dance. It amazes me how many young, All-American athletes can't keep a beat! My dog has more rhythm in his tail swing than most of these kids have in their feet—and I begin by telling them so.

My own journey into the world of alignment coaching was both accidental and predictable. I was 4 years old when our family doctor diagnosed me with juvenile rheumatoid arthritis (JRA). Ballet dancing did nothing to stop the destruction of joints and soft tissue, but it did produce a muscle structure strong enough for me to live a fairly normal and active life. And although my years of study and dancing were riddled with surgery and rehab, I managed to dance my way into musical theatre, and regional, national, and international ballet companies, as both a dancer and a teacher.

It was this unusual blend of dance and physical challenges that brought me to alignment coaching. When I was not able to dance, I apprenticed with some of the most brilliant and renowned Russian and European dance masters in the world. I also worked with physical therapists who specialized in weak or injured dancers. Starting at age 12, the doctors and surgeons involved in my case invited me to medical school seminars where they openly discussed my surgeries and rehabs, then loaned me medical books to learn as much as I could about my unusual and numerous surgical situations. In addition to all of this, I was one of the privileged participants in J. B. Rhine's parapsychology labs at Duke University. There I learned the mental skills and visual skills called "mapping" and the electrical behavior skill called "gyroscoping," all of which will be discussed later.

After years of dancing, teaching, and rehab, I developed a keen eye and was able to point out the misaligned areas on a dancer's or athlete's body and determine how to realign them. When teaching at dancing schools or guest-teaching at universities, I often invited athletes to one of my beginning adult alignment classes, and encouraged them to stay and dance. When they saw immediate changes in their flexibility and balance, they returned as often as their schedules allowed. In time, they encouraged athletes they knew to take my classes. Coaches who saw me working with their athletes and noticed the positive differences assumed athletic alignment was what I did for a living and spread the word. The truth was, there wasn't a single problem facing an athlete that I myself had not faced either as a ballet dancer or because of JRA. I fell in love with the athletes' passions and desires, and they found someone who could truly say, "Sure I can help. I've been there, and this is what I did."

I am still fighting JRA and still facing surgery and rehab, but my love and appreciation for athletes continue to grow. I am forever finding newer and better ways of reaching in and coaching out their extraordinary talents.

ALIGNMENT COACHING

Alignment coaching is on the rise. It is no longer enough to be talented, physically capable, and well-trained to be a professional athlete. Today's athletes are facing much longer and far more competitive careers. Biomechanical alignment produces not only a unique physical strengthening that promotes longevity, but also the kind of correct movement that allows the body to thrive throughout the sport instead of becoming the victim of wear and tear. Athletes' mental, emotional, and physical training must be not only meticulous in its development, but the coach must also continue to guide athletes through the changes that longevity in the sport has created. Biomechanically aligned athletes are known for their long, healthy, and high-performance careers.

My first course of action when taking on a new athlete is to shadow him for several weeks. I watch practice sessions, I observe how he handles pressure and competition, and I witness his behavior when recognized in public. Having been a ballerina, and presently a recognized children's author, I know firsthand some of the unusual situations an athlete may face. Part of my program is to meet with each individual athlete several times a week and discuss these issues. Even though athletes' visions and destinations differ from one another, I believe they all need to keep one thing in mind. Each individual is both "the athlete" and "the athlete's care-taker." Although "the athlete" may want to party, the "caretaker" should make a decision based on the "athlete's" well-being.

Because biomechanical alignment is about centering the physical body, I begin at the feet and work up. By observing the athlete in dance class, I can identify problems such as pronating or supinating, uneven hips, mis-aligned knees, and other structural deviations.

At the beginning of my alignment career, I restricted my coaching to physical alignment, such as lengthening the tendons in the back of a knee, stretching the ligaments that surround a rotator cuff, or teaching a tech-nique called "spotting" for quicker eye and head movement when turning. It was only after six years of apprenticing with masters of gyroscoping (a technique used to quiet the heart and bring it further back in the chest cavity) and mapping (visual, tactile, and verbal exercises using theta waves) that I included these additional alignment-coaching techniques.

Together, biomechanical alignment, gyroscoping, and mapping train athletes to focus on the moment, keep their hearts and "nerves" quiet, and call on their peak athletic abilities day after day, and year after year. The centered athlete, referred to as "elite" within the biomechanical definition, is one of the most remarkably consistent and psychologically sound ath-letes in any sport.

Biomechanical alignment builds the athlete from the inside out. By defining, strengthening, and developing soft tissue and under-muscle, it creates a bracing system for the joints and heavier outer muscles. The sport itself should define the outer muscles. Alignment coaching is less effective with athletes who bulk up with heavy weights. If the tendons and ligaments that surround the major joints can't support the demand of the heavier muscles, the athlete loses flexibility and speed and risks stress fractures. Some of my toughest exercises are as simple as lifting a straight leg two inches off the floor and holding it there, motionless, for six minutes. Without a fully developed under-muscle, the leg will shake and cramp while top-muscle strains to be supportive.

Two other skills I spend a great deal of time on are spotting and "eye links." Spotting is a skill used by dancers and athletes while turning or spinning so they don't get dizzy and can focus properly on their next move. "Eye links" is a unique way of focusing the eyes to increase an athlete's running speed.

None of these skills are achieved overnight. Alignment changes take both time and patience, two things that can't be adapted to this microwaveable world.

ALIGNMENT TRAINING SCHEDULES

Because my time spent with athletes is during their off-seasons, I create intense training schedules. We spend three days a week in the dance and alignment studio. After 45 minutes of stretching on mats, the athletes move to the ballet barre for 40 minutes of strengthening, flexibility, and footwork. At the completion of the barre work, the athletes move to the center floor to work on lateral and quick-step movement, spotting, jumping, and endurance. All work is done to music to encourage rhythm.

Although formal classes are three days a week, the athletes do mat exercises on their own during the remainder of the week. Mat work begins with an exercise called the "horseshoe," a method of stretching and aligning the body that places the feet, knees, hips, back, and head in a specific position. From there, I can see if their backs and necks are centered, whether their hips, hams, and groins are too tight, and whether their knees, ankles, and feet are pointed incorrectly. By the completion of the horseshoe exercise, I have enough information about the individual athletes to give a class that addresses each of the specific problems. All exercises are geared to advance and strengthen the athlete, so performing an exercise, even if not specifically needed, is always beneficial.

Exercises called "knee locks," "torking," and "pulls" help correct the weak ankles, bowed legs, misaligned knees, and weak joist areas. How quickly corrections are made depends on the athlete's condition, how long the problem has existed, and the athlete's diligence. The whole point of biomechanical alignment is to strengthen and build the athlete, utilizing the actual sport as a form of rehab. Over the years, I have had hundreds of athletes complain about knee problems caused by their sport. By teaching them specific exercises and a new way of straightening their legs using their feet as the main thrust and not their knees, their knee joints and cartilage gain strength and dexterity, and they become pain free. The same skills heightened one basketball player's jump by six inches.

Arielle is a 12-year-old ice skater who has set her sights on the 2006 Olympics. I not only coach her in the ballet studio, but I also have her on ice skates utilizing customized exercises such as practicing jumps and turns with her elbows locked behind a broomstick. This is to teach her the *feel* of an aligned spine, straight shoulders, and jumps landed directly over her skates. In the swimming pool she memorizes the feel of spinning in the air before landing. In the mapping room, she closes her eyes and calls upon the feel of a movement while visualizing her routine on the ice. In time, Arielle will understand that a movement, once spent, can never be duplicated. But the *feel* of that movement, once memorized, can be duplicated for the rest of her skating life.

Following alignment class, I accompany several of the athletes to a school track or to a local park for running and sprinting skills. Running is not appropriate for all sports, or when addressing specific alignment problems such as bowed legs or mis-aligned knees called chrondromalacia patella. After stretching, the runners begin with paced jogging to a waltz count. Jogging to a rhythm not only produces a better gait, but also helps the athlete pattern out his breathing, blood flow, and electrical flow. The athletes are required to run every day, whether or not there is class.

Sprinting skills, however, are designed with each individual sport in mind. Sprints that are good for one type of athlete could be counterproductive to another. When everyone has completed his running skills, we go in separate directions. According to the day and rotation, one athlete will come back to my office for mapping and gyroscoping. Both of these skills are practiced privately and individually. (Not all alignment students study mapping and gyroscoping, but *every* mapping student must take alignment.)

Other days, I split the day between the mapping room and an athlete's sports arena. The arena might be another ballet studio or the bottom of a 70-foot rock climb. Here, the athlete and I will *apply* what is being learned in alignment, mapping, and gyro classes directly to his sport.

My coaching is limited to the alignment of an athlete's body, the instruction of how an athlete's brain thinks, and the calming of the electrical system to quiet the heart and stop anxiety. I accompany the athlete to his arena in order to instruct him on how to plant a foot correctly; lift off the ground safely; reach for overhead objects consistently without stressing a rotator cuff; or how to spot in order to speed up a turn. My job (thankfully) does not require me to slide into third base. It does, however, require me to train the baseball player to slide into base without risking a pulled hamstring or Achilles tendon.

SPECIAL PROBLEMS

More importantly, however, the job of any good coach is to solve puzzles and help secure the athlete. Recently a basketball player asked me for help. He had never had any serious injuries. Landing on the floor or being slapped around the court was simply a part of the game. Yet he complained of intermittent dizziness, some loss of balance, and difficulty in focusing. After watching him in class for a few weeks, I saw him waver now and then, but soon regain his balance completely. I had him checked out by orthopedic surgeons and neurologists, who gave him a clean bill of health.

The problems, however, continued. I asked him if he had trouble remembering things and did he use post-it-notes as reminders. He looked at me as if I had three heads, but answered yes to all questions. If things did not improve, he would be forced to retire.

This was not the first athlete I had encountered with these symptoms, and not the first athlete discharged from a specialist's care thinking nothing more could be done to help. Physical contact, banging into a wall, tumbling on the ground, and whipping one's neck is a part of just about every sport in existence. Yet, they can, and do, cause concussions and inner ear tears that go completely undetected and can make an athlete's life miserable. Several years ago, a similar case introduced me to neurotologist, better known as the "dizzy doctor." A neurotologist is a specialist in vestibular disorders such as perilymph fistula, a tear or defect in one or both of the small, thin membranes between the middle and inner ears. This has proven to be a serious problem in some athletes, but most athletes go undiagnosed because they do not know this form of therapy exists. A neurotologist has a system for evaluating balance problems. Through a series of specific tests, the neurotologist can evaluate a number of possible causes and arrive at a course of action, sometimes surgery. When I took my basketball player to the dizzy doc, he passed most of the tests with flying colors. But when he was asked to put one foot in front of the other, cross his arms across his chest, then close his eyes, he fell sideways and landed on the floor. This gave the doctor enough information to warrant a more thorough examination, and discovered the answer deep in the middle ear. With surgery, the dizziness was stopped, balance was restored, and his career took on a whole new life. I ask all coaches and therapists to remember that if after the doctors have dismissed athletes from their care and there are still symptoms concerning balance, dizziness, and random anxiety, there is still one more place to look.

GYROSCOPING

Other problems, far more common to athletes and equally as worrisome, are noticeably elevated forms of anxiety and a racing heart. Although commonly linked together, anxiety and a racing heart do not always go hand in hand when concerning a specific group of athletes called hyperkinetics. For these athletes, it is not enough to consider their systemic, psychological, and musculoskeletal problems. Biomechanical alignists must also take into consideration the unique electrical systems that set them apart from the nonathlete. This is where gyroscoping and mapping have become increasingly important in the athlete's overall alignment.

Athletes with hyperkinetic electrical systems maintain an output of electricity that is faster and hotter than that of the nonhyperkinetic. When tapped into, this hotter form of electricity can be harnessed and aimed, surpassing the power normally initiated by adrenalin. It is the presence of adrenalin that can undo a hyperkinetic athlete.

For the hyperkinetic athlete, the feeling of anxiety is not always anxiety. It can also be an electrical response to his environment. We are all bombarded with electrical waves produced by everything from the lights in our living room to the satellites circling the earth, and we are all affected by the heat and electricity that emanates from other people, much the way an invisible virus can transfer from person to person. The hyperkinetic brain processes these electrical waves to a greater extent than the nonhyperkinetic, and therefore reacts more intensely in certain environments. Ask most baseball players how they feel about crowds, and they'll tell you they feel more comfortable standing on a field with twenty or so players and coaches than they do seated in the stands with 50,000 people talking, cheering, and acting . . . well . . . hyper. The electricity surrounding the stands is far too frenetic for most of the athletes to handle.

In addition to feeling anxious when his electricity is affected, the athlete may experience heart irregularities, including racing, palpitations, fibrillation, and missed beats, among others.

One of the easiest kinetic skills to learn is "astroturfing," a way of focusing the eyes on a single blade of grass until all of the grass around it appears as uniform as artificial turf. Using this soft stare as a part of a specific sequence, the trained athlete will experience an immediate drop in tension and blood pressure, and the resulting calm allows him to find center.

After the athlete has mastered astroturfing, we move on to gyroscoping to teach the heart to behave. Gyroscoping has been a well-kept secret. It has always been taught to the select few who surfaced to the top of their sport when they were lucky enough to come across a coach familiar with the skill. I am trying to change that. I have now taught genetic gyroscoping (a very basic level of gyroscoping) to hundreds of athletes and coaches on their way up the alignment-coaching ladder. Even if we only get as far as calming anxiety and quieting the heart, it has already made a huge difference in athletes who once thought they had unconquerable hurdles.

In order to teach a young child or a puppy to behave, they must first misbehave. It is when they are noisy that they can be corrected and taught to be quiet. This concept applies to an athlete's heart as well. Athletes, or hyperkinetics, often discover that their diaphragms are located higher in their body than in others. Cardiologists have pointed this fact out to many of the athletes I send for echocardiograms before I begin my work with them. I always have an athlete examined by a cardiologist in order to rule out any problems I am not trained to handle. With an elevated diaphragm, and a heart forward and pumpy, it can feel like the heart is in trouble, or at least misbehaving. When examined, however, most hearts are given a clean bill of health. Why then, do I hear so many concerns about the heart hurting? Easy—the lack of room in the chest cavity. Because the diaphragm is elevated, it bangs into the heart muscle causing discomfort. By using mapping skills for teasing the brain, breathing skills for opening the back, and gyroscoping for literally pulling the heart back in the chest cavity, we mentally and physically create room.

If you put a dozen fleas in a jar with a lid on it, the fleas will soon figure out how high they are able to jump. Once they learn this behavior, you can remove the lid and they will continue to jump only as high as they have learned to go. Gyroscoping utilizes the same trick. If an athlete teaches his heart to pull further back in the chest so that it stops banging into the diaphragm, adheres to a specific rhythm, and responds to a few vocal demands, it, too, will behave. The process takes three to five years to learn, yet the benefits while learning the process begin immediately.

MAPPING

Mapping skills teach the athlete and the sport coach how the hyperkinetic brain thinks. What makes them so effective is that they are aimed at the part of the brain that is still open to learning.

Have you ever seen a baby wave "bye-bye" for the first time? He waves to himself. That is what the baby has seen. People say "bye-bye" and wave with their fingers pointing toward the baby, so the baby automatically couples "bye-bye" with his fingertips pointing toward himself. This is the part of the brain referred to as the mapping brain—the part that has not been compromised or prejudiced by background and education, but is still responding instinctively.

The mapping brain can be taught to believe almost anything if the story is convincing enough and can be supported with physical proof. One of my clients was an athlete whose racing heart did not allow him to run. After each paced walk, he was instructed to tell me how great his run was. By the time he upped his walk to a jog, his jog to a slow run, and his slow run to a fast run, his brain was already programmed that he had been running for nearly a year and that one run was no different than any other. He now runs 10k races with a heart that purrs. This is a form of a particular mapp called "ladders." But be careful: Because the mapping brain is so open to suggestion, it can also be quite damaging. Here's an example: If a baseball umpire calls, "Strike one!" the athlete's brain is quick to ask, "Is that what you want?" If the umpire then shouts, "Strike two," the athlete's brain is sure to think, "I guess that's what you want." So the brain actually helps the player achieve "strike three" by neuromuscularly setting up the athlete to ensure the fact. To prevent such a fact from occurring, I teach the player to step out of the box, run a short mapp in his head that we have practiced in the mapping room (a quiet room set aside for learning and running maps), then step back up to the plate and hit as if it's the first pitch of the next inning.

I often talk to athletes about "trees and roots." I am referring to opposites in life that help keep a balance. While hyperkinetic athletes quickly process electricity, often they process their new alignment skills quite slowly. It is important that they understand the way their brain works and learns so that they do not get frustrated when things don't come to them immediately. Golfers are famous for needing to wait several days for something they have learned to finally process through their bodies and minds, thus the often-used quote, "duh."

Alignment coaches must also work with the athlete on what *not* to let in. I teach all athletes a "not me" rule. If an athlete is listening to a negative conversation concerning the team or another player's performance, I instruct him to say quietly, "not me," so as not to carry the idea of the conversation into his subconscious thought. Other, "not me's" might be seeing someone on the street corner with a broken foot, and, most definitely following "strike two." It is an important rule, and one that helps the athletes feel a bit more in control of outside influences than they normally would.

There is a lot of bad information and bad athletics out there. Coaches and athletes must be alert and discriminating. College parents beware. I have been told, up front and personal by coaches themselves, that they often push athletes way beyond their physical, emotional, and mental readiness in the hopes of a winning season or a winning couple of years. What becomes of the athlete does not concern them. In many situations, sport is for profit, with integrity left out entirely. The injuries these tired, overworked youngsters sustain keep them from promising careers later. Even in professional athletics, the individual is often sacrificed if he or his coach is not his own best advocate.

The main philosophy behind mapping—teaching "mapps" (mapping ability and parapsychological potential) and running mapps—is that there is no such thing as backwards. No matter how good or how disastrous yesterday's game was, yesterday is over. An athlete must never carry anything done prior into the next situation, good or bad. There are no "streaks" allowed in alignment coaching. As I mentioned earlier, the athlete must learn that it is impossible to duplicate an action, and therefore he must learn to duplicate the *feel* of an action time after time after time. Everything said and done in the mapping room helps the athlete to continue evolving and growing throughout his career.

Being a good athlete isn't just about having a good day. It's about calming the fear, quieting the heart, and partaking in the joy of the sport. It is the amazing ability to find center so that the same athlete can take command of home plate, own the diving board, or fly off a snowy mountain, making consistency the athlete's middle name.

Alignment coaching considers the entire athlete. It is as tough as standing with your arms stretched out to the side for an agonizing six minutes, and as rewarding as stopping a home run by jumping higher than the back wall. It produces graceful movement, quick feet, and unequaled alertness. To me, there is nothing more pleasing than witnessing an athlete doing what he does best. The moment the athlete accomplishes something unique, something he has striven for all year, I am swept away by emotion.

Being an alignist is a privilege. It is about sharing secrets, keeping promises, and, above all, leaving one's own ego in check. A good coach is not in competition with his athletes; he is inspired by them.

PRACTICAL INFORMATION

ADVICE FOR NEW ALIGNMENT COACHES

1. Biomechanical alignment is divided into three equal parts. The alignment of the skeletal and muscular systems, the alignment of the electrical, or kinetic system, and the centering of the athlete—physically, mentally, emotionally, and psychologically. It is vital to know how the athletic body moves, and how the athletic brain learns and thinks. Because my education was through apprenticeships that are not available to most coaches and therapists, I would suggest a course of study in kinesiology, biofeedback, and Cecchetti ballet. Help keep each of your athletes grounded, centered, and balanced in his sport and in his everyday life by focusing on his point of reference. This will strengthen his trust in you, and help him gain a sense of belief in himself.
2. Observation is the key to beginning any alignment program, whether addressing an individual athlete or an entire team. Always begin by observing the very best. Purchasing videos of Olympic athletes and watching them over and over again, in slow motion if possible, is an excellent way of gaining a sense of comparison between your athletes as they stand now, and what they want to achieve through training.
3. Approach high school and amateur teams and offer to teach them how to stretch. Hang around and talk to them about alignment and strengthening exercises and see if anyone is interested in learning. I never offer and then ask for a fee. If I am asked about classes, I then explain my fee schedule, but I never invite an athlete for that reason. Because athletes learn at different paces, it is important to have classes that are available for the various levels. Once a class is formed, however, make a definite time limit

for newcomers to be allowed to join. When you expand your alignment work to professionals, give them the courtesy of their own class.

ADVICE FOR NEW PEAK-PERFORMANCE COACHES

1. Listen to the things you tell your athletes, and ask yourself if they are the things you would want to hear come out of your coach's mouth. Telling your baseball player, "It's a good thing you can hit, 'cause you sure can't throw," is not going to inspire self-confidence. Be a coach, not a critic.

2. Understand that it is not the job of the athlete to heal bad feelings among coaches, or feel guilty for outgrowing coaches. Nor is it his job to get caught in the politics of the sport. On the other hand, remind your athletes that they are living the life and doing the things hundreds of thousands of people wish they could do. Instruct your athletes to have fun. That's why they're called *playing* fields. If they are not in a sport for themselves and are driven by people who want to participate vicariously, you might help them best by acknowledging this and perhaps giving them a way out.

3. Interview athletes. Most athletes are more than willing to talk about themselves. Finding out what they think made them more successful than others can be very helpful in understanding their point of view. Observe and interview coaches. It is easier to see ourselves in others than it is to look at ourselves. In observing and talking to athletic coaches you are certain to hear and see things that appeal to you, and things that appall you. Never waver in the confidence you have in both your style and technique of teaching.

MY FEES

I take into consideration what I believe to be my value and the pay scale of the athlete I have taken on. In a few years, or a few months, when their pay scales are elevated, so are my payments. I have the advantage of a second career, so I can be far more financially flexible than other coaches. The ultimate payment comes when one of your athletes does something spectacular, seeks you out of the crowd, points to you, and yells, "We did it!"

WHAT I KNOW NOW

If I have learned anything over the past thirty-some years of coaching, it is to be more patient with myself. I used to believe that my athletes deserved immediate attention the moment they called. I thought I owed them immediate answers to all of their problems and I would jump at the challenge. I jumped until I became too ill to work for several years.

It takes time, effort, and patience to develop a talented athlete, and time, effort, and patience to develop a talented coach. Respect what you know and continue to learn. Athletes evolve. So must we.

A BRIEF BIOGRAPHY

I originally began my career as a ballet dancer. I performed and taught throughout the United States and Europe with such groups as the Washington National Ballet, Maryland Ballet, New York City Ballet, and Stuttgart Ballet. I also studied jazz dance with Luigi and spent much of my rehabilitation time with Zena Rommett.

While teaching ballet and jazz in Carnegie Mellon University's theater department, I was invited to teach stretching and basic movement to members of the Steelers Football Team. From there, invitations came in from The White Socks, professional golfers, track and field teams, and (my personal favorite!) a women's roller derby.

In the early 1970s, I served as a dance coach to the U.S. Figure Skating Team for both the Pan American and World Games and to the Women's Gymnastics Team. This work was done while on hiatus from dancing or during times of illness.

In 1994, I opened my own studio for biomechanical alignment in my hometown, Olney, Maryland. Word of mouth had baseball players, track and field competitors, dancers, ice skaters, climbers, and martial artists attending the same classes. Athletes from all over the world come for a now-and-again check-up, or move into an apartment nearby for months at a time to perfect their alignment and improve their sport. Many study mapping and some add gyroscoping to their education. Often, alignment is taught while I am standing on two crutches. This is one class where athletes know better than to complain.

CONTACT INFORMATION

Audrey Penn
Box 1
Olney, Maryland, 20832
Phone: 301-774-1896
E-mail: elitesonly@aol.com

Part IV

Special Niches Coaching

13

When the Therapist Needs a Coach

Lynn Grodzki

When Amy left her secure agency job of 10 years and went into full-time private practice, free of managed care, she felt liberated and excited. Now, the 41-year-old clinical social worker could set her own hours, earn more money, and practice therapy on her own terms: no agency paperwork, no managed care reviews, no endless staff meetings. It was what she had always pictured herself doing with her professional life. She already had a small, part-time private practice of three or four clients two evenings a week, and assumed that running a full-time practice would be the same as running her part-time one, only more so.

But after two years of struggling to keep her practice afloat, Amy was discouraged. Although she was confident about her skills as a therapist, she felt overwhelmed by the inevitable tasks her private practice required—organizing her time, setting business boundaries, networking, marketing, budgeting, and collecting fees. She had sent a letter to colleagues announcing the opening of her private practice, printed up business cards and brochures, given two free lectures on depression at her local public library, and even placed a six-month ad in the local paper. While these efforts did generate a few client referrals, her appointment book was full of holes. Of the 10 clients she saw every week, 5 were sliding-scale clients and 4 owed her money. At the agency, she had never had to worry about collections. Now, her anxiety and uncertainty about how to talk about money with clients resulted in her avoiding the subject. In the meantime, she had bills to pay and felt increasingly stressed and resentful. She was starting to think about dusting off her resume and reapplying to agencies, but decided to see me for business coaching first.

"I feel like a failure," Amy said as she sat in my office one cold, spring afternoon. "I'm making $10,000 a year less than I made at my old job. I don't know where to go from here. Is it me, or is this the future of private practice?" I hear this question from therapists just starting out as well as 20-year veterans in private practice. Is it possible, in the current economic climate, for therapists to work the hours they want, attract enough clients, stay in charge of their clinical treatment, reduce their administrative over-load, and make a good living? I believe the answer is yes. However, there are specific things we therapists need to know and ways we need to change in order to become proficient business owners—without compromising our clinical work in the process.

Before becoming a therapist, I worked in a family business and was trained in management. After going back to graduate school and becoming a therapist, I opened my own private practice. I never thought twice about applying standard business practices to my burgeoning enterprise—right away I created a budget and marketing plan and set income goals, a fee schedule, and payment policies. After a few years I had a thriving private practice. When colleagues complained about how hard it was to keep their practices going, I asked them what I thought were basic questions about how they ran their businesses. I was shocked at how few of them thought of their practices as businesses. In fact, most bristled at the word "busi-ness." They reminded me of the spiritual calling of their work, the art of being a therapist, or the profound connections they forged with clients, as if these things had no place at the same table with the dirty work of "busi-ness." The ambivalence about making a profit in our profession runs deep, particularly among women, who generally feel less entitled than men to be financially successful. To many therapists, profiting from people's pain is the height of callousness.

On the other hand, everyone wants to make a good living. This paradox leaves many therapists feeling stuck. Perhaps because of my own lack of ambivalence about financially succeeding in business as a therapist, col-leagues began to seek me out for advice on how they could boost their practices. After a few years of giving informal advice on business development to therapists, I went for training in business coaching and now divide my practice between coaching and therapy.

THE ARCHITECTURE OF A SUCCESSFUL PRACTICE

As a business coach, I am part therapist, part co-strategist, and part role model. Looking for a metaphor that therapists could adopt for building a successful practice, I borrowed one I often hear from my husband, an architect. Since almost all of my clients have seen a house built, I explain the similarities between the three stages of building a house and building a practice. Before a builder picks up a hammer and nails to build a house, there is *preparation* to do. In the preparation stage, the builder surveys the site—looking for weaknesses in the property that might undermine the building, such as hidden streams of water under the property or the lack of a level site. The land has to be strong enough to hold the weight of the house. A private practice carries substantial weight and burden too, and a therapist needs to survey his or her emotional site. A therapist wants to have sufficient professional and personal support in place to handle the pressures that owning a small business brings.

The builder also prepares by using a design for the house, rather than trying to build without a detailed plan. Although many therapists build their practices by circumstance instead of by design, taking the time to formulate a business vision will give them direction and focus. The builder then lays a strong foundation, to secure the house and give it stability. The foundation that gives a therapist business stability is a mental foundation of knowing about business. Therapists need to adopt an entrepreneurial mind-set, so that they can think and behave like successful, savvy business owners. Fortunately, this mind-set is one that can be learned. A lot of my time coaching therapists is spent helping them become expert entrepreneurs, teaching them to think with a combination of optimism and pragmatism.

In the second phase, *building blocks,* the builder finally picks up hammer and nails to do the actual construction. For the business owner, this stage draws on the tools, strategies, and essential information needed to construct a well-run business. I like therapists to have dozens of strategies in every category of practice-building so that they can pick and choose from many ways to generate referrals, create a menu of services, or make a small practice look larger, and in effect custom-build their practices.

In the third stage, *finishing touches,* the builder adds the polish and detailing that makes a house distinctive. In this stage a therapist adds polish to a functioning practice by looking at futuristic models of operating a practice that keep the therapist and the practice full of passion and promise for years to come.

Therapists like Amy—and even ones who have been in practice longer than she was—often need to go back and revisit the preparation stage. Without the right emotional and cognitive beliefs in place, even the most well-meaning business plan easily gets undermined. How could Amy set a firm policy regarding fees if she felt ambivalent about money or her right to make a good living as a therapist? How could she uphold her business boundaries if she thought that doing so weakened her compassion for her clients? I believe there are numerous ways for a practitioner to set up a business that are harmonious with her values and principles. Amy was relieved to hear that there was no one right way to run a private practice. Her personality and context necessitated a structure and emphasis that would make her comfortable and strengthen her ability to do the best therapy possible. My job was to help her find a natural and enjoyable fit for herself as a therapist and businessperson.

PREPARATION

In the preparation stage, I focused first on assessing Amy's business practices—hearing how she actually ran her practice. Did she have a business plan or business vision, utilize a professional support system, have clear policies and procedures in place?

We then explored the personal blocks that kept her from achieving the kind of success she wanted, which included examining the role models and experiences that defined her image of "success." I was most interested in understanding her comfort level with business and whether she had or could adopt an entrepreneurial mind-set.

Amy was distinctly edgy and insecure when her answers to my specific questions about her business revealed the lack of a business plan, poor boundaries, few set policies, and uneven marketing strategies. She had no vision other than not going bankrupt. She became more thoughtful and relaxed when I brought her back to familiar, family-of-origin turf and asked about her childhood beliefs about business, money and success.

Her mother had not earned an income, and her father had been a low-paid teacher. Her mother was often angry and bitter about her father's lack of financial success, and Amy vividly remembered the scathing comments her mother would make to her father about his lack of ambition. When Amy married, her husband, a college professor, handled the finances and for a few years she was a stay-at-home mom. She went back to graduate school in her forties and became a therapist, and soon after they divorced.

After telling me her history, Amy returned to her present dilemma. "I can talk to my clients about any subject under the sun except the money they owe me or that I'm raising my fees." At the slightest hint that a new client might not be able to pay her fee, Amy would immediately offer to reduce it. While I acknowledged that her family history contributed to her discomfort with money, I also explained that becoming entrepreneurial is a learned skill, one that we could work on together.

Amy, like other therapists I coach, would need more than just good advice to become successful. Even with a dazzling business strategy, she would not be able to follow through on the series of action steps required to achieve her goals until she dealt with her underlying negative beliefs about succeeding in business. I asked Amy about her favorite therapist role models. Like many clinicians, she had no problem describing the people who had inspired her to enter the field—a kind and caring therapist who had treated her, and a brilliant teacher she had looked up to.

But she drew a blank when I asked her whom she wanted to emulate as a business woman. "I guess I assume that people who do well in business are ruthless, rigid, and exacting," she said and then described an uncle who owned a chain of furniture stores and had done well financially, and who fit this description. As she got in touch with her negativity about business and her family-of-origin experiences around money, Amy decided to see her former therapist for a few sessions to look more deeply at these issues; therapy can be a wonderful complement to business coaching, and something I will encourage for a client who is stuck.

BUILDING BLOCKS

Although she had not resolved all of her uncertainty about business and success, she was working on it, so I moved our coaching sessions on to the building blocks stage and how to change some practical aspects of Amy's business. She was anxious about how to collect unpaid fees without alienating existing clients. "What if I get so focused on collecting my fee that my clients experience me as greedy?" she asked. Rather than give her my answer, I gave her two homework assignments: to talk with colleagues whom she respected—and who were doing well in their practices—about how they resolved this issue; and to read books about value-based business practices, such as *A Search for Excellence* by business guru Tom Peters; *The E-Myth Revisted,* a classic text for small business owners by consultant Michael Gerber; and Linda Stern's *Money-Smart Secrets for the Self-Employed.* I also asked her to remember what her own therapist had said and done around money that had either contributed to the therapeutic relationship or diminished it.

"How did you learn to be so comfortable discussing money?" she asked me. I told her a story about my father, who was one of my business role models. My dad was great at running his successful scrap metal business. Soon after I started working for him as his assistant general manager, he asked me to call a steel broker to collect an overdue bill of $15,000. I felt anxious—wouldn't the client be angry? I was relieved when the client breezily told me, "I'll be happy to put the check in the mail." Two weeks passed with no check. I called again and had the same conversation and got the same response. My father shook his head and suggested I listen while he made his regular collection calls. In each call, he asked to speak to the business owner, made cheery small talk, and then purposefully brought up the overdue amount. He asked specific questions in a friendly tone: Exactly when could he expect the check? Who in the company would be writing it—the owner or the bookkeeper? Could he have the bookkeeper's name, because his secretary would call on that date to make sure it had, in fact, gone out. If he didn't receive it by that date, how did the customer want it to be handled? My father never lost his even tone of voice and in most cases, the checks came in as promised. I learned from him that the financial details of business can be discussed in a conversational tone, without anger, anxiety, or upset.

In the next two sessions, Amy rehearsed how she would talk to clients about their overdue bills in a friendly and gentle tone. Sometimes, therapists ask me for a script of exactly what they should say, but I encourage them to find their own words. Amy developed her own script that matched a gentle verbal style she was comfortable using. To the client who had owed her the most money for the longest time, she said, "I have enjoyed our work together, but now it's time for you to catch up on the balance due. Here are two payment plans I am comfortable offering clients. Which would you prefer?" and then "I will write this down and next week when you come in, I'd like you to initial it, so we can both refer back to it. Each month I suggest we review how this plan is working. It will help keep us on track. If you have feelings that talking about money brings up, I will want you to bring your feelings to our sessions to process with me." She sent letters to past clients who still owed money in which she calmly reminded them of her effort and goodwill in providing service based on the mutual understanding that she would get paid.

In the next 90 days, she collected $3,000 of unpaid bills—including the total balance from the one who owed the most. She was ecstatic because she had asserted herself and effectively said, "I deserve to be paid for my work," yet had done this in a gentle relational style. No clients left therapy as a result of this approach. The remaining $800—owed by two past clients—proved uncollectable and on an attorney's advice, she eventually wrote it off as a bad debt. Even this decision empowered her; she was able to finally put her debt to rest and move on.

Another key component of her business plan involved setting a fee that she could confidently uphold, instead of being so quick to use a sliding scale. I coached Amy to evaluate the current market forces, factor in her years of experience, and also look at the perceived value of her services. After she came up with a fee she thought was her "right" fee, I asked her to practice saying it with a smile and in the same tone of voice she might use to state her name. Amy had decided on $90 an hour, but when she tried to say it aloud, she literally cringed.

"It's too much," she explained.

"Drop it by five dollars," I suggested.

"I charge $85 an hour," she said, again pursing her lips.

"Go lower," I said.

"I charge $80 an hour," she said and smiled easily. There is no "right" fee, just one that matches our internal values. Amy's body language showed that, for now, $80 was her fee.

FINISHING TOUCHES

At the end of two years of bimonthly business coaching sessions, Amy had increased her practice from 10 clients to 17 clients a week, all paying her full fee, more than doubling her income. In the finishing touches stage, we reevaluated her new policies and procedures, and refined some of the ways in which she was generating referrals. For example, instead of continuing to give free lectures at her local library, Amy began to market half-day seminars on divorce, an area in which she was building a specialization. Amy kept her business plan and her business vision on her desk and referred to it every week. "I might never love the business side of things the way I love clinical work, but I love feeling successful," she told me in our last business coaching session.

All business owners—therapists included—need a picture of where they want the business to go and what they want it to achieve, but this business vision needs to be flexible, because dreams and goals change over time. While I try to help my clients figure out how to refresh their practices so that the ratio of onerous business details to satisfying work is favorably balanced, I also encourage them to examine their strengths, talents, and passions, and think creatively about how to incorporate them into their business. This generates a new and stronger foundation for a different style of practice.

COMBINING A MANAGED CARE PRACTICE WITH PERSONAL VALUES AND PASSIONS

Sandy, a 55-year-old psychotherapist from California, called me on the phone for business coaching. She sounded alternately defiant and collapsed; she waxed poetic about the heart-warming work of psychotherapy and then complained about the rigors of licensing and insurance changes affecting her practice. She fantasized about early retirement, but didn't want her years of experience and wisdom as a clinician to go to waste. I asked her to tell me what her dream practice would look like. At first, all she could say was, "No managed care!" "No paperwork!" "Clients who never cancel and always pay on time." But I invited her to think bigger. What was she passionate about? What did she really love to do? If she could do anything at all, what would it be?

I want clients to answer this question for a practical reason: Running a therapy business is hard work, and therapists need to find a reliable source of energy to fuel the day-to-day grind. I want clients to tap into the natural source of energy available from feeling passionate. In a shy, hopeful voice, Sandy said what she loved best was being in nature, going on adventure vacations, and working for environmental causes. I suggested that instead of focusing on how to make her work life bearable under managed care, we focus on creating a diversified practice. One part of her practice would have nothing to do with managed care, but be totally focused on her values and passion.

For the next few weeks, we mapped out a financial plan that would allow her to cut back on her individual sessions and run retreats that combined an adventure experience in nature with psychotherapy. Every once in a while, Sandy's excitement gave way to fear and lack of confidence in her dream, and she needed to hear me say, "Yes, it's possible to do what you love and make a living at it. Others do this and you can, too!" We talked about her concerns that she would be seen as "flaky" by colleagues, and that she would lose referrals. I assured her we could reevaluate the plan and adjust it if it became necessary.

Having drawn up a budget and a timeline, Sandy promptly felt over-whelmed. How would she make it all happen? Now we were into the build-ing blocks stage. When I suggested that she begin with a marketing strategy, which involved doing research by asking therapists running similar kinds of retreats what they charged and where they advertised. Sandy did this, but balked at further assignments regarding marketing. "I hate marketing. It's a form of selling. I think it's wrong for therapists to par-ticipate in commercialism." I proposed she think about marketing by attraction: How could she get the word out without being self-promotional or commercial, so that the clients who could benefit from her services would naturally gravitate to her?

Sandy decided to take two actions: She became a model of her services as a leader by organizing several rigorous nature hikes for a group of friends for free, to test herself. These hikes were well received and built her passion and confidence to a higher level. Then, with her passion and confidence fueling her, she told the president of her hiking club about the new direction of her work. The club president agreed to sponsor a half-day workshop for couples and list it in their monthly newsletter. When only two couples signed up, Sandy was discouraged and considered canceling. I strongly urged her to follow through to get the experience and develop a track record with the club, and explained that she would likely need to repeat this workshop several times before it would result in a good turnout. Starting something new requires sufficient repetition, and Sandy's negativity or disappointment could easily sabotage her goal by making her stop too soon. Over the next few months, I coached Sandy to hang in there and take daily action toward her vision. By the end of the year, she had held four workshops, and each grew slightly larger until she finally had 16 participants, and another eight signed up for a longer retreat with her in the mountains.

In this last phase of our work together, we were ready for finishing touches. She began to write a journal of the retreats, which she envisioned turning into a book someday. We revised her original plan to include postretreat reunions and a quarterly newsletter to keep participants in touch with new programs she was developing.

She still grumbles from time to time about the paperwork demands in the managed care part of her private practice, but feels energized and happy with the nature retreats aspect of her business.

PRACTICING WITHOUT MANAGED CARE

Given the changes in the insurance marketplace, even if veteran therapists manage to maintain their client hours, their income may have dipped dramatically. Many therapists I coach are looking for a magic formula for ditching managed care altogether. It can be done, but there isn't one formula for doing it. Every clinician's path to achieving that is going to be unique. The trick is finding out the path that best suits each client.

When Ted, age 60, came to see me, he had been working at an exhausting pace for 30 years. After a decade of seeing clients, he was worn out and, in his words, "spiritually depleted." Like Sandy, Ted complained that being a therapist was no longer fun. Hoping to reverse the downward trend of his client hours in the early 1990s, Ted had signed on with several managed-care companies. His client hours surged back up, but he was collecting lower fees, and hated battling with managed-care officials who disputed his treatment decisions. "I would love to stop having anything to do with them, but then my practice would crumble," said Ted. "What else can I do?"

Like Sandy, he needed to go back and refurbish the preparation and building blocks stages for his practice, and to do that we worked on a business plan to eliminate managed care altogether from his practice within one year. To counter his feelings of spiritual depletion, I asked Ted to begin to develop an "abundance mentality," an entrepreneurial belief in plenty—that there were plenty of clients, plenty of opportunities, and plenty of room for his practice to succeed on his terms. Abundance requires getting into the flow of life. I wanted Ted literally to get out of his office and notice how much activity was happening all around him. I requested that he immediately join a local entrepreneurial association, not for marketing opportunities, but to be around people who were used to seeing opportunity every where they looked—other successful entrepreneurs. He found a group through the business pages of the newspaper and joined. The group was full of energetic men and women and Ted felt invigorated after their weekly meetings.

We addressed his fear of losing his income by coming up with a menu of services Ted would offer, the types of clients to whom he might offer them, and put a price tag on each service to each type of client—individuals, groups, agencies, and supervisees. We also discussed how he would talk to his clients about his new business.

Ted gave his current managed care clients several months of warning that he would be resigning from their plans. He offered to continue to see them, but reminded them it would be at his full fee. He talked about the range of services he was ready to provide and helped them select a package that would work for them, both therapeutically and financially. He stopped accepting any new managed-care clients. Three months later, Ted resigned from all his managed-care panels. Five existing clients had decided to terminate based on his decision to stop accepting managed care. He was understandably nervous about the loss of income, but I coached him to be patient and to keep going with the steps of the plan.

Revitalizing a practice requires committing time, energy, and money toward growth and change. I encouraged Ted to think about what form he wanted that investment in growth to take. He decided to focus on training, simply for his own pleasure and enrichment. He had always wanted to learn improvisation and psychodrama, and decided to take trainings in both and weave them into his work.

Ted complained that his old network of colleagues, most of whom were also struggling with burnout, left him feeling more drained than supported. I encouraged him to seek out new professional groups that would allow him to feel positive about his professional future. He was so enthusiastic about psychodrama that he and two others from the training sponsored a day-long workshop for clinicians, which put him in touch with a wider network of like-minded therapists. They created a monthly psychodrama peer group, which he loved, and which helped him polish his skills and techniques. Through a contact in that group, he joined a community theater group and met local businesspeople, which resulted in more referrals.

Building a strong practice to house the important work of therapy can only improve the overall product. All of the coaching I do with therapists is to further this goal, to help therapists provide the best services possible by having solid, viable private practices. I want them to learn not only to tolerate, but also to love the business of therapy. By taking a frank inventory of their practices and making some necessary shifts in their thoughts, feelings, and behaviors, therapists can become savvy, skillful businesspeople. From this position it is easier and more natural for them to take the steps to create the private practice they desire.

PRACTICAL INFORMATION

ADVICE FOR BUSINESS COACHES FOR THERAPISTS

1. You need to walk your talk in this niche. It's essential that you be suc-

cessful in private practice as a therapist yourself in order to coach others to success. One reason that I am good in this area is that I have never stopped being a therapist in private practice, so I know the daily challenges of the business of therapy.

2. It's not unusual for this type of business coaching to be mixture of business consulting, personal coaching, and clinical supervision. Some of the coaching relationship will include talking about the personal life of the therapist, about the state of the therapist's practice, and about clinical cases. I like the fact that coaching therapists involves a blending of several disciplines for me, as the coach.

3. Be patient. Therapists are notoriously shy about disclosing issues regarding money, finances, and business. Coaching a therapist to become highly profitable takes several months, and may require a year or two. The joy of this type of coaching is to see more therapists build ideal practices, so that the therapy profession continues to flourish, regardless of economic healthcare challenges.

ADVICE FOR NEW THERAPIST-COACHES

1. Get coached for at least six months from a strong business coach, and get your life and practice into good shape.
2. Don't scrimp on your coach training. This is an investment that will pay off in many ways, including helping to develop your professional community.
3. Join the International Coach Federation and attend their national conferences or local meetings to connect with the upbeat coaching community.

MY FEES

I charge a monthly fee of $325 for phone coaching (two 45-minutes coaching sessions per month including e-mail support.) I charge my regular hourly therapy fee of $110 per 50-minute session for those who come for in-person coaching sessions. My fees are higher for phone coaching because the phone sessions require additional time outside of the session to read and reply to the e-mails, and for other types of follow-up.

WHAT I KNOW NOW

I worked really hard to be a "smart" coach when I started out, but I have since learned that my effectiveness is not based on the amount of information or ideas I provide (although I can strategize with the best of them). My value is better defined as the fact that I am able to hold a strong vision of success for my clients, even when they can't see how things will ever work out. I am amazed at how just holding this vision, week after week, month after month, even in the face of setbacks and challenges, can result in my clients being brave and persistent, taking difficult steps, and accomplishing great things for themselves. If I had understood this earlier I could have relaxed a lot more along the way.

A BRIEF BIOGRAPHY

I am a licensed clinical social worker working as a psychotherapist in private practice since 1988. In 1996, I diversified my practice and added "business coach" to my business card. As a business coach, I work with executives, entrepreneurs, and therapists. In 1977, I developed the Private Practice Success Program™ specifically for therapists and healers, and eventually wrote a book based on it—*Building Your Ideal Private Practice: A Guide for Therapists and Other Healing Professionals,* which has become a best-selling practice-building text. I give workshops based on my practice-building approach internationally, and continue to write articles on this topic for psychotherapy and trade magazines. I also write a free monthly e-mail newsletter, "Private Practice Success," available by subscription at my Web site for therapists, coaches, and other entrepreneurs.

I am a graduate of and certified teacher/trainer for Coach University, primarily teaching "Coaching For Therapists Only," a course I co-created with my friend and fellow CoachU trainer, Harriett Simon Salinger. I often mentor new therapist-coaches, and find that my style of coaching has been influenced by several master coaches, most notably Thomas Leonard, Pam Richarde, and Jeff Raim. I have also been deeply influenced by Marilyn Ellis, LCSW, who has been my therapist, supervisor, and mentor for almost 20 years.

CONTACT INFORMATION

Lynn Grodzki, LCSW-C
910 La Grande Road
Silver Spring, MD 20903
Phone: 301-434-0766
E-mail: lynn@privatepracticesuccess.com
Web site: www.privatepracticesuccess.com

14

The Money Coach
Lynne M. Hornyak

I love dealing with money. I always have. As a child, I enjoyed tracking my allowance and seeing how carefully I could spend for what I wanted *and* have some left over. Now I balance my business accounts as relaxation between sessions. I love to reconcile my bank accounts and feel a spurt of pleasure when I pay my bills. When I mention things like this in conversations with friends and colleagues, I often see that familiar "What planet are *you* from?" look come across their faces. But it's true.

I love to talk about money. So, what did you learn about money from your mother? Your father? Did your family *talk* about money? *How* did they talk about it? What kind of a relationship do you have with money now? There are hundreds of questions to be asked, clarified, understood. That's what I do as a money coach. I don't analyze clients' investments. I help them to analyze their beliefs, attitudes, and habits so that they can make better choices and develop an abundant life.

While animated discussions of stock market trading and the economy are standard party fare these days, conversations about one's personal finances in the "real world" are rare. Think about it. Do you know how much your closest friends or your siblings earn? Do you know how they budget their money or how much they put into their retirement fund each year? Do you know who is in debt and exactly how serious their situation is?

Taking it one step closer, there are many partners—spouses, unmarried couples living together, business partners—who rarely talk about money. They may fight when a financial problem arises but this is not the same thing as communicating about money. This "money talk taboo" can result in some relationship-shaking consequences, particularly when one partner has been designated as the "financially smart" one and the other agrees, explicitly or implicitly, to let him or her handle the "big decisions." This situation arose for Teresa who sought money coaching after a major crisis. Teresa and John had been married for six years. John took over all their investment decisions, to Teresa's great relief. She didn't like to deal with money and felt that John was much more savvy than she in the financial realm. A crisis resulted because John had been daytrading for about 14 months, using their mutual savings. He hadn't told Teresa until he'd lost over $35,000, and they had no financial cushion left. Needless to say, marital counseling was in order, and Teresa began working with me on her money avoidance.

When I decided to focus on money as my coaching niche, I wondered how making the unspoken spoken would work out. If money is such a loaded topic, would anyone admit that they wanted or needed money coaching? Would people really want to analyze themselves, rather than expect me to analyze (and take care of) their finances? And, even if they did, would they want to pay for it? Could I really make my living doing my passion?

Working with a client like Becca encouraged me to push forward. Becca was referred by a friend who knew of my money specialty. In the first session she said, "It's a relief to know that you actually coach on money. I've been in therapy three times over the past five years for various reasons. Twice I ended therapy over the phone without much notice. I was taking out cash advances on my credit cards to pay my bills, and the balances got way out of control. The third therapist carried a balance for me for a while. But eventually he brought up the issue, and we decided to take a break until I paid off my balance."

I asked her how she had talked about her money problems with her therapists. Becca responded painfully, "The first two never asked me about my financial situation. And besides, I felt that it wasn't their problem. They deserved to be paid their fee. Like I said, the third therapist did raise the issue; he wondered if I was expressing my dependency on him by getting behind in my payments." While dependency may have been an issue for her, as we discussed her situation it became clear that Becca felt incompetent in her money life. She was raised in a family that lived from paycheck to paycheck, so she didn't have a healthy model for managing her money. When we decided to work together, Becca indicated that she couldn't afford to pay my full fee. I asked her, "What could you afford per month right now?" Becca responded, "I don't know." I replied, "You don't know because?" inviting her to explain further, to which she said, "Actually I don't have a clue about how much money I ever have. I deposit my paychecks when I get them, then just write checks unless I check my ATM and there's nothing in my account. That's when I use my credit cards."

This exchange became the entry point for defining her first financial goal: to assess her monthly income and determine where she spent her money each month. We negotiated a starting fee that was manageable for her. Accomplishing these initial tasks gave Becca enough confidence to tackle other areas of her money life. The gratification I felt when working with clients like Becca, helping them to break through money taboos and take charge of their financial lives, convinced me that this coaching niche could be my passion for a long time to come.

THE MONEY RELATIONSHIP

Everyone has a relationship with money, even if they haven't thought about it that way. How we think and feel about money has a relationship to the actions we take, such as how we earn our income, save, budget, and invest, as well as how we react and interact with others around financial matters. Understanding our relationship with money is empowering. Once we understand it, we have the power to make choices, develop healthy attitudes, and learn to deal with money in a way that is consistent with what we truly want. That integrity results in a sense of abundance and satisfaction—what I term "wealth health."

There are as many ways to look at one's relationship with money as there are ways to look at one's personal relationships. Olivia Mellan, in her book *Money Harmony,* talks about five money types: hoarders, spenders, money monks, avoiders, and amassers. Kathleen Gurney, in *Your Money Personality,* discusses nine money personalities: entrepreneur, hunter, high roller, safety player, achiever, perfectionist, money master, producer, and optimist. Some clients find that identifying their money type using Mellan's book enables them to take that essential first step toward greater self-awareness. Teresa, mentioned earlier, began her coaching that way. Knowing that her feelings and behavior were shared by other "avoiders" helped her to surmount the feelings of embarrassment and insecurity that had kept her stuck for years.

Since my philosophy focuses on helping clients to achieve satisfaction and abundance, I developed a survey that people can download from my Web site. The survey asks specific questions, such as: Does the word "wealthy" have a positive meaning for you? Are you making enough money for the type of life you want to be living? Are you spending money faster than you are earning it? Do you dread looking at your checkbook or bank statements? Do you have a budget? If you have a budget, do you follow it?

Celia became a coaching client after finding my Web site and taking the survey. She described her current relationship with money as conflicted. While she had minimal bad debt, kept up her checkbook, and contributed to her retirement account regularly, Celia felt that she worried too much about money. She was uneasy about taking much financial risk and felt guilty about spending money on clothes and vacations, although she could well afford to spend money this way. Celia wanted to feel at peace with money, which for her meant being financially secure and enjoying the benefits of this security. We agreed that looking at her money messages would be her initial goal. To prepare for our next session, I asked Celia to think about how money was handled in her family.

In the next session, Celia reported that she had thought a great deal about her family history but wasn't sure where to start since there were no earth-shaking money-related events in her past. I asked her if she'd be willing to do an exercise: "If you and I were watching a videotape of what impressed you the most about money as you grew up, even if the events weren't earth-shaking, what would we be seeing and hearing?" Celia imagined the videotape as a family home movie, commenting that "we wouldn't hear much" because her family didn't talk about money per se. Her parents were hardworking and responsible people. Celia remembered her mother sitting quietly at the dining room table paying bills with a worried look on her face. Her family had no credit cards; they paid only with cash and checks. She remembered her father saying, "You should buy only what you can afford."

Celia also had memories of high school, a time when she realized that the world was a much bigger place, meeting peers of diverse ethnic and economic backgrounds, and attending extracurricular activities such as drama club, horseback riding lessons, and ski trips. Celia recalled wanting to take horseback riding lessons and to go on a ski trip during her junior year. When she mentioned this to her mother, her mother responded "Dear, I don't think so. What if you got hurt? And, we're going to take a trip to the lake this year, so we'll save our money for that. Remember how much fun we have there?" I asked Celia how she felt as she recalled that memory. She replied, "Crushed," and fell silent. When I invited her to note what feelings she had, she said, "Mixed feelings. I knew that my mother was working so hard to make ends meet and doing her best, and I felt bad about wanting so much. On the other hand, my friends were doing these things and I had to make up excuses why I couldn't go." I asked Celia if she would stay with that awareness for a moment and write down what she came to believe about money and her relationship to money from that experience. Celia wrote down: "I can want things but I'm not meant to have them. " I then asked her to write down how she thought that belief currently influenced how she earned and spent her money. "Do you see some old patterns in your current thoughts, feelings, expectations?" Celia wasn't sure, so I suggested that she pay attention as she went through her week to situations that involved spending money or other money decisions.

At our next session, Celia excitedly reported her discoveries. "Wow, when I began paying attention, I noticed how I put blinders on myself. Even in the grocery store. I walk past the yellow peppers and mixed field greens that I really love, and buy the head lettuce and mushrooms because they are cheaper, not because I like them better. The same with watching TV. The minute the commercials come on, I start reading my book. I don't want to be tempted to buy something that is being advertised. I think I must make a lot of decisions that way. I feel good for being responsible, yet it makes life bland. And it's not like I can't afford to buy field greens and yellow peppers, and it certainly isn't being wild and crazy to spend money on them."

I then asked Celia to replace the money message from her past: "What would be a more realistic, believable image or thought for yourself at this time in your life?" Celia liked the sense of responsibility that she learned in her family; it was a value she wanted to keep. Since she wasn't in the same financially tight situation as her family apparently was, we talked about the concept of abundance and what that could mean for her. Celia decided on a new message: "I can be a responsible person *and* have abundance in my life." She decided to post the statement on her bathroom mirror so that she could read it each morning at the start of her day.

When I proposed the idea of practicing abundance thinking over the following week, Celia responded enthusiastically. Anticipating that this exercise might bring up a variety of reactions, I introduced the concept of "gremlins." Developed by Richard Carson in his book *Taming Your Gremlin* and discussed by Laura Whitworth, Henry House, and Phil Sandahl in their book *Co-Active Coaching,* the concept represents a constellation of thoughts and feelings that maintain the status quo in our lives. The gremlin seems protective, yet keeps us from moving forward to attain what we say that we truly want.

For example, Celia had commented that she felt responsible when she overrode small pleasures. One way to depotentiate the gremlin is to identify it, notice when it is operating, then consciously choose another, more effective course of action. I find that the gremlin concept is a respectful way to talk about fears and self-sabotaging patterns. It is also useful to present the message that our gremlins commonly appear when we start working toward something that is important to us, so that its appearance is a sign of movement forward rather than something to feel bad about. Celia liked the image, and named hers "the frugal gremlin"; it was concerned about her financial security, yet was overly cautious.

Celia reported that her gremlin appeared a number of times as she worked on her abundance perspective, but she felt better knowing that it was a sign of taking action. She decided that she would simply continue to do this exercise for the next few weeks. Celia wanted another goal to work on during this period as well, and decided to define her vision of a "wealthhealthy" life. Celia tried to visualize where she wanted to be in five years, but had difficulty coming up with anything more specific than to be married and in a satisfying job. It seemed that her frugal gremlin was interfering with a more expansive, detailed image of her future. I suggested an exercise called Pillars of a Balanced Life to provide a more structured way she could have a big picture view.

The pillars look like a bar graph in which each column represents an essential life area. The pillars that we selected for Celia included career, health, significant other\intimacy, family & friends, physical environment, fun, personal growth, and wealth. Celia rated her level of current satisfaction in each life area on a scale of 0–10, which gave her a clear visual representation of her life. She gave high ratings to health, significant other\intimacy, family and friends, and personal growth, and ratings of 5–6 to the others. As we discussed what influenced her ratings, I had the impression that her frugal gremlin was present, so I asked her if we could push the envelope a bit. She said, "Sure."

I said, "Imagine that you are walking through a field of abundance. It's a beautiful day. The sky is clear and brightly blue, and it feels like the world has opened wide up. Anything is possible. (I paused a few seconds.) And the frugal gremlin is nowhere in this picture. (Celia chuckled.) Okay? (She indicated yes with an "mmhmmm.") So look again at your pillars, and imagine what would really make each pillar a 10, the greatest 10 that you can imagine, no holds barred." Celia came up with a host of possibilities, ranging from taking horseback riding lessons to going back to school for an advanced degree. However, she noted that she was quite uncomfortable with the notion of wealth as an essential pillar.

"Celia, what does wealth mean to you? What images and thoughts does it bring up?" I asked. She thought briefly then said, "Being a snob, getting obsessed about making money, living in a different social world." We spent the remainder of the session discussing her associations. It became clear that Celia feared that she would feel different and alienated from her family and friends if she was wealthy.

Discovering her inner conflict proved to be highly valuable for Celia. Over the next few weeks, Celia defined her picture of a financially satisfying life that could embrace family and friends. She addressed each pillar in a stepwise fashion: If fun was a 6, she looked at what it would take to make it a 7, which resulted in specific action steps. Celia assigned each step two values: (1) the dollar cost of expenses necessary to take that action, and (2) the dollar value to her of taking that step. In this way, she could responsibly weigh the costs and benefits to her of taking each risk.

Over time, Celia's confidence increased. She designed a budget that included line items for weekly fun and vacations. Finally, Celia decided to consult a financial planner to develop her investment plan. Before ending her money coaching, we brainstormed interview questions. The last I heard, she was happily working with a well-respected financial planner.

FROM DEBTS OF THE PAST TO INVESTING IN SELF

In contrast to Celia's frugality, other individuals overspend. They may seek out a money coach when they feel out of control or their spending has had some serious consequences. Libby was an overspender. In our initial phone consultation, Libby rapidly told me about her history. She was an independent child from an early age, with a chronically ill mother and a father who seemed overloaded with both work and family responsibilities. Bright and engaging, Libby easily made friends. Hanging out at the mall after school, she would spend her allowance on the latest CDs and treats for her friends. Libby went away to college, then attended law school. Earning a good salary as an associate in a mid-sized law firm, she developed the habit of shopping after work. She enjoyed buying suits and matching accessories, accent pieces for her apartment, and expensive wines. Libby said, "I probably wouldn't have called you except that my boyfriend, Todd, told me that he had concerns about our getting married since I was out of control with my money." When I asked her what had precipitated this comment, she said, "I came home with three terrific designer suits. Todd got upset since I'd just bought two suits a few months ago. But, they were on sale and I couldn't decide which I wanted so I bought them all."

From our conversation, it seemed that Libby relished the notion that, since she earned her money, she could spend it in whatever way she wanted. I asked her what most concerned *her*—what made her decide to seek money coaching. "I love Todd and want to be married. And, he's right; we can't put a downpayment on a house if I don't have any savings. But, I don't want to feel deprived or that Todd is looking over my shoulder." In wrapping up our conversation, I reflected Libby's ambivalent feelings back to her. I suggested that, if we worked together, we first look at her relationship with money—her beliefs and attitudes about money and how these influence her spending behavior. We could then look at the pros and cons of making any changes in her money style. Libby agreed.

Before ending the phone call, we discussed my monthly fee to which Libby replied, "Wow, I can't afford that much each month." Aware that one designer suit with accessories probably cost the same as a month of coaching, I posed: "Well, I invite you to think about it. And, would you mind if I suggested a way to think about this important decision? She indicated yes, and I explained:

> I'm going to suggest an exercise that I use with many clients who are working on money issues. One night this week, set aside 20 minutes and sit someplace comfortably, with a piece of paper. Near the top of the paper, write: "If I say yes to 'blank,' I say no to 'blank'." Then halfway down the sheet, write: "If I say no to 'blank,' I say yes to 'blank'." Now, I can estimate that the price of one suit by that particular designer, a scarf, and shoes probably cost the equivalent of one month of coaching with me. And you're right—if you are paying for coaching, that probably means you won't be able to buy a suit each month. I'd really like you to think about that—*really* think about what that would mean. So, in the top sentence, you'd write: "If I say yes to coaching, I say no to a suit." And what you're to do is to think about what it *really* means not to buy a suit, for example, feeling deprived like you said earlier. Try to be as specific as possible, for example, in what ways you'd feel deprived. And write down everything that comes to mind that you'd be saying "no" to, even if you think it's silly or trivial. Now, for the second sentence, you'd write: "If I say no to coaching, I say yes to the suit."

This time, think about what it means to not look at your relationship with money, both pro and con. Write down everything
that comes to mind. For example, you would face Todd's
concern about your spending on your own—which might be a
pro or con depending on how you view it. Does this seem like a
useful exercise to you?"

Libby said yes, and I then asked her how long she thought it would take
her to complete this exercise, and she agreed to call me in a week with her
decision.

Libby did call and contracted for short-term money coaching. As part of
our work, I introduced a concept of debt, budgeting, and investing that I
frequently use with clients. Debt refers to the past; it may be actual monetary debt or emotional debt that we carry that keeps us stuck in old patterns. Budgeting is living in the present. It involves trade-offs suggested by
the "If I say yes" exercise that are part of everyday life. Clients frequently
begin coaching with the view that budgeting is a burden. However, an alter-
nate view is that budgeting is about choices. Making choices can be
empowering when we are the ones actively making the decisions about our
own money. Finally, investing refers to the future. We invest in our future
when we take the time to define our desires and goals, which then typically
translates into various monetary investments.

DEVELOPING A COLLABORATIVE PRACTICE

I have been contacted for financial coaching by women and men ranging
from entrepreneurial professionals, to the recently divorced who are
rebuilding or building a financial life for the first time, to individuals with
lengthy histories of money disasters. This breadth of money-related issues
provides for a richly diverse and stimulating coaching practice. It also
means that many clients need specialized financial information and assistance. By collaborating with financial planners and advisors, I am able to
provide my clients with valuable and timely resources. Collaboration is

valuable to growing my coaching practice and prevents the sense of isolation that can come with coaching primarily by telephone.

When I initially contact financial professionals, I typically explore the nature of their financial services, their philosophy of working with clients, as well as their ideal and most difficult clients. Most financial advisors that I've met have a commitment to fully servicing their clients, which means understanding their personal needs and interests, educating them, and researching and developing their financial plans and portfolios. And most acknowledge that it is a challenge to provide ongoing financial counseling as well as extensive financial analysis in the amount of time that they can devote to any particular client. Consequently, my services can be an added value for their clients. I am the resource that they offer clients who need to overcome blocks about making money decisions or understand their spending patterns that interfere with implementing an effective investment plan.

My e-mail newsletter offers another avenue for collaboration. I regularly feature articles or commentaries by financial professionals, which gives them exposure to my readership while my readers get practical financial information that complements the psychological focus of my newsletter. Currently, I am in the process of extending this collaboration to teleclasses that I typically provide for free over a bridge line that allows up to 75 people to be on the call. A financial advisor and I are offering sessions on special money-related topics such as inheritance, divorce and money, and money issues in widowhood.

I believe that everyone has a relationship with money, satisfying or not. If it's not satisfying, there are ways to improve it. If it is satisfying, it is possible for the relationship to be even more rewarding. As a therapist, I was trained to be an expert in the area of relationships; as a therapist-coach I contribute as much as I can to the arena of financial well-being.

PRACTICAL INFORMATION

ADVICE FOR NEW MONEY COACHES

1. While financial health and success require practical knowledge about money matters, the vast majority of people deal with money from a psy-

chological place. Consequently, therapists have substantial knowledge and skills to contribute to the arena of behavioral finance.

2. The financial arena is ripe for collaboration between therapist-coaches and financial advisors and managers, particularly given the current downturn in the economy.

3. Facing money beliefs, attitudes, and habits can arouse strong emotions and other personal issues. It is helpful to anticipate this, and to predict to your clients. It is also helpful to have analyzed and worked on your own money attitudes and habits.

ADVICE FOR NEW THERAPIST-COACHES

1. It may take a few trials to find a coaching niche that you are passionate about and that is financially viable. Be patient with yourself and persist until you find it.

2. For many therapists, certain aspects of coaching such as marketing are foreign or uncomfortable. Perhaps some people are born with the confidence to "just do it," but my experience is that confidence comes from taking calculated risks, actions that stretch us enough to gain and integrate new experience. I believe this process is part of becoming a coach.

3. Take time to figure out a fee structure that respects your personal, professional, and financial needs. It will then be easier to communicate and negotiate your fees with potential clients.

MY FEES

I started off with fees that were similar to my psychotherapy fees: I charge $125 for a 45-minute session. Early on, I willingly reduced my fee to get the experience of coaching. As I gained experience as a coach, I developed a fee schedule that offered five options ranging from $200 for two 25-minute sessions per month to $650 for four 60-minute sessions per month. I have since simplified my fee schedule to the following: $500 per month, which is based on four 25-minutes sessions with e-mail and fax contact between sessions. I bill clients at the beginning of the month, and accept payment by credit card or check. I always offer a half-hour initial consultation at no cost to the potential client–except what they are charged for a long-distance call by their telephone company.

What I Know Now

The line between coaching and psychotherapy is blurry regardless of what some folks say. With experience, I grew more comfortable with the lack of clarity, and knowing when someone needs psychotherapy rather than or in addition to coaching.

To the uninitiated, coaching may seem like a unitary field. Yet, there are many approaches to coaching just as there are many approaches to psychotherapy. The time that I took to read widely in the field, attend coaching workshops, and network was both invaluable and essential to developing my own coaching style.

Developing a coaching practice takes time and effort, like having a second job. This is particularly important to take into consideration when you are working full-time in your current profession.

A Brief Biography

I began formally coaching in 1998 after completing the MentorCoach Program (MCP), a six-month program specifically for therapists training to become coaches. During my training, I had wonderful experiences of coaching individuals, leading virtual groups, and being coached myself. Those experiences, in addition to the similarity of coaching to the clinical work I had done in the areas of stress management and performance enhancement, convinced me that coaching was my ideal mid-life career transition. I've continued to stay involved in MCP as a member of the training faculty. I am also a member of the International Coach Federation.

I was trained as a psychologist, graduating in 1983 from Catholic University of America in Washington, DC with a Ph.D. in clinical psychology. I began full-time private practice in Washington, DC in 1985, specializing in women's health and empowerment issues. Early on, I became fascinated with people's relationships with money, food, and their bodies. I developed a specialty in clinical hypnosis and related methods, which I apply in both long-term as well as problem-focused therapy, including stress management and performance enhancement. I train other professionals in clinical hypnosis through the American Society of Clinical Hypnosis and the Society for Clinical and Experimental Hypnosis. I continue to have a psychotherapy practice along with my coaching practice, anticipating that I will be coaching full-time within the next six months.

Several individuals have had a significant impact on where I am today as a coach. Ben Dean was my first professional coach. He was incredibly generous in sharing practical ideas and technical information as well as in his ongoing support and encouragement to reach for my dreams. With two friends, I hired Judy Feld as a business coach. Judy was a terrific role model; she was not only professional, business-oriented and successful; she also spoke our language. During this time I developed my money niche, and began marketing my business, WealthHealthy.com. I continue to meet twice monthly by telephone, as a peer brainstorming and support group, with my two colleagues who have also been instrumental in encouraging me to develop my own coaching style and pursue my professional vision.

CONTACT INFORMATION

Lynne M. Hornyak, Ph.D.
1731 Swann Street, NW
Washington, DC 20009
Phone: 202-387-5923
E-mail: LMHornyak@worldnet.att.net; Lynne@WealthHealthy.com
Web sites: http://WealthHealthy.com; http://Hornyak.com

15

Celebrating Success with Special College Students

June Bond

My coaching office is like the refrigerator door that parents use to recognize and honor the drawings, writings, and grades of their children. My office at the community college posts and boasts the achievements of a unique population of college students. For many of these students, this is the first such celebration in a lifetime of frustrations and failures.

I am a consulting psychologist at the Community College of Baltimore County Essex. I work three days a week in the Office of Special Services as a coach, providing support to individuals who have psychological disorders. The community college setting has an open door policy and welcomes anyone who wants to take classes. I have found that today's medications and therapies have enabled individuals with psychological disorders to integrate successfully in the community. These citizens often have untapped reservoirs of brilliance and talent that have been dormant for years. My coaching provides the support, acknowledgement, and accountability necessary for many of them to stay balanced and on track.

Each semester, I schedule weekly coaching appointments with individuals and pairs. As they enter my office, the window view of trees captures the season, while my rock fountain trickles softly in the background. A homemade quilt on the wall enhances the warmth of the setting; classical music is sometimes added to the peaceful milieu. My students come from places that were not so peaceful. Each has a story to tell but we leave the past behind as we build their futures. They process their pasts with therapists in the community. Some had horrendous school experiences. Others were quite successful in business or school before an illness disrupted their lives. By the time they reach my office, hopefully they have progressed in treatment to a point of readiness. For many, it is the first time in years that they have stepped outside of the hospital or day program. They enter the college community with trepidation and awe. Through coaching, they find acceptance in a small segment of that world, which they can carry with them into the community at large.

Many students directly or indirectly received the message that they were failures and would never amount to anything. They will never hear that from me. We adorn the refrigerator door as we discover hidden sparks of wonderful qualities, long neglected. As we uncover these inner qualities, the students begin to evolve into the individuals they were meant to be. Their souls are nourished, and my soul is as well.

CELEBRATING REALITY

Ruth was the only one to raise a hand to ask questions about special services when I made a presentation at her community rehabilitation program. Her questions were concrete but appropriate. Most of the clients appeared to be listening to my short speech about going to college; Ruth, however, was raring to go. If I had a van and announced, "Come with me," she would have been in the front seat. She followed up the presentation with a phone call and an appointment with me.

At the age of 40, Ruth spent almost half of her life in a state institution. When we met, she was receiving support in an apartment with another rehab client and she attended a day program that was within walking distance from the college. Her psychotic disorder was effectively treated by one of the newer medications, and she was responding well to agency supports in the community.

The community college provided a safe, normalized environment in which Ruth could spend time with a wide range of models for communication and socialization. Someone with her history, however, does not "wake up" with skills. As her coach, I became teacher, interpreter, and cheerleader.

In some ways, Ruth mirrored a typical coaching client. She knew that she wanted her life to be different and that she could not do it on her own. When faced with choosing classes, she had a long list of possible interests. She was like the proverbial "kid in the candy store." She had no idea what her strengths were or what she might be able to achieve. She needed structure and support to set reasonable goals.

With coaching, Ruth started slowly, taking only one or two classes at a time. Initially, she audited an academic class and a physical education class. This gave her intellectual stimulation and physical exercise without the pressure of grades. Although she audited, she took her education seriously. She purchased and read required texts, accessed additional resources from the library, and completed assignments. And Ruth rarely missed class. Eventually, she was able to take classes for credit but continued to attend part-time and to maintain her primary roots at the day program.

Together, we built skills that addressed the negative symptoms of Ruth's illness. Her eye contact was an empirical measure of our success. Initially, her eyes were averted from mine. Gradually, without directly addressing the topic of eye contact, she frequently met my gaze and sustained it for many brief periods. Ruth shared that she was afraid to socialize in class because she might misinterpret the interactions. At one point, she became attracted to another student and had to choose between focusing on her romantic thoughts or her academic goals. She knew if she obsessed on the thoughts she would fail the class. Eventually, in another class, she was able to connect intellectually with a study partner to prepare for tests together in the library. Although Ruth's affect was usually flat, she demonstrated a dry sense of humor. With her, my humor had to be based on concrete, observable facts and events because subtleties and ironies escaped her. It was essential not to treat her like a child, although some aspects of her personality were quite childlike. At one point, she announced, "I don't have a child's mind no more." And she was right.

Sometimes, coaching Ruth involved clearing misperceptions and reframing distortions. If she became agitated about something that occurred in class, she described her perception of the event. We discussed whether her agitation might escalate and create a threat to others. The records did not indicate that she had a history of aggression and Ruth convinced me that there was little likelihood of such behavior. She built social skills as she learned to consider the alternative explanations. She calmed down as she expanded on her possibilities and broke through old habitual patterns of rigid thinking. With the interpretive role of coaching, she could avoid the problems of confusion and frustration that had previously plagued her, and stay in school.

Ruth was fairly stable when she arrived on campus. As long as she remained on her medication and maintained her community supports, she was able to capitalize on her strengths in school. In reflecting upon what it was like to be finally stabilized on medication, Ruth profoundly explained that in the past, unreality—the world of delusions and hallucinations—had become her reality. The loss of those symptoms was scary because she had to redefine what was real. I believe that matriculating on a college campus helped her with this redefinition.

A thank you from Ruth came in the form of a card, not words she formulated but words she chose: "The world's a better place because of people like you." She signed with a unique icon that she invented so that no one could copy it.

CELEBRATING SELF-ADVOCACY

I looked at my appointment book and noted that a new student named Albert had an appointment at 9:00 a.m. My secretary handed me the intake form that was completed by the person who arrived at 9:00, but when I went to greet him, the only person waiting was a middle-aged woman. I wondered, "Could this be Albert?" and "How could I handle this sensitively?" I approached the woman and said, "Albert?" She smiled and said, "No, I am Al's mother." We proceeded to my office and Al's story unfolded through his advocate.

At 18 years of age, Al had just graduated from a school that was located on the grounds of a psychiatric hospital. He attended that school for the last two years, following a year at home, because his anxiety was too severe to attend public school. Now, Al wanted to go to college and had the intellectual ability to succeed. His disorder paralyzed him. He was isolated and withdrawn, struggling with obsessions, ritualistic compulsions, and panic attacks. Although he survived the years in the special school, his attendance was poor because he felt safe and grounded only at home.

In the initial interview, Al's mother stated that Al wanted to start college by taking courses through the computer and television. Distance learning was designed for individuals who have jobs, disabilities, or family responsibilities that make it difficult to travel to campus. It was an ideal place for Al to start. In his isolation, he had already become comfortable with the technology necessary to learn at home.

Following the interview with his mother, I contacted Al by phone. In fact, all of our contact during the first year was through the phone and e-mail. Our first conversation revealed that Al was bright and motivated. He felt he had the self-discipline to stay focused if he did not have to struggle with the social aspects of school. He tolerated his anxiety to come to the college to take his placement tests. We arranged for him to do so when the college was not crowded and he was tested in a room near the outside door. His scores indicated that he could proceed with college classes without reviewing his basic math, reading, and writing skills.

Al was comfortable sharing the ramifications of his anxiety disorder with his teachers during the time he learned at home. He maintained contact through the technology at his fingertips. I coached Al on an as-needed basis while he remained at home. With his focus on school, Al completed three courses each semester. His As were a testimony to his ability and his compulsivity. For the first time, with the social stressors removed, Al was achieving at the level of his intelligence. The success rippled into his emotional health, motivating him to commit to therapy and medication regimes in order to pursue the challenge of college.

His call came as a surprise one day. After much thinking and processing on his own and in therapy, Al wanted to attempt taking a class on campus. We started with a face-to-face meeting with me. It was summer, so the campus was not busy with matriculating students. Meeting him was delightful. We celebrated the progress he had made to come this far, figuratively and literally. It was stimulating to spend time with someone as bright and interesting as he was. As we planned for the fall semester, Al decided he would take one class on campus and two at home. He registered for an honors class. The honors classes are limited to 15 students and are taught by instructors with great passion for their subjects. Although the class size was ideal, the consideration of himself as an honors student was foreign for him. As his coach, I acknowledged his strengths and his abilities.

Weekly coaching sessions with Al facilitated his learning process as we celebrated accomplishments and tackled dilemmas. Al recognized that his previous pattern of procrastination was an avoidance of rituals. He broke down long-term assignments into manageable steps and imposed mini-deadlines on each step. He used a word processor to overcome his hand-writing imperfections. If something unexpected and intolerable happened, we explored solutions and active steps he could take to solve the problem. Once, Al agonized over a short paper for history class only to have the instructor misplace it along with the papers of several other students. At first, she suggested that he redo the paper. Al obsessed on the unfairness of this, and was unable to proceed with other schoolwork. With coaching, he considered another strategy for dealing with his frustration. He called the instructor who agreed that since it was her fault she would not include the paper in his grade for that class. With coaching, Al felt empowered to take steps on his own behalf.

Eventually, I coached Al together with another man who had similar goals. The camaraderie was poignant as they became a support system for each other. I sometimes saw them together at an isolated table in the cafe-teria or a corner of the library, talking. On coaching days, they greeted each other in the waiting room and "started without me." It was apparent that eventually these gentlemen would not need me as their coach. They would coach each other.

CELEBRATING BALANCE

Daniel represented those students who, despite rigorous treatment efforts, could not be medically stabilized. If I could guess a diagnosis from a tran-script, I would have surmised that he had a mood disorder. His transcript reflected that he tried several semesters in school, each time registering for 16 to 18 credits, and then failing or withdrawing from all of them. In desperation, Dan decided to register with the Office of Special Services. After making and breaking several appointments, he finally came to see me. He walked into my office and at first I only saw his multicolored hair, body-piercings, and black clothing. His dress and demeanor were my first indication of the internal conflicts he struggled with, as he tried to manage the cycles of mania and depression that affected his life and his learning. In his own words, Dan experienced "ricocheting bullets of brilliance interrupted by moments of gloomy silence."

Dan arrived for our first appointment loaded for bear, defensive and agitated. He said he had programmed his mind for years to "observe, report back to the brain, and prepare for battle." My gentle demeanor and direct manner disarmed him. He agreed to weekly coaching and he left with a glimmer of hope of survival in college.

Dan's disorder was resistant to treatment. At 35, he had spent two decades on a roller coaster. Beginning in high school, he medicated himself with alcohol to numb the feelings, his attempt at controlling his mood swings. Eventually, he spent time in hospitals and jails until he was accurately diagnosed and treated with mood stabilizers. He had been sober for 10 years when we met. He attended several meetings of Alcoholics Anonymous each week and making sure he could attend meetings was his first priority when scheduling his classes.

Dan learned to maximize his productivity when his mood was high. He used periods of hypomania to stay up all night and produce excellent term papers and creative art projects. At these times in class, he was exuberant, raising his hand frequently. His speech was pressured and he could be somewhat aggressive. Dan used coaching sessions to monitor his moods, to reframe misunderstandings, and to modify his behavior.

At the college, the code of conduct applies to all students. Anyone who is disruptive to the learning process is subject to disciplinary consequences that range from a meeting with the instructor or dean to expulsion from the school. In order to address this directly, I explained the code to Dan early in our coaching relationship. He chose to meet face-to-face with the director of campus security, to explain his disorder, and form a link with another potential helper on campus. Dan expressed that he did not want to scare people. In reality, although he looked and sounded tough, he felt quite small.

Knowledge of the consequences, acquaintance with security, and the alliance with me helped Dan to make healthy decisions related to school. When he felt rageful, paranoid, or depressed he retreated to his houseboat. We decided that "hospitalizing himself at home" was his safest choice on those days.

When Dan was depressed, he stayed home for a week at a time with no contact. I left e-mail and phone messages to encourage him to respond when he was able. In the past, without this safety net he would become hopelessly discouraged and give up on school. With coaching, he eased back as soon as he was chemically stabilized.

During coaching sessions with Dan, it was crucial for me to maintain an even mood. I never knew how he would act when he arrived, but it was essential to our coaching relationship for me to be predictable. My consistency and predictability grounded Dan when his own system could not. He could depend on my unwavering belief in him and his gifts. I believed in him from the day we met. At times, he thought I was "crazy" for this. He came to accept my belief in him and eventually he believed in himself.

Dan developed the confidence to open his own business selling his artwork. He worked when he was able and rested when he could not work. Self-employment afforded him the flexibility necessitated by his disorder. Dan wrote a letter that applauded some of the people who helped him in school. He described us one by one. In his description of our coaching sessions he stated, "She knows things sometimes before I do. She has personally taken problems that always used to compound in my head, and showed me new ways to view them. She really cares about how I feel. That has probably been one of the key factors why I am still in school today. I have met with her once a week since the day I enrolled. Truth is, if she hadn't been there for me, I wouldn't be here at all. I owe her."

Dan did not realize that he did not owe me anything because he had already given so much. The connection between a coach and client is a two-way connection in which both give and receive. The intangible gifts of coaching keep me coming back.

CELEBRATING PERSEVERANCE

When I first met Anna, she walked timidly into my office with her shoulders forward and her head down as if she was trying to be invisible. She appeared to be much younger than 28, the age stated on her intake form. The paperwork said that her legal name was Karen but she did not use that name anymore. Anna had first attended college after high school graduation. Her transcript showed As, FXs (failures due to nonattendance), and Ws (withdrawals). During our first interview, she stuttered and would not look at me. She vaguely remembered going to school 10 years ago but did not remember which classes she had taken. She did not remember what she had learned, not even in the classes she aced. The period of time since her withdrawal from school was a blur of hospitalizations, day programs, psychiatrists, and medication trials, until she finally received a suitable diagnosis. She had been discharged from the trauma disorders day program and wanted to return to college to have a reason to get out of bed in the morning and to have some structure in her day.

Weekly coaching sessions were an essential element in Anna's development. She found a safe place in Special Services as she ventured onto the campus. It was absolutely necessary that she continue intensive outpatient therapy and a regime of medication. She was in and out of the hospital, and each time she was out, she returned to academia.

Coaching goals involved attendance, self-advocacy, networking, and symptom management. When Anna was at school, she learned to control the power of her past by staying in the present and projecting into her future. At first, she focused on seemingly small goals, which were huge for her.

Showing up was an initial objective. As Anna began to attend regularly and experience success, this step became more manageable. In the letter we wrote to her instructors each semester, she requested flexibility in attendance policies. She could not attend college when she was hospitalized. Sometimes, during a difficult bout of illness, she was housebound and could not drive safely. Anna maintained our coaching by phone, kept up with her schoolwork, and eventually returned to her schedule. She learned when to withdraw from a class before failing, and when to negotiate with her instructors to make up tests. Sometimes, she would return from a hospitalization ahead of the class on assignments. She also gave my number to other inpatients who were curious about her schoolwork. At one point, we laughed about whether it was written in the graffiti on the bathroom wall of the hospital unit: "For a good time in school call June." Through coaching, Anna obtained the support necessary to take responsibility for the ramifications of her disorder. School became her reason to live.

For a student like Anna, who has a trauma-based disorder, there are constant triggers that can create upset. Literature is replete with tragic stories. Photography class has a dark room. In art class, you draw nudes. Psychology openly discusses disorders. Criminal justice speaks of rapes and murders. Swimming class requires you to undress in a locker room and wear a bathing suit. Math anxiety is rampant. Speech requires you to get up in front of the class. Biology lab dissects living creatures. Our coaching provided reframing for these situations so that she could proceed with assignments. On one occasion, Anna and I talked about her terror of the revolving door that led into the photography dark room. When she was able to reframe a childhood nightmare into "the doorway to my future" she could go in and out of the darkroom with ease. When faced with an assignment to write fiction for her composition class she felt she was "telling lies." When coached to understand the lies as "art," writing flowed more easily.

Dissociation significantly interfered with the learning process. An instructor told one class to "pretend that we traveled out the window to a desert." Anna followed the instruction very well but later chuckled when she told me that he never told them to return. She remained on the desert until class was dismissed. Another instructor gave a gentle verbal prompt to Anna's class to look at the blackboard when he noticed she had lost her focus. At times, Anna studied extensively and mastered material that she could not internally access on the day of the test. A memorized piano piece looked foreign when placed on the classroom piano. Anna's instructors were more willing to accommodate for these lapses if Anna's other work was satisfactory and if they understood the phenomenon of dissociation. My proactive and open dialogue with them was an essential part of her program.

Hypervigilance and hypersensitivity were also obstacles to school success. Anna would be startled by common noises in the hallway. Any negative feedback from her peers or instructors set her back. She arranged for a special parking permit so that she could feel safe going to and from her car. One day, I came to work following a family emergency, masking my own feelings. No one noticed except Anna. She came into my office and immediately asked, "Are you all right? I walked in and got sad. I didn't know if it was you or me." When I explained briefly, careful not to dismiss her while maintaining appropriate boundaries, she offered to "fluff my aura."

It was apparent that an element of Anna's struggle came from the unclear boundaries between herself and other people, and within her own psyche. Anna learned to come to see me in between our coaching sessions if she became overwhelmed. We wrote protocols for dealing with her sense of overwhelm. One semester, her goal was "not to cry in class." She fulfilled this humble expectation.

Anna attended the college for several years. One day at a time, she built a future based on school success. She wrote a poem that stated, "I am creating me." Another poem boasted, "I have angels inside me, who are finally in charge." Invisible no more, Anna discovered her brilliance and graduated with an Associate of Arts degree. She made a special request for me to present her with her diploma. The administration responded by inviting us to be distinguished guests at a brunch with the president. In a letter Anna wrote to me following graduation, she saluted the substance of coaching: "Thank you for all the support and encouragement as well as the praise you've given me. I didn't think I'd make it but I did. Thanks for believing in me."

THE BIGGER PICTURE

As a coach within a college, working with students who are in treatment in the community, I cannot work in a vacuum. It is important that I interact with the treatment team on behalf of a student. The level of communication needed is individualized and any contact I make is with permission of the student. In the initial interview, I obtain names of therapists, psychiatrists, and agencies working with the student. The student signs a release form so that I can send for documentation of the disabilities and recommendations concerning college attendance. I cannot work with someone who does not provide documentation. Additional contact with people within and outside of the school is arranged as needed. Some students require little communication between me and other professionals; others require frequent interaction between me and an instructor, therapist, or parent in order to facilitate success.

If a student chooses to disclose his or her disability to instructors, we write a letter to appropriate faculty. The form letter contains general information about the legal requirement to make reasonable accommodations for people with disabilities, the need for confidentiality, and the services of my office. We insert a paragraph or two about the needs of the individual student. A student may disclose his or her diagnosis or state nonspecifically that he or she has "a documented disability." We then explain the impact of the disorder on educational endeavors (academic, social, and behavioral). The letter also includes reasonable accommodations. Ruth wanted her instructors to know that she might misinterpret social interactions so that they could respond appropriately. Al wanted to have his panic attacks explained so that he could take unscheduled breaks. The fluctuations in Dan's symptoms were described, because if an instructor witnessed the bullets of brilliance, it was difficult to understand the weeks of gloomy silence. Anna needed extended time on tests and someone to give her copies of class notes to accommodate her periods of dissociation.

Interactions with faculty also take place by phone, e-mail, and meetings with the student and me. Collaboration is essential in programming for a student with complex needs.

I also maintain periodic contact with service providers in the community. I visit agencies, and telephone case managers, therapists, and doctors. Ideally, we work together toward the same goals. Most of the time, students have worked in therapy toward college attendance. The transition to the community college is a big step in recovery. I am a guide through that step.

A student with a disability can attend school without disclosing to anyone. If they disclose to me and provide documentation, they are entitled to services. I provide regular coaching to students who demonstrate a need for the service and an ability to benefit. Coaching is a proactive approach to school success. It is an adjunct to therapy for my students.

A student does not have to be in treatment or on medication to receive my services; however, the ability to benefit is related to the bigger picture. The disorganized, unstable, or untreated student presents an array of issues on campus and is essentially uncoachable. One such student experienced a "black cloud" upon entering my office. Others frightened the staff, wrote letters to Protection Services about delusion-based concerns, and wrote papers in class that had nothing to do with the assignment. Those students required intervention, but were not appropriate for coaching. Usually, they do not last long on campus.

The primary responsibility for treatment rests in the community, and treatment frequently interferes with school. Medication trials, hospitalizations, and crises disrupt school attendance and the ability to learn. If I have concerns about treatment I feel free to discuss them with the clinician. Some observations can be shared with some students carefully in order to avoid "splitting," or setting up a conflict between the clinician and myself. Some students keep their worlds chaotic through splitting, so I try hard to stay out of that position. I try to help students take responsibility for their recovery, which includes helping to structure an open network of resources.

I call therapists if I think a student is a threat to himself or others. In a crisis situation, a therapist is frequently contacted to provide direction to the student or to me. I have participated in a three-way contract for safety with a student in my office and her therapist on the phone. I have walked students to the emergency room of the hospital that adjoins the campus. Students carry wallet cards that I designed to provide instructions related to school if they are hospitalized during a school semester. The folded business card contains information for reaching the coach and spaces for names and numbers of instructors. The student is encouraged, "Do not postpone necessary medical attention—your health and safety come first." The list of instructions includes notifying the coach and keeping in touch while in the hospital, working on assignments if able, discreetly notifying instructors, bringing a discharge summary to the coach, and finally making a plan with the coach and instructors for completion or withdrawal from classes. The card finally quotes a Japanese proverb that encourages the student to "Fall seven times, stand up eight."

When people work together headed in the same direction, goals can be reached. It is imperative to be flexible, cooperative, and focused when working with this population.

Coaching provides me with daily opportunities to fulfill my life purpose, "To touch souls deeply while honoring mine." My refrigerator door is covered with the accomplishments of students like Ruth, Al, Dan, and Anna. I am both touched and honored to be invited to their celebrations.

PRACTICAL INFORMATION

ADVICE FOR NEW COACHES OF SPECIAL COLLEGE STUDENTS

1. Accept that we all have gifts and a life purpose.
2. Realize that people with disabilities frequently have untapped resources that can be cultivated through coaching.
3. Understand that people in recovery can be coached concerning concrete goals about their present and future circumstances, as long as their therapeutic needs are being met elsewhere.

ADVICE FOR NEW THERAPIST-COACHES

1. Consider intensive coach training in order to define the differences between therapy and coaching, to learn about marketing, to explore your own goals, and to practice coaching skills.
2. Network with other coaches so that you are not alone. In this relatively new profession, it is easy to become isolated. Colleagues can be a support system for a new coach.
3. Hire a coach to mentor you through the transition period. There are a lot of factors to consider and details to organize. My coach kicks me in the rear but wears a slipper. Subsequently, my new business shaped up more quickly than if I had tried to formulate it alone.

MY FEES

I have been working as a coach in the community college for six years; the college pays me $27.43 per hour for 24 hours of coaching time per week. These hours include telecoaching, face-to-face coaching, consultation with therapists and instructors, and other duties. The service is free to the students. In my private practice, DreamCatchers Life Coaching, I charge a monthly rate that is paid at the beginning of the month. I provide telecoaching or face-to-face coaching at the rate of $100 for two meetings, $150 for three meetings, $200 for four meetings per month. Rates are based on 30- to 40-minute contacts. Brief calls and e-mails are made in between meetings.

WHAT I KNOW NOW

I can have a satisfying career and make good money too. I was a teenager during the love and peace era of the 1960s, raised by parents from the Great Depression. I am gently shifting my goals toward prosperity without compromising my core values. I have been coaching for years in my role as a therapist. With formalized training as a coach, I am expanding and enhancing my repertoire of skills without abandoning my life goals and purpose. Coaching challenges me to become a more fulfilled and balanced person.

A BRIEF BIOGRAPHY

I have a B.A. in biology and psychology; an M.A. and A.G.S. in school psychology; an Ed.D. in human communication and its disorders; and a C.A.S. in neuropsychology. I have worked for 27 years as a therapist in both public and private settings. My approach is based largely on a cognitive-behavioral paradigm.

Early in 2000, I attended a one-day workshop on coaching, and I realized I had been coaching for many years within my experiences as a therapist. I subsequently pursued training through The Institute for Life Coach Training (formerly TherapistU), which trains therapists to become coaches. I continue to learn through teleconferences, newsletters, books, and mentoring. Later that same year, I established DreamCatchers to formalize coaching as a separate entity within my array of private counseling services. Pat Williams, president of the Institute for Life Coach Training, continues to mentor me as my private coach. His support has helped me make significant changes in my life and the lives of others. Jennifer Johnson, my coaching buddy from class, continues to be my friend and my biggest cheerleader.

Working as a coach is invigorating. I am honored to be an invited guide on someone's journey. I get a natural high when I participate in the unfolding of a life as brilliance and talent are recognized and realized. If you can conceive it, perceive it, and believe it, you can achieve it.

CONTACT INFORMATION

June O. Bond, Ed.D., CAS, NCSP, LCPC
CCBC Essex
7201 Rossville Boulevard
Baltimore, MD 21237
Phone: 410-780-6741
E-mail: jbond@ccbc.cc.md.us

DreamCatchers Life Coaching
9618 Belair Road
Baltimore, MD 21236
E-mail: Dreamcatchers123@aol.com

16

Coaching Lawyers

Ellen Ostrow

As soon as I heard Steve's voice on our first coaching call, I felt like a scared novice. All the confidence I'd built over 20 years as a psychologist and 3 years as a professional coach drained out my toes. He'd heard that I was an experienced coach and clinician who was interested in working with those in the legal profession. I wanted to develop a niche of coaching lawyers, but, truth be told, he was my first.

His deep, resonant voice and polished, professional manner sounded commanding and in control. As a partner in one of the largest and most prestigious law firms in the country, he was an expert in his field. I'd never gone to law school, much less practiced law. What did I really know about being a lawyer except what I'd read or heard? Would I really know how to coach him?

I asked him to tell me what was on his mind and then listened intently. He'd been at the firm for 20 years and his youngest child was leaving for college. He still wanted to practice law and didn't want to reduce his income. However, he'd been having increasing difficulty working in the firm. There had been a lot of changes—the field had become far more competitive. From his perspective, younger attorneys failed to exhibit his own level of commitment to the work, so he rarely delegated. As a result, he spent most days just putting out fires. He missed doing the kind of legal trouble-shooting and advising he really loved, but his time was consumed with work that had long ceased to be a challenge. He complained that with fewer attorneys practicing in his area of specialty, he felt increasingly isolated.

Steve said he worked too much. This wasn't really a new awareness—

he'd always known that his work demanded so much of his time and energy that his life felt out of balance. As a result, his relationship with his wife was strained and it had been years since he'd done any kind of regular exercise. And just the other day his secretary had mentioned that he was wearing the same suit he'd worn the day before. He wondered how often he'd done that.

For years he'd been telling himself that he'd address all of this—but he wasn't sure what the solution might be. Now time had passed and nothing had changed. It was getting harder to do work he didn't really enjoy. He wondered how he could he step out of the whirlwind long enough to get some kind of handle on the situation. Someone had suggested coaching. Did I think I could help?

I took a deep breath and realized that I was certain I could. Listening to him dispelled the doubts I'd had about the necessity of being a lawyer in order to coach a lawyer. The memory of an old clinical supervisor came to mind: "You don't have to be schizophrenic to help one," he'd advised.

The skills needed to help Steve seemed well within my repertoire. I felt engaged, energized, and focused—my signals that I wanted to work with him and that I could help him. As an attorney and close friend had said to me before my first speech to a large audience of lawyers, "Don't worry—they really need what you have to offer them."

DEFINING THE NICHE

The coach training program I completed offered this list of criteria as necessary to developing a coaching niche:

1. There must be a problem or some kind of need for which coaching would be an appropriate intervention.
2. The population should be currently underserved, in terms of help for this particular need.
3. These people should have sufficient discretionary income to be able to afford coaching services.
4. The people in the niche should be accessible, via the Internet or fax.

5. The population should be sufficiently large.

6. The coach should have a passion for working with these people.

To define my niche, I started with the last criteria and thought about my passion. I considered which clients I liked working with best over my 20-year career as a psychologist. The Washington, DC area is full of lawyers, so over the years I'd counseled a lot of attorneys—and enjoyed it. I particularly enjoyed working with women lawyers. They tended to be exceptionally smart and verbal, very tough and determined, yet tender and creative beneath their left-brained veneers. These women had given me a good education in the stresses of their jobs.

Next, I began to research the psychological literature for studies about lawyers, and broadened my search to data and surveys from the work of sociologists, feminists, legal scholars, and various divisions of the American Bar Association. I learned that several industry changes had made practicing law increasingly stressful: The legal profession had undergone a transition from being a profession to a business, the market had become fiercely competitive, and expectations for responsiveness had accelerated due to electronic communication. As a result, high rates of dissatisfaction among lawyers have consistently been documented.

For example, a variety of surveys have indicated that lawyers suffer from depression at rates almost four times higher than non-lawyers with similar sociodemographic characteristics. Lawyers have elevated rates of anxiety, substance abuse, suicide, divorce, and stress-related medical illnesses. ABA surveys indicate that approximately 30 percent of lawyers are dissatisfied with their jobs. Lawyers in private practice in large firms appear to be the most dissatisfied and this trend has been increasing over the past decade. Women lawyers, in particular, report high levels of dissatisfaction, especially in large firm settings.

In an effort to attract and retain legal talent, starting salaries in large law firms in major metropolitan areas have soared to $125,000. But in order to support these salaries and maintain partner profits, billable-hour expectations continue to spiral upward. Law offices have increased billable-hour requirements—typically to minimums of 1900 or 2100 hours per year, per lawyer. Under all this pressure, the emotional climate of law firms has become increasingly short-tempered and hostile. Having a life outside of the office has become much more difficult for those engaged in law. But once you're on a runaway train, it's hard to get off. Walking away from a $125,000 salary when you still have $60–70,000 in law school debt to pay, or children to put through college, is difficult.

These issues are heightened by subtle forms of gender discrimination for women in childbearing years. With the increase in billable hours, work/life balance issues have become overwhelming. It's not possible to work 80 hours a week and be a mother, too. Often, if women complain, they are told that they simply aren't tough enough. On the other hand, if women lawyers attempt to promote themselves in their firms, they are frequently labeled as too aggressive.

The more I thought about these issues, the more they stoked the embers of my '70s feminism. I was becoming genuinely passionate about the professional issues facing women attorneys and discussed them with a woman judge I knew personally. When I described the coaching I wanted to do, she encouraged me. Countless women lawyers had talked to her, wondering if they'd ever have time to find a partner, have a baby, spend time with their children, or have any kind of a life outside of work. She'd said exactly what I'd needed to hear. I made the firm and deliberate decision to make attorneys, and especially women lawyers, my coaching niche.

Marketing the Niche

The judge generously introduced me to the editor of a bar association publication who invited me to write an article for an issue she was planning on work/life balance. I went to work. My Web site, LawyersLifeCoach.com, went up in a flash; after all, having a Web site is the electronic-age age equivalent to hanging up a shingle. I researched and wrote as if I were studying for my Ph.D. comprehensive exams and submitted my article. In the article I quoted Joan Williams, a professor of law at American University Law School who had written *Unbending Gender: Why Family and Work Conflict and What to Do About It*. Williams had recently received a grant from the Sloan Foundation to study the high rate of attrition among women attorneys in Washington, DC law firms. Her co-investigator was a woman attorney working in a DC firm, who also edited the Women's Bar

Association newsletter as well as an information Web site for women lawyers, www.womenlawyers.com.

As a result of this article, some good connections emerged. I requested that www.womenlawyers.com establish a reciprocal link with my Web site and I provided a copy of my recent publication to establish my credentials as a resource. They agreed, and I developed an association with them that has informed my work immeasurably, as well as provided several other marketing opportunities for my coaching practice. Meanwhile, I kept networking—attending more bar association meetings, meeting more lawyers, and in the process, growing more passionate about my niche.

A CASE EXAMPLE

One of the most gratifying experiences I've had coaching an individual attorney was with a fourth year associate in a large firm who had heard me speak at a bar association event. Gifted and brilliant, she was having difficulty dealing with the angry outbursts of one of her firm's partners. She enjoyed working in her area of the law, but the level of distress she felt as the object of these rages had her thinking she might not be tough enough to succeed. She was also afraid that this partner's anger reflected other partners' more general dissatisfaction with her work and that she would not be offered a partnership.

In addition to these concerns she knew she wanted a family, but since breaking up with her boyfriend there were no prospects on the horizon. She let me know that her biological clock was ticking loudly. Working well into the night and weekends did not provide her much opportunity to date.

We contracted for three 45-minute coaching calls per month. I chose not to begin with "big picture" issues, such as how she wanted her life to look in 20 years, her sense of mission, or purpose—she needed some immediate trouble-shooting to handle the office crises she faced. We quickly jumped into a discussion of how to deal with the angry partner. She described the firm's culture and why she didn't think she'd ever be viewed as partner material.

Though bright and self-motivated, she was unable to position herself in opposition to a critical and angry superior. Unlike many of the other attorneys in her firm, she did not come from a long line of lawyers. In her middle class family, women were expected to marry and have babies. Her traditional, patriarchal family did not understand her desire to have a career.

She revealed that she was not sure why the firm had hired her, despite her stellar law school record. For her, not having gone to Harvard meant that she wasn't really the "best and the brightest." We spent considerable time examining her assumptions about her work situation and how these influenced her behavior. My role as her coach was to question her about the validity of her beliefs and to invite her to imagine how she might behave if she gave credence to some very different notions.

For example, I asked how might she respond if she was certain it was absolutely unprofessional and never acceptable for a partner to scream at an associate? What if "tough" meant standing up for yourself, rather than withstanding all blows in silence? Why was emotionality bad in a lawyer? Wasn't anger an emotion?

I felt like I was walking through Wonderland with Alice. As each constricting assumption lost its "truth" value, she was able to open up an entire range of new possibilities. Even over the phone, I could "see" her face—first puzzled, then wide-eyed. One of the aspects I most love about coaching, after having done psychotherapy for 20 years, is that I empathize with a client's excitement instead of her suffering. At the conclusion of each of my calls with her I felt energized and excited, too.

Questioning her limiting beliefs was just a beginning. It was one thing to believe the senior partner was behaving inappropriately; it was quite another to face this partner and challenge his behavior. We brainstormed about what pressures he might be facing and she considered his behavior over the course of the time she'd known him. It occurred to her that he might not even realize the impact of his behavior. She imagined many possible scenarios for dealing with him—writing a script, rehearsing her behavior, visualizing his reactions, and experiencing her emotional response.

In spite of her intention to be proactive and approach him at the time and place of her choosing, the partner surprised her by talking to her unexpectedly. Though somewhat nervous, she ad-libbed her response and handled it beautifully. The partner responded reasonably well. She sent me an e-mail describing the interaction; I could hear how proud she was. The fact that she had managed the conversation unscripted made it all the more successful in her eyes. Our next call began with a celebration of her victory. She'd had her first glimpse of becoming empowered and was ready for more.

Now she had another situation to talk over with me. One of her clients had recently put his arm around her and called her "sweetheart." She'd felt furious but paralyzed. When she mentioned this to a lawyer in her firm, she was criticized for "overreacting." We discussed this incident in broader terms and I suggested some books and articles she might read. Seeing commonplace behaviors in the firm as reflections of unconscious gender discrimination, rather than as personally addressed to her, gave her the distance she needed to consider an entirely new range of potential responses. At my suggestion, she joined her local women's bar association and decided to participate on a committee examining diversity issues in law firms.

Another situation arose. She sent me an e-mail the moment she heard that her firm had won a very significant case that she'd been working on for almost a year. But this was soon followed by another e-mail: The managing partner had omitted her name from the memo he'd sent around the firm congratulating all of the participating lawyers.

We were scheduled to talk the next day and spent our time discussing how she might handle this situation. What would it mean for her to just let it go? If she didn't fight this battle, were there implications for her career? If she did protest, what did she stand to gain? Fourth year associates didn't typically challenge managing partners. Was there any way she could receive the credit she both deserved and required if she was going to advance professionally—without inviting trouble?

She decided to challenge the lack of recognition by sending an e-mail to the managing partner asking that the error be corrected. Not surprisingly, he told her that she was behaving like a "prima donna"—but when a new memo came out the next day, she enjoyed receiving her share of the congratulations.

As her successes accumulated, I could hear a fascinating transformation taking place. In the beginning, she'd sounded young and timid to me, although I knew she could act tough and lawyerly when necessary. Within a few months she'd matured 10 years. She now had a calm and confident presence. She spoke in a stronger, clearer voice and stated her opinions without qualification. She trusted her judgment and asked me less often if I thought she'd done the "right" thing.

Feeling more in control of her current situation in the firm, she shifted her coaching to another aspect: her future. She wanted to focus on how to establish contacts with potential clients and bring in new business. Like many attorneys, she hated the idea of marketing, believing that it required a kind of hard-sell pushiness. As an introvert, I could well identify with her feelings. But during the course of developing my coaching practice I'd learned how to market in ways that suited my personality. The literature on marketing professional services validated my thinking: If she could identify the ways in which she was comfortable telling others about her expertise, and if she was genuinely enthusiastic about her work, she'd be able to market effectively without being "pushy."

Since she was most comfortable talking to people she knew, we began by listing everyone in her current network so that she could identify potential clients and considered possible connections between the people she knew and her prospects. She began to attend professional meetings in the industry she represented. We designed a system for her to alert current clients about legal news affecting their industry. Increasingly, clients with whom she worked began to request that she do new work for them. She was establishing herself within her niche, which would not only increase the likelihood of making partner in her current firm, but also open up many other opportunities if she didn't, or chose not to continue there.

The more we discussed her professional aspirations, the clearer she became about her core values. Recognizing that part of her motivation for becoming a lawyer was to prove her strength and independence to herself and her family enabled her to see that she'd accomplished this goal. It became easier for her to acknowledge her needs for connection—but this intensified her experience of the empty, non-work side of her life. To change the emptiness she'd need to set boundaries around work.

Initially, she could see no way to reduce the number of hours she spent at the office. On one call she mentioned that she'd had to work all weekend because the client had absolutely needed the document by Monday morning. I expressed curiosity about the definition of necessity. Recalling the various times this client had labeled a task "urgent," she realized that not all emergencies were equal. Sometimes a brief had to be filed according to the court calendar—and this had to be done on time. But on other occasions, the client simply wanted the document finished so he could leave it on his desk and move onto something else. She became quite adept at differentiating between these. The first time she told him, "I can't have it to you by Monday, but I can by Wednesday," she held her breath waiting for his response. He agreed to Wednesday.

She and I talked about the many ways in which language influenced behavior and how she might have different definitions for terms like "urgent," "success," "strong," and "enough." As she took greater control of her work by setting priorities for herself and setting limits with other people, she noticed that her feelings of urgency lifted. At first she worried that she wouldn't be able to work successfully without the motivation of these feeling and missed the adrenaline rush of working under intense pressure. We discussed alternative sources of motivation and excitement other than work, which further pinpointed the lack of balance in her life.

It was finally time to address her personal life and specifically her loneliness. She wanted to find a loving partner and have a family, but she was inhibited by the emotional messages she received from her family, who valued this above all else. She needed to claim this goal as her own.

I asked her to describe to me how she socialized; she said that her social life mirrored her work routine. She often went bar-hopping with other associates and recognized that the level of urgency she felt during these social outings, as she evaluated the men she met in bars as possible life partners, was like the urgency she had brought to the workplace. She complained that the men she met weren't seeking a permanent, committed relationship. So we designed a relationship search, much as we would a job search.

I asked her to visualize her "ideal" relationship—how she would feel and behave; the quality of intimacy it might have; how differences and problems would be addressed. Through this process she became aware of how vital it was to her to have a partner who completely accepted her. Together, we brainstormed ways in which she could increase the likelihood of meeting an accepting and appropriate man.

However, I soon learned that not every coaching goal gets accomplished according to design. On a business trip, she began talking with a man while waiting for a table in a restaurant—and he was the one! Now our sessions focused on her relationship—how to take those personal risks that would establish the kind of intimacy she wanted. She said that nothing at the firm had frightened her quite as much as trying to communicate her needs to her new boyfriend. Due, in part, to our coaching, she knew how to push herself outside her comfort zone and keep taking risks.

And like many of my coaching stories, this one has a happy ending: They're now husband and wife.

EXPANDING THE NICHE

One of the things that struck me most about coaching this woman was that in spite of the fact that many other women lawyers were struggling with similar challenges, she felt so isolated and alone in her struggles. The literature on women lawyers indicates that this isolation is commonplace, which fits with my experience as a coach in this niche. The fear of being criticized and the need to appear confident and strong makes lawyers, especially women, circumspect about revealing their professional concerns. Often, as I coached this woman, I wished I could introduce her to other women lawyers I was coaching. It seemed to me that the sense of universality would help them.

I've recently developed a strategy that enables me to expand my niche into group coaching for women lawyers. Each time a bar association accepts one of my articles for its print publication, I offer to provide six *free* group coaching sessions as an exclusive member benefit. It's a way to market my services where everyone wins. The association and the members enjoy the free sessions, and I've learned so much from leading these groups it more than makes up for the unpaid time.

Topics I cover include "Defining Success On Your Own Terms" and "Marketing Your Services When You Have No Time." Women lawyers call in from all over their state and take part in a virtual telephone group. Almost every group begins with at least one person telling me they don't like "touchy feely" exercises. But by the end of the first call, most are saying that the experiential coaching exercises were the most powerful for them. On every single call in every single state, the participants have expressed how relieved they feel to discover they're not alone with their thoughts and feelings. They really didn't know that women lawyers throughout the country are struggling with many of their same issues.

Sometimes the group participants call in separately; sometimes they call in as an established group, seated around a conference table. The classes work within a wide variety of settings. But when I invite participants to talk about how to succeed as an attorney and as a parent, they speak with one voice. Senior members on the call offer stories about what's worked for them, mentoring younger associates who despair of ever having a life while practicing law. During one group, one member offered to meet another lawyer on the call who worked in another firm across town, so they could establish a regular exercise program together.

These groups, more than any other experience, have convinced me that I chose the right niche. I love empowering lawyers, because they are in a position to effect significant change in the world. These lawyers have taught me many lessons about possibility and transformation—and I'm looking forward to learning more.

PRACTICAL INFORMATION

ADVICE FOR NEW LAWYERS' COACHES

1. You don't need to be a lawyer, but you do need to know what it's like to be one. Talk to attorneys; learn about different practice settings and the culture of each; read their publications (e.g., *Legal Times*)
2. Explore the Web sites of the ABA and the NALP. There are a number of excellent books written about the profession and career-related issues. Establish credibility and expertise and then find ways to demonstrate your expertise; lawyers in particular respond better to face-to-face marketing.
3. Lawyers are trained to be analytical, to minimize risk, to be alert for potential problems, and to be problem-solving and solution-seeking. Consider this as you choose your approach to coaching a lawyer.

ADVICE FOR NEW THERAPIST-COACHES

1. As a therapist, you already have many of the skills needed to be an excellent coach. Your ability to listen deeply and to ask questions that facilitate self-awareness are well-honed. The biggest leap will be shifting the focus from psychopathology, problems, and repair to facilitating growth in healthy, well-functioning people. Completing a coach-training program is probably the best way to make this transition.

2. If you plan on a virtual coaching practice, you will need to learn how to adapt your skills to the absence of visual information. This is especially crucial when facilitating virtual groups. A coach-training program and a lot of practice can help you to develop these skills.

3. The most difficult transition for many therapist-coaches is from clinician to entrepreneur. Unless you are already very skilled at Internet marketing and marketing in general, you'll have a lot to learn about niche selection, positioning, writing for the Internet, publishing an e-mail newsletter, Web site design, and marketing professional services. Working with an experienced coach is probably the best way to develop expertise and comfort in these areas.

MY FEES

Most of my coaching is conducted over the phone. For individual/private coaching, my fees range from $400–$750 a month, depending on number and length of calls. For small-group coaching, my fees range from $195–$400 per client per month, depending on number and length of phone calls and number of clients in the group. I charge $299 per client in the LawyersLifeCoach Group Coaching Program for six one-hour calls.

WHAT I KNOW NOW

I understand the concept of "branding" much better—I know it's far more effective to be identified with a specific issue and a specific group of professionals rather than trying to be all things to all people. I've also learned about the pros and cons of marketing to individuals vs. marketing to businesses.

A BRIEF BIOGRAPHY

I am the founder and owner of LawyersLifeCoach.com, a professional coaching firm specializing in providing virtual coaching (by phone with e-mail and fax back-up) to lawyers trying to achieve professional success without compromising the quality of their lives. I received my Ph.D. in psychology (clinical) from the University of Rochester in 1980. I have held faculty positions at three universities and staff psychologist positions in the counseling centers of four universities. I entered full-time private practice in 1987 and am a founding owner of Metropolitan Behavioral Health Care, LLC, a multispecialty firm providing psychotherapy and consulting services in Washington, DC and suburban Maryland.

I developed my coaching skills in the MentorCoach Program. Given the number of attorneys in the Washington, DC area, I had an opportunity to work with many lawyers in my years as a psychotherapist. Coaching lawyers seemed like a natural niche, given my years of experience working with lawyers as therapist, consultant, and expert witness.

I publish a free e-mail newsletter, "Beyond the Billable Hour," which is available at my Web site. My work has been reprinted in numerous Bar Association publications and my coaching groups are offered as a special benefit to members of many Bar Associations. I have been invited to speak at a variety of lawyers' meetings, including the 2001 Annual Bar Association meeting.

CONTACT INFORMATION

Ellen Ostrow, Ph.D.
8811 Colesville Road, Suite 104
Silver Spring, MD 20910
Phone: 301-585-5539
Fax: 301-585-7392
E-mail: Ellen@lawyerslifecoach.com
Web site: LawyersLifeCoach.com